FRIENDSHIP AS SOCIAL JUSTICE ACTIVISM

Friendship as Social Justice Activism

CRITICAL SOLIDARITIES IN A GLOBAL PERSPECTIVE

Edited by

NIHARIKA BANERJEA

DEBANUJ DASGUPTA

ROHIT K. DASGUPTA

JAIME M. GRANT

Seagull
BOOKS

LONDON NEW YORK CALCUTTA

Seagull Books, 2018

Text © Individual authors
Photographs © Individual photographers
This compilation © Seagull Books, 2018

ISBN   978 0 8574 2 443 3

British Library Cataloguing-in-Publication Data
A catalogue record for this book is available from the British Library

Typeset by Seagull Books, Calcutta, India
Printed and bound by Maple Press, York, Pennsylvania, USA

CONTENTS

x
Acknowledgements

1
INTRODUCTION
Why Friendship *as* Social Activism?
*Niharika Banerjea, Debanuj Dasgupta, Rohit K. Dasgupta
and Jaime M. Grant*

9
CHAPTER ONE
Friendship, Affect, and Capitalism
Kaciano Barbosa Gadelha

21
CHAPTER TWO
Enqueerying Friendships: Radical Ramblings
Paramita Banerjee

34
CHAPTER THREE
A Love Note to OUT! DC: My First Radical Queer Affinity Group
Amelie Zurn

38
CHAPTER FOUR
rwethereyet: A Conversation
Ajamu, Jane Standing and Marai Larasi

53

CHAPTER FIVE

Kinship, Friendship and Researching Queer Digital Media in India
Rohit K. Dasgupta

65

CHAPTER SIX

Global Day of Rage in London: Reflecting on Queer Activisms,
New Media and Friendship
Rohit K. Dasgupta, Sunil Gupta and Rahul Rao

79

CHAPTER SEVEN

In Terms of 'the Excess'
Akanksha and Sumita Beethi

92

CHAPTER EIGHT

'Baar Baar Sakhi': In Search of the Queer Temporalities of Sakhya
Torsa Ghosal and Kaustavi Sarkar

115

CHAPTER NINE

the circle of friends
Aulic

117

CHAPTER TEN

The Unruly Grammar of Friendship
Debanuj Dasgupta

128

CHAPTER ELEVEN

Life-Making
Niharika Banerjea

135

CHAPTER TWELVE

'I Get by With a Little Help from My Friends': Ending Domestic
Violence One Friendship at a Time

Shannon Perez-Darby

141

CHAPTER THIRTEEN

Seven Is a Prime Number

Sumita Beethi

145

CHAPTER FOURTEEN

What Happens in My Body When I Choose You

Susan Raffo

151

CHAPTER FIFTEEN

Friendship Is Not Magic: Online Echo Chambers in the 2014 Scottish
Independence Referendum

Jeremy Matthew

162

CHAPTER SIXTEEN

Con Viviere: Friendship as the Means to Live Fully

Nila Kamol Krishnan Gupta and Shamira A. Meghani

171

CHAPTER SEVENTEEN

Friendship Is an Invisible Blood that Keeps Us Real

Ma Mercedes Alba Benitez

173

CHAPTER EIGHTEEN

Thinking the Relational Character of *Commoning* to Understand
Political Activism

Cesare Di Feliciantonio

187

CHAPTER NINETEEN

Friendship As a Mode of Sustainable Change in the Ready-Made
Garment Sector in Bangladesh

Lipi Begum and Maher Anjum

199

CHAPTER TWENTY

Personal and Political: Friendship as a Feminist Methodological Tool
in the Recovery of Anandibai Jaywant's Life and Writing

Varsha Chitnis

209

CHAPTER TWENTY-ONE

Conflicts and Intimacies: Rethinking Friendship and
Transnational Solidarity

Sam Bullington

216

CHAPTER TWENTY-TWO

My Summer in Cape Town: Or, I'm Sorry for Losing You

Alok Vaid-Menon

219

CHAPTER TWENTY-THREE

On the Path of Friendship

Mary Adkins-Cartee and Karni Pal Bhati

245

CHAPTER TWENTY-FOUR

Kissing Friends

Ignacio Rivera

250

CHAPTER TWENTY-FIVE

Untitled

Alexis Pauline Gumbs

256

CHAPTER TWENTY-SIX

Jack and Jaime: Making Love, Making Revolution

Jaime M. Grant and Jack Harrison-Quintana

268

CHAPTER TWENTY-SEVEN

Concluding Conversation

Niharika Banerjea, Debanuj Dasgupta, Rohit K. Dasgupta and Jaime M. Grant

279

Notes on Contributors

ACKNOWLEDGEMENTS

NIHARIKA would like to thank all her queer kin and friends, including fellow editors, for making her feel 'this is where I want to be!' This book is dedicated to all of you.

DEBANUJ acknowledges the editorial team for their love and support. This book could not have been possible without the support of Sunandini Banerjee whose friendship and creative work has been a lifelong inspiration. I would like to thank my parents, close friends Leslie Lord Humphrey, Bill Humphrey, Dr Ila Nagar, Mark Roberts, Kelle Avilla, Naman Mody, Sridevi Thakkilapati, Archana Venkatesh, Siddharth Singh, Nitya Rajan, James Vincent Cooley and James Talbert for surrounding me with everyday care in Columbus, Ohio. Special thanks to Nicholas Flores and our cat, Stella. I would like to dedicate this book to Audre Lorde, June Jordan, Gloria Anzaldua, Sushama Sen Sharma and all the queer, transgender, feminists of colour whom we have met in the course of this journey.

ROHIT would like to thank his parents, sister and colleagues at Loughborough University for their support and, most of all, his friends and fellow activists across several continents for their critical solidarity and friendship.

JAIME is grateful for the incredible diligence and brilliance of the editorial team, and the great love that has flowed throughout our collaboration. This book is a brazen love letter to all my friends. And a prayer of unending faith in our movements for justice.

Why Friendship *as* Social Activism?

NIHARIKA BANERJEA, DEBANUJ DASGUPTA, ROHIT DASGUPTA, AND JAIME M. GRANT

This anthology brings together essays, brief memoirs, poems and art-work by contributors working in academia/activism. We reflect upon friendship *as* social justice activism. Recent scholarship in different disciplinary fields as well as activist literature has brought attention to the political possibilities within friendship. Women across the globe have been organizing under contested banners such as feminist move-ment sustained through relations of friendship. Intimate relations are mobilized within movements based upon sexual identities and sexual health (Bose and Bhattacharya 2007; Bhaskaran 2004; Ekime and Abbas 2013; Nagar, 2015; Shah 1993). A plethora of literature focus on friendships among activists involved in social justice movements. Poems, films and short stories about love, friendship and desire are being circulated as activist materials, modes of performance and different forms of protest. Friendship as a mode of disrupting hetero-normative ordering of life is being written and re-written through the lens of Michel Foucault (1981), Audre Lorde (2007), Adrienne Rich (1995), June Jordan (2002), and diverse spiritual-religious traditions around the world. Friendship is critically re-visited as activism within religious traditions (Sankar 2011), and traced through intimacies across difference within libidinal economies of friends that resisted the British Empire (Gandhi 2006) and US imperialism (Wu 2013). We bring together academics/activists in order to push ourselves into thinking how we have been experiencing friendship as a mode of activism in our quotidian lives, politicking and thought; friendships that may otherwise not be documented or recognized as activism per se. For us, friendship as social activism is about the renewal of our imagination about who we are and who we wish to *become*. Friendship as social activism is also about being in discourse and engaging in praxis about others and us. To be or to want to be entwined, in allegiance, in resonance with those who are border-crossers, un-/misrecognized, silent, departed, awkward misfits, un-aligned souls.

Two years ago, when we began the search for contributors to this volume, we had the following questions in mind which we had also forwarded to our prospective contributors: What does friendship and love mean for those involved in social justice movements? How has friendship and love constituted and helped activist struggles, organizational conflicts, heartbreaks, meltdowns for movements? What are the life-worlds of friends and lovers involved in social justice work? In what ways are friendship and love spatially organized within social justice movements? How are friendship and love constituted within transnational movement spaces? How do forms of kinship and care inform social justice work? What are the forms of formal and informal accountability within friends? How are desires lived and mapped within social justice work? When contributions started coming in, and we began reading them, we realized that more than looking for direct answers to these questions we, and our contributors, were engaging in a kind of ethico-political exercise through the writing-and-reading process as it is played out within different rites of friendship within the context of gender, sexuality, ecological and economic justice movements. Hence, we believe this project to be a document of love, a document filled with dreams, and about dreams. Through this project we hope to insert ourselves in the crucial conjuncture of risk speculations, ecological devastations, perpetual wars and annihilatory regimes in order to paint 'revolutionary dreams' and utopian projects. We are all dreamers.

This collection is an outcome of a lifelong, transformational project of finding and cherishing our friends. It is a love letter to the people who have entrusted us with their spirits, and in doing so, enlarged our hearts and our sense of what is possible. Friendship is integral to vitality. Friendship stokes imagination. Friendship fires rebellions. Friendship provides testimony. Our friendships witness the negativity of desire, by struggling through our attachments, the ambivalence of desire and our insecurities. At the same time, friends remind us of the positive potentials, holding us accountable and, in this way, push us through negativity towards creative possibilities. All of these crucial attributes of friendship may be found here in the pages of this book. We are honoured to think through and write with our contributors, to feed us, to make visible the 'sacred', revolutionary work of friendship in such a violent and riven world.

Our contributors are academics, activists, academic/activists located across countries around the world, working on issues that cut across the boundaries of the Global South and the North. We have worked across continents through various digital platforms. This book appears as a screen and a mirror especially since the faint blue screen of our laptops continue to operate as our psychic horizon while working on this anthology. Each of us is entangled in diverse friendships. While reading our contributors pieces, we felt as if we were travelling through their words to spaces that we had not been to before, or wish we had. As editors we have consciously refrained from analysing these pieces in the introduction. They will speak for themselves. Hence what could we say to 'tie up' and/or 'introduce' the varied voices in this volume? And then it struck us that making a departure point—as is the case with academics—is not the goal here. Yes, but we can discuss how the pieces resonate with each other, a resonance that is not merely about conversing with each other but trying to find ways of being together that is *within and outside* the heteropatriarchal ordering of things.

The voices in this anthology are not isolated but, rather, speak to each other without actually having met. Our contributors highlight the productive power generated between and through bodies engaged in resisting/questioning the insistence of a kind of regime ultimately positing certain ecologies of sex, gender and survival as illicit. Instead of focusing on questions of legal recognition or misrecognition, we talk about: (1) the new orders of sex, gender and economies of survival being created and re-created through activists; (2) the relationships that are formed as activists attempt to address the law, but are not necessarily a product of law. We collectively reflect about the life-worlds of friends as vital spaces of productive power.

The Appearance of Friendship as Social Activism

Friendship, in our minds and hearts, is a word that associates itself with other words (not necessarily in a particular order): desire, object, consumption, attachment, assurance, resonance, belonging, dissonance, silence, entanglement, love, incompatibility, future, difference, political, loyalty, heartbreaks, gossip, uncertainty, etc. Each of these words evokes feelings, ideas and faces around various relationalities that are within the luring and dangerous spaces of the filial and the non-filial, producing and being produced through death-inducing norms and life-inducing opening up of those norms. Friendship is believed to be something common, yet something familiar, banal, or even mundane, it is almost taken for granted and overlooked as an inescapable, recognizable truth of life. Friendship evokes something about the other, relationality with the other, a process that is forged perhaps throughout one's lifetime, involving modalities of awareness, of unlearning with self and others—acknowledgement of which is merely the first step—and pain and loss as part of its temporality, and hence the desire to endure, almost obsessively.

We do not mean to temporally fix friendship and social activism, but to welcome friendship's appearance whenever, wherever and with whomever it arrives *as* social activism. The life-worlds, words and images in this anthology are reflections about such moments of appearance. Containing complex and, at times, contradictory gestures that are based within reciprocity and unanimity, friendship becomes a mode of social activism when singular selves try to find connections beyond commonalities and sameness in order to create diagonal relationalities and differential alliances across gender, sexuality, race, nation, age (Kaciano Barbosa Gadelha; Paramita Banerjee; Amelie Zurn; Rohit Dasgupta). Friendships such as these are queer, breathing new life forms through rage, anger (Rohit K. Dasgupta, Sunil Gupta and Rahul Rao), a politics and relationality of excess and pleasure (Akanksha and Sumita; Torsa Ghosal and Kaustavi Sarkar) and 'breaking open' (Aulic).

Friendship as social activism appears as an ethico-political relation with the self and with others through pleasure, affect, devastation, violence, support, loss (Debanuj Dasgupta; Niharika Banerjea;

Shannon Perez-Darby), unclassifiable as a single state, except as a thing or a process (Sumita; Marai Larasi Ajamu and Jane Standing; Susan Raffo). Such ethico-political relations thrive within the realization of activist goals (Jeremy Matthew) and through activist engagements (Nila Kamol Krishnan Gupta and Shamira A. Meghani), helping to keep those bonds real (Ma Mercedes Alba Benitez) and provide a counter to capitalist modes of governance and coercion (Cesare Di Felicantonio; Lipi Begum and Maher Anjum).

Friendship is brought into existence through the construction of an ethics around writing, research and pedagogy that has the potential to disrupt institutional spaces and temporalities (Varsha Chitnis; Sam Bullington; Alok Vaid-Menon; Adkins-Cartee and Bhati). Such 'callings' are at times, pleasurable and at other times, painful, involves transforming intimate selves and others into a productive play of power (Ignacio Rivera) deeply inflected by estrangements around gender and race (Alexis Pauline Gumbs). Indissociable and yet separated, friendship appears as social activism when work is never complete and thus dead, but a living practice, refusing assimilation (Jaime Grant and Jack Harrison-Quintana).

Capitalism, racism, sexism, ableism and ageism, all collude in selling romantic attachment as the scarce and penultimate brass ring of life. This book is a vigorous counterpoint to that fantasy and a fierce claiming of the power of friendship in our lives. Being an outsider to one or most recognized communities of belonging, we have sought belonging, renewal, resonance with fellow 'misfits', the expression of which has revolved around different forms of collaborative work, thought and praxis. This anthology is an outcome of the collective. Our commitment to friendship *as* social activism therefore lies in a gesture towards documenting and writing with and about the unassimilable. What does documenting and writing with and about means? Rather, what does it yield, other than a collection of essays, artwork and poems that make up this volume? Are we (the editors) committed to friendship *as* social activism because we want to offer examples of and possibilities for non-communitarian forms of belonging or are we also *seeking to create* forms of belonging through this process of documenting and writing? Hopefully our anthology is a concrete example of a search for a non-communitarian form of belonging that while acutely aware of the logic of the same in politics of community, is also about asserting such politics without a representational base.

To conclude the brief introduction, a few customary points need to be articulated. First, how is an academic/activist anthology a piece of research? This is because, while academic/activist productions are well recognized within the genre of participatory research, an anthology that emerges through different kinds of writing practices and creative outputs are typically not classified as academic research. More so when we did not restrict the contributors in terms of their writing style and chose to retain the original style as much as possible, rather than polishing or correcting them to fit the needs of an academic readership in general, and an English readership in particular. Many of our contributors do not have English as their first language, and hence the style may not conform to known structures. We have deliberately preserved the overall style of the individual contributors, editing occasionally and only for clarity. We resist the neoliberal metric that measures research success (the REF system in the UK, the tenure system in the USA and the API points system in India). This book attempts to bring together creative practices, activism and academic research in transformative ways which address the role, implication and power of friendship and kinship.

So readers, fellow travellers, friends, acquaintances, lovers; we bring herstories of living, loving, thriving and heartbreaks within our friendship networks. Just as the grass that has no roots is carried away by the wind, and grows wherever it falls. The grass dances in an ever-changing pattern with the rain, thunder, sunshine and drought to create a fresh cover, a design, a kind of mosaic. Grass has no origin, no end, just a milieu, and thrives in the middle of multiple life-worlds. Our friendships, too, have developed amid multiple life-worlds, diverse ecological conditions and each network has bent/broken /re-made our bodies, helping us, enabling/disabling us. Across the universe our life forces fly and thrive. Life after all is an unruly vector, always escaping empires, biopolitical attempts to discipline and regulate our bodies and pleasures. Let us pour our hearts and souls in the following pages. Let us collectively create and experience a mosaic of words; a milieu; a potentially new order of things.

Works Cited

BOSE, Brinda and Subhabrata Bhattacharya. 2007. *Phobic and the Erotic: The Politics of Sexualities in Contemporary India.* London: Seagull Books.

BHASKARAN, S. 2004. *Made in India: Decolonizations, Queer Sexualities, Trans/national Projects.* New York, NY: Palgrave Macmillan.

CHEN, Ching-in, Jai Dulani, Leah Lakshmi Piepzna-Samarasinha (eds). 2011. *The Revolution Starts at Home: Confronting Intimate Violence within Activist Communities.* Cambridge, MA: South End Press.

EKINE, Sokari and Hakima Abbas (eds). 2013. *Queer African Reader.* Dakar: Fahamu Press and Pambazuka Press.

FOUCAULT, Michel. 1981. 'De l'amitié comme mode de vie' [Friendship as a Way of Life], interview in *La Gai Pied* 25 (April): 38–9.

GANDHI, Leela. 2006. *Affective Communities; Anticolonial Thought, Fin-de-siècle Radicalism, and the Politics of Friendship.* Durham, NC: Duke University Press.

HERNANDEZ, Daisy and Bushra Rehman. 2002. *Colonize This! Young Women of Color on Today's Feminism.* Berkley, CA: Seal Press.

JORDAN, June. 2002. *Some of Us Did Not Die: New and Selected Essays of June Jordan.* New York, NY: Basic/Civitas Books.

LORDE, Audre. 2007. *Sister Outsider: Essays and Speeches by Audre Lorde.* Berkley, CA: Crossing Press.

NAGAR, Richa. 2015. *Muddying the Waters: Coauthoring Feminisms Across Scholarship and Activism.* Champaign, IL: Illinois University Press

RICH, Adrienne. 1995. *On Lies, Secrets, and Silence: 1966–1978.* New York, NY: W.W. Norton and Company.

ROACH, Tom. 2012. *Friendship as a Way of Life: Foucault, AIDS, and the Politics of Shared Estrangement.* Albany, NY: SUNY Press.

SHAH, Nayan. 1993. 'Sexuality, Identity, and the Uses of History' in *Lotus of Another Color* (Rakesh Ratti ed.). Boston, MA: Alyson Publications Inc.

SANKAR. 2011. *The Monk as Man: The Unknown Life of Swami Vivekananda.* New Delhi: Penguin.

WU, Judy Tzu-Chun. 2013. *Radicals on the Road: Internationalism, Orientalism, and Feminism During the Vietnam Era.* Stanford, CA: Stanford University Press.

CHAPTER ONE

Friendship, Affect, and Capitalism

KACIANO BARBOSA GADELHA

> A way of life can be shared among individuals of different age, status, and social activity. It can yield intense relations not resembling those that are institutionalized. It seems to me that a way of life can yield a culture and an ethics. To be "gay", I think, is not to identify with the psychological traits and the visible masks of the homosexual but to try to define and develop a way of life (Foucault 1997: 138).

Following Foucault's argument, the question should not be "how to be gay?" but, rather, "how to become gay?" This is a question I put to myself in order to consider even personally the role friendship played to me and how friendship is connected with my experience as a young queer of color researcher. Re-reading this interview blew my mind in many ways. First, it was an interview that Foucault gave to the gay magazine *Le Gai Pied*, founded in 1979 in France, where Foucault expressed skepticism about a gay magazine, considering its existence important and relevant, but also trying to address the limits of the construction of new relationships, and for new ethics. Foucault's rationale about the restriction of the question of homosexuality implies that it is a question of *being* rather than a question of *becoming*. This question for me is very persistent and relevant as my research and personal experience bring me to encounter the limits and struggles of identity politics on a daily basis. I would like to propose a recovery of this idea of "friendship as a way of life" to our contemporary practices; practices not only in the domain of political activism but also in our personal experiences with love, frustration, and pleasure, and how friendship can be articulated with it. Second, I reckon that the diagonal relations can offers us the possibility of recognizing difference in the field of politics than horizontal relations of commonality, "we are all gays," or "we are all women," or vertical relations of power and supremacy, for example, white feminisms x black feminism. With diagonal relations, I would like to direct my view into the breaking of problematic commonalities that tends, at the end, to block companionship, dialogue, or simply assume the tension as something taken-for-granted that could be not overcome, since two groups with different identities can only communicate with each other by reinforcing those differences. I recognize that this is, at times, very problematic especially if you are a queer of color who has to deal with various versions of gay identity that racialize your body and exclude you from some hegemonic representations of the gay identity.

I see myself crossed by many lines, and I cannot ignore that my *ex-is-tence* steps further away from different places of comfort and well-established positions. What is the relevance of friendship when you are always moving from home to home? What does friendship mean beyond the idea that only in the commonality can we understand each other? Is friendship as way of life beyond sisterhood, brotherhood, or other *same*-hoods possible? I would like to share some thoughts with you.

Sharing the (Un)common

While talking about friendship, I intend to question the idea of something linear and coherent about identity: what is supposed to be personal; what belongs to me and does not belong to others; what makes me successful. I'll take another route. In addition, I am not alone. It is not entirely personal but, rather, shared with many other similar lives that I have come to know during these years.

A sequence of *mis*fittings and failures moved me in many ways. The first one was to be a black working-class boy, born and raised in a Brazilian *favela*, till I began studying at the university. I have been raised as someone who was sold the dream that "personal dedication" could change life; education could work for social mobility if you were very clever, that means, it hangs only on your personal efforts, what implies a focus on individual aspects rather than to think about the social structures, or the social constellation in which one lives. By that time, we had to believe in the equality promoted by education. My parents believed that and they made me believe in it as well. Later, when I saw myself being one of the two black students in my first class in the Bachelor in Psychology in Fortaleza, Brazil, I really felt proud of myself, believing in the sold dream of "personal achievement" without asking what happened with my peers, what happened with my friends from Pirambu (the *favela* where I was born): Weren't they as much dedicated as I was? Could they not overcome the similar struggles that I have? So, the success of personal achievement was involved with illusion, and my first failure was to see that the educational system in my country does not work toward inclusion of black people. Moreover, the idea of "personal achievement," of the individual overcoming all challenges to reach the goal, was the best ideology to make up black people trajectories that failed in reaching this goal as the excuse of their lack of effort.

It is very important to enunciate this now, in a text about friendship, because this search for the (*un*)*common* in me and in others has triggered me many times. Firstly, in the difficulty to find my place in various spaces that have opened to me because of my entrance in the academic world. These spaces moved in me the sense of field, a sense that crossed me, my body, my history, that I felt vibrating in my soul but still could not articulate properly. I was aware of being in a battlefield. And what happens when one meets other people that have another history, other battles, and other ways of life? We have an ideal representation of friendship with people sharing similar experiences, the same social background, and an experience of the common. When friends appear showing their difference to each other, this moment is faced as a proof, as the ritual moment in which friendship can survive or not—overcoming differences. I think this is very problematic because we still insist in an imagery that regulates friendship and affective bounds by the principle of the *uno*, the "common": the overcoming of what is *trouble-making* by the disruption of difference.

By that time, I do not remember being too much active. I just felt uncomfortable with what was called the gay scene or LGBT activism in Fortaleza, my home city. I was aware of the people's struggles in

Fortaleza, I just could not find a place in the political discourses and, in a certain way, I was in agreement with Foucault's thoughts on gay identity. I went to the clubs, to the cruising areas, to the prides, and what I saw most of the time was the reflection of a society marked by a strong class division and the heritage of colonial times that makes the gay scene a much more contradictory space to the visibility of Brazilian social wounds. However, I learnt a lot from my friendships from that time, when I came out in the gay scene. I was member of a mIRC channel called #zonagls, and through it I began my virtual contacts with other guys. Although the real spaces of clubs and bars were still visually divided in terms of race, class, sexuality, and gender, online was much more mixed and my friends who promoted this channel were great people who really took care of the bonds that started to form there. I discovered that I was not alone and also how diverse it could all be. One of the best memories I have was to see friends starting the drag performances, what was for me formidable. One of them was thrown out of home when *his* mother discovered he was gay and did drag. He got help from other more experienced drags who were not living in any better conditions, with precarious work and performances in discos which they did much more for the show, for their existence as drags, for money. I remember us sharing a lot of things, my first encounter with sex workers, with friends who did it, with other ways of life and I was just okay with them. They were my friends, my colleagues, we were gays and lesbians, we were active in our affection for each other. Today I know that is activism . . . to run away from home and find someone to take care of you, to be robbed in cruising areas and have a friend come over to save you, to be brave and confront every time people threw their prejudices on sex workers, just because your friend is one and it has opened your mind. Many of the things on drag performance, sex work, and intersexuality, I would not have learnt in an undergraduate degree in Gender Studies, if I had the chance to, but on the streets, clubs, porn cinemas, public bathrooms, and cruising areas. Mostly in places beyond the walls of academia and because of this, I am coming back to connect with these people again.

What keeps the bond of friendship strong and what changes the process of being someone from an identitarian community to the terrain of *becoming other* is the singularity of encounters. I think about it in a very Deleuzian way—that the encounters of two things cannot not be anticipated, there is always a virtuality which is unpredictable and which makes us connect with a certain sense of queerness and opens the space for *short-circuit* relations. Whether these moments can challenge heteronormativity and social structures at a macro level, remains the question. I would like to explain this further by talking about diagonal relations of companionship that made it clear for me how friendship and affection can open the path to other ways of life and resistance. This is possible when the virtual dimension comes up as diagonal relation, when people encounter solidarity by sharing their (un)commonalities.

In 2014, the British film *Pride*, directed by Matthew Warchus and written by Stephen Beresford, recovers one of those historical moments in which an unlikely friendship emerges between two groups that normally would have different political agendas in the UK in the 1980s: on one side, gay and lesbian activists; and on the other, striking miners under the austerity of the Thatcher government. The film recounts, mixing fiction with real events, the history of a group of gays and lesbians activists on the signa LGSM (Lesbian and Gays Support the Miners) that decided to raise money to support the miners' strike in 1984. The group traveled from London to the South of Wales in order to give their support, without knowing if they would be accepted by the group of miners, having to deal with an scenario of alleged homophobia or austerity toward them. The film is quite clear in showing, by that time, the differences between these two groups, and the development of a friendship between both sides in this historical moment, without advocating a total coincidence of their agenda which would point to a clear association between them. A lot has been said— that this union occurred because both groups had common enemies: the Thatcher government's austerity that failed the two groups both in economic terms, and in terms of a moral conservadorism that would have been challenged by LGBT activism.

I would like to distance myself from the common-enemy thesis as the main factor that contributed to the building of their friendship. I argue that the film has enough elements to think about how this happened in a singular fashion, related not only to central aspects of macro politics but also to micro politics of affection and companionship, inasmuch as it shows the internal tensions between the two groups. Not all the miners were in favor of accepting the support of the LGSM; within the LGBT movement there were also doubts and uncertainties about the risk of this alliance. The film actually shows the meeting of some actors in a production of an event. This event reached greater proportions than expected, challenging some assumptions that issues of sexuality and class were split and were represented separately by one group. The assumption that all the miners were heterosexual, or that there was absence of class issues within the LGBT movement would serve for an inaccurate consideration of the film (here the miners would represent the class issues while the LGSM would represent the gender and sexuality issues). This could result in a reductive interpretation of the film, attaching the two groups to an identity dimension without intersectionality. Yet the film can show at times this union of agendas without questioning class issues inherent to the LGBT movement, which are much more strongly accentuated when you think of the context in which the film takes place by the absence of other actors, especially migrants and people of color.

Given these caveats, no longer relevant, the film shows the unusual and extraordinary aspect of this encounter. On the one hand, it portrays a class movement which often excluded issues of race and sexuality from its agenda. On the other, it offers an example to a LGBT movement that still has difficulty with intersectional agendas, when race, sexuality, and nationality cross each other in problematic ways, posing the question of to how to be supportive to others who do not share the same privilege as you, or how to deal with subjects that are not posited yet. For example, some contemporary aspects of LGBT agenda bears a certain assimilationist aspect, reinforcing state policies that often appear linked to anti-migration discussions, given the case of contemporary advance of homonationalism in the Global North. What one might observe in the film points to a micropolitical aspect that involves sympathy and the development of a friendship between actors from both groups, especially between gay men and the wives of the miners, as long as the events are depicted. In those events, the moments of solidarity between miners, lesbian and gay activists became more evident. The LGSM was the group that raised more money to support the striking miners in 1984. In 1985, the Gay Pride in London had the support and the participation of miners, a proof of the unlikely friendship that developed between the members of both groups. Here it is important to consider the significance of this event in the history of labour movement in Britain, in the context of the changes during the Thatcher era. As Diarmaid Kelliher observes, a much more complex picture of this event should be explained, actually in the changes that occured in the 1970s which created the pre-condition for the openness of striking minors for gay and lesbian groups. Firstly, the sense of community shared by both groups, decentering the focus on class to identity politics:

> This approach obscures the importance of solidarities in con-structing relations between places, activists, diverse social groups. This can be 'about the active creation of new ways of relating' . . . LGSM's attempt to create a new way of relating partly relied on an appeal to likeness. While the solidarity of many other groups was based on the common interest of the working-class, LGSM had to take a different approach. By providing an understanding of oppression that highlighted the commonality of experience between mining and lesbian and gay communities, they sought to undermine divisions between class and sexuality-based politics (Kelliher 2014: 248).

With all the problems and criticisms that one can raise against the film, it does not cease to be valuable; the film brings some affirmation of the power of affecting and being affected by others. A power that can be stated for other fights. Thinking about what happened at that time does not cease to be significant when we rethink our forms of actvism today, especially when we face a lot of strategies of exclusionism in some representations of gay and feminist actvisms. With the advance of the neoliberal politics implemented by Thatcher, which weakened the labor movement and gay and lesbian activism not only in the British scenario but also in various countries, part of the Global North is deadlocked over issues of race, class, and ethnicity, especially after 9/11 and the discourse of the war on terror. This makes us reflect today how many of us became impervious to others, to their difference, their power of trouble-making, with few exceptions in the LGBT movement, especially with the advance of various right-wing movements in some countries in contemporary Europe. It would be necessary to review *Pride* as an effective experiment that can be useful to revisit history and examine what has already been done in terms of politics of friendship within the context of LGBTQI activism that can inspire us to revitalize our current strategies. I think that unlikely alliances appear as challenges to contemporary micro and macro political spheres. One would have to go back in the direction of the diagonal relations discussed by Foucault, and to rethink the idea of crossing over, of intercections, such as in Gloria Anzaldua's feminism.

I think what is positive in *Pride* is that it relies on showing an experiment to cross borders, to open connections in areas that could deter the emergence of new forms of friendship as ways of life. For this, I would return to Giorgio Agamben's text that can elucidate what happens when some forms of activism seem to have been crushed or have hit a dead end with neoliberal forms of assimilation. These assimilationist strategies resulted in recovering the differences in a representational model producing pret-a-porter identities in alliance with the demands of the market, and consequently diluting markers that were important for the affirmation of some fights. This aspect became, in my opinion, very clear when, for example, some people argued the class idea as obselete to contemporary struggles. On the contrary, we need to cross borders and be crossed by them—it is necessary to exercise an ethics from the outside.

> In Kantian terms this means that what is in question in this bordering is not a limit (*Schranke*) that knows no exteriority, but a threshold (*Grenze*), that is, a point of contact with an external space that must remain empty. Whatever adds to singularity only an emptiness, only a threshold. Whatever is a singularity plus an empty space, a singularity that is *finite* and, nonetheless, indeterminable according to a concept. But a singularity plus an empty space can only be a pure exteriority, a

pure exposure. *Whatever, in this sense, is the event of an outside. What* is thought in the architranscendental *quodlibet* is, therefore, what is most difficult to think: the absolutely non-thing experience of a pure exteriority. It is important here that the notion of the "outside" is expressed in many European languages by a word that means "at the door" (*fares* in Latin is the door of the house, *thyrathen* in Greek literally means "at the threshold"). The *outside* is not another space that resides beyond a determinate space, but rather, it is the passage, the exteriority that gives it access in a word, it is its face, its *eidos*. The threshold is not, in this sense, another thing with respect to the limit; it is, so to speak, the experience of the limit itself, the experience of *being-within* an *outside*. (Agamben 2007: 74–5)

From the Outside, Many Days and Some Nights

In *The Coming Community* (2007), Agamben points to an ethical, aesthetical, and political review of what is defined as "common." By defining the outside as "external immanent," Agamben reviews the ethical thought in Kant's philosophy. According to Kant, it is unthinkable to affirm a position of subjectivity that is not entered in space and time. Time and space are aprioristic categories that shape thinking, and consequently give the path to the experience of subjectivity. The outside is this exteriority to which the subjectivity extends itself, that outside in which the ethics is the ontological condition as being open to the exterior. The subjectivity is a position in-between, this means, subjectivity can only be defined in ex-tension to space, to the other world. We, as ethical subjects, are always being part of that outside. This ontological condition bears an ethical consequence: we are always at someone else's door.

I would like to conclude my considerations with this metaphor of being at someone else's door as a condition of affection and ethics. When I read Agamben's text for the very first time, I remembered two moments I experienced. The first, when I decided to not come back to my country after finishing my PhD in Germany without any prospect of a new position after receiving my diploma and even refusing some invitations to return. This decision was for me very personal and affective, having to do a lot with the new connections with friends, projects, relationships, and desire; things that I consider really mattering as, for example, the fact of being part in a collective to curate an exhibition (What is Queer Today Is Not Queer Tomorrow). The experience of being in this collective, in working together, in producing this event, bringing local artists from the queer scene that were sharing with us, collaborating with us, and giving their efforts to make this event possible, even if we did not have enough finances to support them, this experience of sharing and collaborating moved me and pushed me to think critically of the demands the academic world puts on young scholars in terms of finding a job quickly and being "productive."

I was in Germany; my parents could no longer support me and the pressure of academic productivity made me sick. I decided to go out again, to go to the streets, to experience, to find new friends, to share new things with them, new affects. From a young scholar with a very good status visa (because the German system of migration has interest in qualified people and I had a proportionate 18-month visa to find a job), I had to face the reality of a common migrant or, to be more precise, a queer migrant. I am qualified but in a minor field, in a problematic field that is queer, gender studies. I do not need to theorize too much about it, just to look around and ask how queer of color scholars have got a professorship in Germany in the last few years. Although, I cannot spend too much time investigating this development . . . I am too busy dealing with other struggles.

I felt like going back to the past, to other spaces, to get in touch with many other queer migrants, most of them from Brazil, who decided to stay here. Artists, students, sex workers, performers, or just gay, lesbian, trans people I met at demonstrations, parties, conferences, exhibitions, sex clubs. From these people I got support for the sadness that affected me every time I got a new letter with a "NO." Among those people I allowed my body to establish new connections, I open my skin and my mind to chemical assemblages: the organic and the inorganic, the prosthetic pleasure invaded me as a new wave of sensations. I was at many doors: at the doors of others looking for pleasure, looking for escape, looking for affect. My skin went beyond my fingernails; my body was extended and diluted in the vibrations of dark rooms, of sweating walls and broken bottles. When the sun came up, it was time to go. In all those moments I experienced another sense of sharing: sharing incommunicable pleasure with strangers, sharing craziness, sharing the bad trip, sharing the precarization of qualified queer migrants of color in the Global North, sharing fierceness and bitchiness . . .This sharing does not invoke a reification of sympathy. On the contrary, this sharing hangs on the capacity of making strange, of trouble-making, of breaking established borders.

Who thinks that activism must be successful in order to be effective? In the queer art of failure (Halberstam 2011), there are many activisms crossing queer lives that just gave up the straight way to *ex-ist*, breaking with the familial order, the success, which has been designed in a very heteronormative fashion. To fail could be sometimes the minor way to resist micro politically the demands of the neoliberal and biopolitical order we face at present. Friendship as way of life could also mean failing together but not by the same mistakes or mis-fittings. Friendship could be to find a "weirdo" recognition and sympathy to other ways of life that bear the potentiality of inverting, shaking and making trouble to our certainties.

Ethics appears when we see ourselves at someone else's door like the character portrayed by Marion Cotillard in *Two Days, One Night* (2014). Directed by brothers Jean-Pierre and Luc Dardenne, this film is the best example of Agamben's metaphor of the door and a crude depiction of a working group that lost the sense of class and solidarity in our time. In the film, Marion plays Sandra, a worker in a factory, who returns to work after being long away due to a depression episode. While she was absent, her coworkers took on her tasks, and now they face a situation in which the factory has promised a 1,000 euro bonus at the expenses of dismissing her. She still has a chance to maintain her job if the coworkers vote in majority to renounce the bonus. She has only one weekend to convince them to support her and give up the money. Then she starts a journey from door to door, calling her colleagues, and facing sometimes the indifference from some of them. In this social film, the Dardenne brothers show a reality of the working class in contemporary Europe that has lost the sense of *class*, being crossed by different lines of segregation. The film does not polarize

Sandra's position as the victim inasmuch as not only everyone has a personal reason to get the bonus. In addition to this, Sandra, as a white Belgian woman (the film is based in Belgium), came to know the reality of other coworkers with a migration background, two of them black, and working extra "illegally" in order to have more money to live and feed their families. There is no friendship in play, and to reclaim solidarity between her and her coworkers involves an ethical problem. The limits of ethics is not be in the position of the other but to be at the door of the other, at the crossing point between me and what is beyond myself, what appears as exteriority in a situation that affects me in a dissonance. One of the most emotional moments in this film occurs when Sandra meets a colleague who is coaching a team. He burst into tears when he saw her and this overacted reaction of solidarity shows the difference of social and cultural backgrounds between them, and how their struggles are in dissonance but it is because of this dissonance that both of them are affected and can support each other.

To sum up, the relation between friendship and activism, in my view, should be a relation of affective dissonance that will make it possible to build other ways of life. Who are most "uncommon" friends now? For what friendship counts when things seem to comfort and sympathy can hide the traps of assimilation.

Works Cited

AGAMBEN, Giorgio. 2007. *The Coming Community* (Michael Hardt trans.). Minneapolis: Minnesota University Press.

FOUCAULT, Michel. 1997. "Friendship as a Way of Life" in Paul Rabinow (ed.), *Ethics, Subjectivity and Truth*. New York: New Press.

HALBERSTAM, Judith. 2011. *The Queer Art of Failure*. New York: Duke University Press.

KELLIHER, Diarmaid. 2014. "Solidarity and Sexuality: Lesbians and Gays Support the Miners 1984-5." *History Workshop Journal* 77 (Spring): 240-62.

CHAPTER TWO

Enqueerying Friendships
Radical Ramblings

PARAMITA BANERJEE

> When we honestly ask ourselves which persons in our lives
> mean the most to us, we often find that it is those who, instead
> of giving advice, solutions, or cures, have chosen rather to
> share our pain and touch our wounds with a warm and tender
> hand. The friend who can be silent with us in a moment of
> despair or confusion, who can stay with us in an hour of grief
> and bereavement, who can tolerate not knowing, not curing,
> not healing and face with us the reality of our powerlessness,
> that is a friend who cares.
>
> Henri J. M. Nouwen, *Out of Solitude: Three Meditations on the
> Christian Life*

It's incredible that more than a year has passed by and I still wake up
every Sunday, thinking about the call that I must make at 10.30 . . . It
still takes me some time to get out of that fuzzy just-awake feeling,
especially since morning is not my time at all, before I remember that
the person to call is no more. One of my best friends, my strongest
anchor for eighteen years of my adult life, a tough time to say the least
and not only because of the transition from middle age to being
'elderly', passed away just like that—exactly as he had wanted to go.
Quietly, by himself, at night. By the time anyone reached him, alerted
by his weekly Man Friday's summons of 'Doctor Saab' not responding
to the doorbells—my friend was already cold to the touch. And no,
my Sunday calls were not a ritual between us, but I'd usually call him

on Sunday mornings if I hadn't spoken to him during the week. His demise threw me so deep into an abyss that I needed to go on medication for acute depression to deal with my near-total dysfunctionality.

So, what was the role of this friend in my life? I am not even sure that I can articulate a communicable answer to that question. I had met him through work connections when I was 38 years old, going through a highly abusive second marriage, which would soon break. The friendship was instantaneous. On the very first day of our meeting, which was incidentally his birthday, our conversations just carried on and on to an extent that my then boss was forced into saying, thinly veiled irritation in his voice, that I needed to be left alone to be able to work—though this man, my newly acquired friend, was the boss' great friend, apparently. I do not know what in me caught his fancy, but he would walk out with me to carry on the conversation even when I stepped out on the balcony for a smoke, though he was a non-smoker. As for me, I was completely mesmerized by his entire personality—his eyes that were piercing even from behind the thick gold-rimmed Gandhi-style glasses that he wore, his erudition, his oh-so-British diction, his somewhat rasping voice and overall—the genuineness of his human warmth.

The adulation and ecstasy, of course, was mutual for that meeting to be cemented into a friendship that would continue literally till death did us apart—but it was NOT an erotic–romantic relationship. It was a friendship that allowed us to accept each other as we are—with all our follies, frailties and failures. There were no expectations, but neither of us would have to think twice to make a demand on each other—however small or great it might be. There were personal stories that we shared only with each other. The empathy was deep enough for us to be able to grieve together when one of us had lost someone special (except, of course, that he had the last nasty laugh in not sharing the grief that I'm still dealing with, post his departure from this world). We had the fiercest of arguments about many things, but that never eroded the deep caring for each other that we shared. And irrespective of how critical we were of each other, how conscious of the vices each one had—a deep sense of mutual loyalty also meant that we would defend the other with ferocity, if someone else was being critical behind the person's back. I can call my friend any names I want, but who the hell is anyone else to do so—that was the unlettered, unuttered understanding.

Let me at least attempt to answer the question stated earlier about his role in my life. The role of friends is difficult to define, since friendship—in my understanding—is the most multi-dimensional and expansive of human relationships. A friend is everything and nothing. Now, why would a friend be considered everything? One might refer to Aristotle in this connection, who has presented one of the most elaborate discussions on friendship in *Nicomachean Ethics*. He argues that: 'Without friends no one would choose to live, though he had all other goods; even rich men and those in possession of office and of dominating power are thought to need friends most of all; for what is the use of such prosperity without the opportunity of beneficence, which is exercised chiefly and in its most laudable form towards friends?'[1] Moving away from the classical, one might also refer to a more contemporary view through Anais Nin, who writes in one of her diary entries in March 1937: 'Each friend represents a world in us, a world possibly not born until they arrive, and it's only by this meeting that a new world is born.'[2]

Nin's assertion is certainly applicable to the friend I've been talking about. Till he arrived in my life, I was unaware of a world where an intellectual-emotional partnership could develop between a bisexual woman and a heterosexual man with no erotic–romantic tensions built into it. I did not know that I could make unthinking demands and behave like a spoilt child; had no idea how much being pampered meant to me. My journey from childhood to adulthood has been one of learning to take responsibility of my own decisions and actions; of being available to kith and kin in crisis; of carrying a chip on my shoulder about changing the world for greater equality and justice. The explicit and implicit norms of a socialization further strengthened by my voluntary enrolment in radical left activism taught me to look at pampering with disdain—it is bourgeois, a sign of decadence. To be soft and vulnerable was a sign of weakness. Just like boys, courageous revolutionaries are not supposed to cry either, which further

strengthened the habit—I learnt this early in life as a naughty, disobe-
dient child—of shrugging off pain and sorrow. To have demands was
to move away from the plain-living-high-thinking lifestyle ingrained
deep in my childhood psyche by academic, left-leaning parents—
which only got further reinforced by the desperate attempts at transcending my petty-bourgeois class location towards a proletarian
lifestyle. So, the charm of being pampered, of making unreasonable
demands and having them met, with a show of irritation that hardly
veiled the warm chuckle that lay behind, of being able to have one's
moments of acute sadness understood in empathy without needing to
utter a single word or shed a single tear—it was a whole new world of
experiences that emerged in my life with the advent of this friend at a
point of time when many face mid-life crisis.

This emphasis on the element of pampering might raise the question as to whether the relationship was one of 'true friendship', if one
goes by the Aristotelian notion of it. He has spoken of three kinds of
friendship: one based on utility; another on pleasure; and the third
one—which, according to him is the 'perfect' one—is based on goodness. Friendship based on utility can only be temporary, argues
Aristotle, for utility is in itself impermanent and time-bound; it
changes with time. Pleasure, too, according to this philosopher, is a
feeling that changes with age and experience, which is why it is mostly
the young who look for friends solely for pleasure—and such friendships break as the feelings of what gives pleasure change.

Aristotle's views on friendship based on goodness offers many
important insights worthy of attention. 'Perfect friendship is the
friendship of men who are good, and alike in virtue, for these wishes
well alike to each other *qua* good, and they are good in themselves.
Now those who wish well to their friends for their sake are most truly
friends, for they do this by reason of their own nature and not incidentally; therefore, their friendships last as long as they are good—
and goodness is an enduring thing.'[3] Keeping aside the issue of the
masculinist bias in his language for the moment, let us concentrate on
what Aristotle is emphasizing here. In stressing the elements of mutual
goodwill among friends where no agenda other than the virtue of
goodwill is important—is he eliminating the elements of utility and

pleasure? Quite on the contrary, he goes on to state that: 'The truest friendship, then, is that of the good . . . for that which is without qualification good or pleasant seems to be lovable and desirable, and for each person that which is good or pleasant to him; and the good man is lovable and desirable to the good man for both these reasons.'[4] There is certainly no denial of the feelings of love and affection involved in friendship, nor of the pleasure that the reciprocity of these feelings generate. He also acknowledges that good men are of use to each other in the material sense also, but that is an incidental quality of real friendship—not the basis of it.

It would be worthwhile to note in this context that Aristotle highlights self-love and unanimity as inseparable ingredients of 'perfect' friendship. 'The bad man does not seem to be amicably disposed even to himself, because there is nothing in him to love; so that if to be thus is the height of wretchedness, we should strain every nerve to avoid wickedness and should endeavour to be good; for so and only so can one either be friendly to oneself or a friend to another.'[5] Referring back to the situation of unreasonable demands and pampering mentioned earlier, it may, then, be argued that these needs arose out of self-love, which is possible only for a good person, and the feeling of pleasure derived was incidental and mutual. Such demands and their fulfilment were reciprocal, but they did not define the friendship. Rather, they could arise because of the nature of the friendship, defined by a feeling of empathy and complete trust in each other, not directed at anything more or less than wanting the other one to be happy. In Aristotle's sense, this quality allowed this friendship to be enduring.

The condition of unanimity laid down by Aristotle seems somewhat more problematic, for we had many disagreements—as already stated—and bitter debates around them. But in retrospect, I realize that there was an agreement of perspectives at a larger level—with reference to a committed belief to the values of equality and social justice, to respecting plurality and differences; a shared sense of responsibility born out of the recognition of the privileges each of us had grown up with; a firm belief that the world can be made a better place to live in than it is currently. True, I was the activist between the two of us— but he had been a staunch supporter psychologically and practically, irrespective of how strongly he criticized many of my endeavours. Constructive criticism that helped me strengthen my logic and egged me on to achieve better results. Maybe this is the kind of unanimity that Aristotle had in mind as a contributing factor to the endurance of friendship between good persons.

Talking about the enduring quality of 'genuine' friendship, I am reminded of other friendships that have stood the test of time, so to say. My school friends, for example. It has been 40 long years almost to the date since we stopped being in school together, but the friendships have continued. Of course, there were variations in the degrees of friendship with different classmates and not all of them were friends. Not all of them are friends even now. Some of us were bosom buddies, so to say, united in everything we did—mischief-making and the norm-breaking. Without quite realizing it, we were transcending gender norms in many ways. Some of that was facilitated by our being in a school where so-called male games like cricket and baseball were available and us best friends were very much into them. But there were also other areas of gender stereotypes that we audaciously broke through. We were a bunch of naughty girls typically called 'tomboys' and many things we did were in the not-done-by-decent-girls list. That bond continues till date and we are still engaged in sharing many moments and activities that 'proper' elderly women with silver strands in their hair are not supposed to be indulging in. We reach out to each other even today, in moments of major crises—emotional or concrete. This is not determined by the others' capacity, especially in situations of practical problems, to take care of the situation—but by the profound inner knowledge that the others will understand and offer the kind of support necessary to calm the mind and console the heart. There is a healing quality in such sharing, for the support offered comes without any agenda attached to it. Flowing out of the goodwill we have towards each other—*a la* Aristotle. We must be good human beings, therefore, to have continued being friends through the trials and tribulations of our lives, irrespective of the very different course each one has chosen and the variations in our lifestyles and priorities. It stands true for our political views and priorities as well. None of these friends have chosen to be a social activist, let alone a queer activist. Changing the world order towards greater social justice and equality is a priority only for me. Of course, I must admit that there is a shared belief in plurality and tolerance, a common loathing against any kind of discriminatory and divisive politics—but that's about it. The news of a child from a red-light area being sexually abused or a lesbian teenager being forced by parents into psychiatric treatment to be 'cured' of her abnormality would have me rush with others to the spot to see what can be done. My friends would just condemn it. Political interference in the field of education would be much more their concern, for that has direct impact on the careers of their children. Yet, these differences in personal political beliefs and choices have not in any way marred the bond that holds us together in joy and sorrow, anger and celebration.

It would be years later that I would confront and acknowledge my bisexuality. Looking back, I would realize that my love and affection for one among our gang of five was more than friendship; there were elements of erotic–romantic feelings that I nurtured for her, which I had not realized back then. Life is not made of what could-have-been; making it pointless, therefore, to speculate on how our lives might shape out to be, had I realized my attraction for her and expressed it to her. But, a feeling of softness continues to linger between us—a reality that I cherish even now. In recent times, when a Bengali film called *Ami ar Amar Girlfriends* (literally, Me and My Girlfriends) was released in 2013, this friend of mine had called me to say that I'm her only girlfriend and she wanted to watch the film with me. A sense of joy and warmth had spread through—almost as if we were back in our school days and she had just expressed reciprocity for the kind of love that I used to feel for her. Had I realized back then the nature of my attraction for her and spelt it out—she might have expressed her reciprocity and our lives might have traversed roads different from how we have lived our lives. But it is equally possible that she might have completely rejected such a declaration and a friendship that has continued for nearly half a century would have died with just that. Neither has happened, however, and the friendship continues with the softness and warmth of what could have been wrapped into it—allowing us even today to tap into each other for emotional and concrete support as and when we need it. Enduring friendship, as Aristotle has maintained, resulting from a feeling of mutual goodwill.

There is a school of thought in sociology and psychology that argues that friendship is felt differently in different stages of life. Around 12, which incidentally is the average age of the onset of puberty for Indian girls, individual friendships are recognized to be part of a larger social network and that perception is carried into adulthood.[6] I had met this set of friends when I was approaching 12, and it is true that similarities in our socioeconomic situations and cultural settings had made it possible for us to be in the same school and become friends. But I must admit that these thoughts were certainly not present back in those days when we became close friends. There were marginal differences in the socioeconomic status of our families, as also the cultural practices within family settings. Where I came from a family of academics, there was one among the five of us who had lost both her parents early in her life and lived with an uncle and aunt; a third one whose father was a drunkard and a debauch (that's how we understood this man back then) and my earliest exposure to domestic violence was through the horror tales we heard from her; my closest friend—closer even than the other four—came from a somewhat lower-middle-class family with her father working as a security guard in a public sector undertaking; and the fifth among us came from the most economically rich setting which would be considered 'Westernized' in many ways. The bonding was determined purely by the cohesion in our common interests and shared personality traits.

In fact, I have an argument with the school of thought stressing that friendships can occur only among people sharing some degree of sameness in socioeconomic status and cultural settings. Graham Allan, for instance, insists that friendship can be viewed as personal and freely entered into—but it is formed in particular social, economic and cultural circumstances, which have significant impact upon the people we meet, and our ability to engage in different activities.[7] My objection does not stem from just the differences as stated above in the life situations of my school friends, which may be considered minor, insofar as they do not affect the class position (in the Marxist sense of the term) that we shared. Rather, my objection stems from my friendship with some women engaged in sex work with whom the only major similarity I share is that of age. Trafficked from poor rural families into prostitution (and I use the term 'prostitution' consciously, since that is how these women describe it) at an age between 12 and 15, they have had none of the privileges that I've grown up with and which largely determine who I am today. Nor can I claim to have any direct experience of what it means to be caught in a situation of being thus betrayed by a father or an uncle or a boyfriend and find oneself in a situation of not just extreme exploitation, but also an occupation that is thoroughly stigmatized in public and self-perception. Despite these differences, some of these women have become friends—entering its fifteenth year this year—taking care of my then rather young daughter on Saturdays when her crèche would remain closed, when I needed to hold sessions with the children of Kalighat, a neighbourhood in the southern part of Calcutta that is identified as one of the oldest red-light areas. They address me by my name rather than as 'didi' (an address for the elder sister, and similar relationships)—ubiquitous in its usage by members of beneficiary communities towards develop-ment personnel, which is how I had met them. Maybe the connection point was being single mothers, I do not know, but I do know that we continue to occupy a special space together where we share personal stories; pay heed to each other's moments of crisis and also have fun together. It is my friendship with these women that has deeply influ-enced my continued connection with DIKSHA, an organization run by the adolescents and youth of the red-light area in Kalighat, many of whom are children of these women. It is this connection that keeps prodding me to look deeper into the issue of the 'prostitution versus sex work' debate and understand the grey areas that challenge the dichotomy of legalization versus rehabilitation; exploitation versus agency. There is enough that these women have shared for me to understand that these binaries are meaningless as the categories are not mutually exclusive. Like most things in life, forced prostitution evolves into conscious sex work over time due to a variety of reasons; what starts in exploitation also help the women gain a sense of agency and autonomy that many women of average families never get a chance to taste. It is my friendship with these women that keeps motivating me to anthologize their narratives in order to problematize the issue that has become so readily divisible into camps in today's prostitution/sex-work discourse.

Talking about my activism, I must refer to my college days, and to my friends thereof. I had joined Presidency College, determined to be a Naxalite (a term used back then for radical leftist politics)—convinced that this college was the venue to access them. This is not the space to discuss the details of that presupposition and its results, but I must refer to the friends I made during this phase. Some of them would help me to carry on my activism by variously supporting the multifarious transitions I was undergoing during that stage of my life. Needless to say, those whom I called friends during this phase all contributed to the 'party fund' through either direct monthly contributions or through buying the party publications, or both. But that's certainly not all. This is also the time when I would leave home, transporting myself overnight from the upwardly mobile middle-class home of my parents to a life in slums. Two of my friends from college would supply me with saris to wear to college and university—saris that I would wear and return without washing them, to receive the next lot that would take care of another two weeks. In a recent conversation, I was stunned to realize that neither of these friends even remembered this help which was so crucial to me during that time. Perhaps the gesture was so natural as friends that it is not something worth remembering for either of them—but it remains etched in my memory because of the enormity of their support in my life at that point of time. I would perhaps not even complete my post-graduation degree if these close friends of mine had not taken it upon themselves to persuade me to sit for the final exam, so disillusioned and distressed I was after being expelled from the radical left political outfit that I was part of, and all because of reasons that I considered extremely patriarchal even then, although my introduction to feminist discourse and movements would happen a couple of years later.

These are friends who have evolved with me. None of them have adopted a queer life, I admit, but they have accepted my bisexuality—which I had myself recognized several years after we had graduated from college and university together—and have made efforts, perhaps solely because of the deep caring they feel for me, to understand non-normative forms of sexuality and gender identities constitute queer politics as well. I derive quite a sense of pride from introducing these friends of mine to my associates from queer-activist spaces, basking in the glory of their acceptance of the different, of the non-normative. Frankly, I feel more accepted in the company of these friends, than at times even in queer spaces—for the simple reason that I have received greater understanding and acceptance from my friends than from many queer spaces that I have been exposed to. Bisexuals are variously labelled as being greedy/opportunistic and/or confused even within queer circles, but these heterosexual friends of mine have not changed their opinion of me after coming to know of my sexual orientation. Not just that, among them is a friend whom I today describe as someone beyond whom I would not look at anyone else, had I known my orientation then. Neither she nor my other friends of this group had felt any reason to either label me anything or sever their connections with me because of my sexual orientation. Moreover, I have confessed my feelings to her, realized in retrospect, but that has not led to any change in how she relates with me. She continues to relate with the same affection and care that she has always done. Even indulges my requests for a meeting over a cup of coffee now and then, without involving the others.

This is exactly why I think friends are nothing. They are nothing because friendship occurs without any particular agenda. It is a bond that defies explanation—but plays a crucial role in offering emotional and practical support and contributes in various ways in cementing one's personal identity. And here, I have a personal position: my personal experiences have taught me to believe that friendship loses its essential quality of unconditional acceptance and support when it changes into a erotic–romantic relationship. There may be elements of romance and eroticism in a friendship—but if the relationship changes into an erotic–romantic relationship, then expectations come in, thereby undermining the quality of agenda-less acceptance and support. A good friend of many years became an abusive husband within just 4 years of conjugality, for example. Another friend with whom I had shared common interests and activism for several years chose to become a stranger when she decided to break our same-sex relationship to enter into one of her several marriages—the friendship that had preceded the relationship was completely forgotten. I have found queer couples, both of whom are my friends, view my relating to any one of them with suspicion—unable to accept that I may perhaps be better friends with one of them.

It is useless to lengthen the list with more illustrations. I would rather conclude on the note that friendship is a deep, fulfilling, reciprocal relationship that exists between two or more people because of reasons often inexplicable. Because of this inexplicability, I have serious questions about Aristotle's emphasis on unanimity and Allan's stress on socioeconomic and cultural sameness as essential elements of friendship. My experiences do not substantiate either of these positions, as mentioned in the context of each friendship talked about in this piece. The concept of difference—as understood in philosophy as a set of qualities/properties/processes that distinguish one entity from another within a relational and/or conceptual framework—is often crucial for friendship. In fact, Aristotle's notion of unanimity becomes meaningful and tenable within the context of friendship not when taken to signify an inevitable unity of experiences, views and reactions—but to denote a meta-level of unity in accepting pluralities and differences, and an agreement to disagree without causing distress/distrust. Viewed from this perspective, Allan's argument about socioeconomic and cultural sameness becomes unsustainable. The strength of friendship lies in the honouring the differences, rather than in the enjoyment of similarities—I would argue. Much like Jacques Derrida's concept of *differance*—simultaneously alluding to both deferring and differentiating, friendship is a kind of bonding that holds within itself a huge world of possibilities since it contains many elements such as affection, care, love, eroticism, understanding, acceptance and so much more. But this quality of friendship—this poignancy of possibilities—gets somehow compromised when the relationship evolves into something else. With the actualization of one or more possibilities, the others die a natural death maybe. Such actualization, therefore, must always be deferred for friendship to continue as a reciprocal celebration of differences that make friendship such a rich human experience.

Notes

1   Aristotle, *Nicomachean Ethics* (William David Ross trans.) (Oxford: Oxford University Press, 1984), pp. 192–247; here, p. 192.

2   See also Anaïs Nin, *Fire: From a Journal of Love* (San Diego: Mariner Books, 1996).

3   Aristotle, *Nicomachean Ethics*, p. 196.

4   Ibid., p. 200.

5   Ibid., pp. 229–30.

6   Ray Pahl, *On Friendship* (Cambridge: Polity, 2000), pp. 99–101.

7   Graham Allan, *Kinship and Friendship in Modern Britain* (Oxford: Oxford University Press, 1996), p. 114.

CHAPTER THREE

A Love Note to OUT! DC
My First Radical Queer Affinity Group

AMELIE ZURN

Dear OUT! DC:

Oppression Under Target, you were my first affinity group of radical queers.

You taught me how to love in a web of resistance and, because of this, my affection for you is deep. You held me as kin and taught me the power of making a revolution with those of you who are in your heart. In you, I found a home, best described as a veritable hot house of possibility and passion. Together, we found mirroring for our lives and validation for our bodies. In this holding, we forged a path to a different world. We took to the streets shouting out desires with our fists held high and delighting in the joy that comes when voices are no longer silenced.

We were a disparate network of lesbians, bisexuals and gay men who formed an affinity group in 1987 until about 1992. Like the growing network of ACT-UP groups we were connected to across the country, OUT! DC was united in our anger at the outrageous neglect of the United States government and general population in the early days of the AIDS epidemic. We wanted health, wellness, and wholeness. We cried out for an end: to AIDS, to the violence against queers, and to the criminalizing of our bodies. Emboldened by our coalitions of radical organizers, we moved quickly to save lives and to spark changes in the healthcare and social support systems that were crumbling around us.

Together, we acted-up while fully aware of our brave ancestors who were civil rights visionaries, peace hippies, radical feminists, women's health activists, butch dykes, and drag queens. We stood there making a scene, forcing a confrontation, speaking out for change, and saving our lives. Justice was our desire and non-violent civil disobedience was our tool. We laid our bodies down in the streets, we disrupted meetings, we attached ourselves to buildings, we tied up traffic, and painted the parade routes red. We did it to save those living and to honor the dead who left us too soon. We did it because "Action = Life" and without it "Silence = Death."

We called ourselves glorious names as we focused our efforts. OUT! DC, aka, "Oppression Under Target" met weekly in Washington DC public libraries and the Washington Peace Center to organize our actions. We birthed smaller groups like the "Safer Sex Sirens" to provide street outreach safer sex education and materials to lesbians and bisexual women. Gender transgressive activists like the "Church Ladies for Choice" came out in drag to confront the anti-woman bigotry of anti-choice champions in power on Capitol Hill. We united gay and anti-violence organizers to create "GLOV: Gays and Lesbians Opposing Violence" together to respond to police brutality, hate-oriented bashings, and interpersonal violence targeting transgender and queer folks.

Arms linked, we stormed Washington, DC with witty chants and fabulous outfits at our rallies, marches, zaps, and takeovers. We had a community-held bullhorn and slogan laden T-shirts to sell to fund our jail/bail funds. We loved agit-prop and we made flyers, press releases, and letters with early versions of PageMaker. We made homemade signs/banners with paint, markers, foam core, and pithy slogans. We used an after-hours "free" copy machine to promote our actions and disseminate our demands.

We were tired but wise radicals, sexy fags, subversive bisexuals, queer feminists, loud-mouthed femmes, and baby dykes. We were federal workers and non-profit junkies. We were monogamous romantics, polemic pluralists, and celibate folks. We were graphic artists, dancers, media strategists, labor organizers, peer counselors, waiters, students, doctors, and lawyers. We blurred gender standards, sexuality norms, and whatever other norm you wanted to find. We talked and processed. We came to consensus, then argued and talked it out some more. By day, we would storm a governmental agency and by night, we would celebrate life together. We ate, danced, drank, and got sober. We kissed, fucked, found peace, traveled miles, and figured it out.

In an era where half the states in the USA still had sodomy laws on the books, a demonstration of queer affection—"read our lips" style—was subversive and shocking. A kiss-in was a defiant act of loving each other and showing the world of our love. We believed that the mere making of our lives visible and without shame might propel forward social justice. We fought: for public displays of homoerotic art, for AIDS services funding, for an end to sex-negative sodomy laws, for the faster release of the experimental drugs which would save our sick, and for our right to choose/self-determine the futures of our bodies. We were up against the growing radical right of the Reagan–Bush eras where old laws were used to terrorize us on the job, blackmail us by outing us to our families, and sabotage our safety in our communities.

OUT! DC, you were so damn sexy. HIV transmission and AIDS had changed all our sex lives. Suddenly, talking about sex was vital to our survival. The haters were clear in the 1980s, they wanted us dead because of our sexualities and gender transgressions. We fought back. We wanted to give out life-saving safe sex information, even if it meant plastering the local buses with condom education ourselves. It was vital to show that our sexualities were not deadly. Therefore, we embodied our demos with kissing, licking, public affection, education, and lots of condoms. Showing off our passion and affection kept us fired up, and brave and were concrete articulations of our love in action.

OUT! DC, you taught me how to shout out loud to startle the world. You taught me follow up my yelling with lists upon lists of concrete demands for lasting change. You held me with compassion when I was confused or unaware or caused hurt or unknowingly furthered oppression. Thus, you taught me how to be a strong ally. My activist self was youthful and evolving when I joined OUT! DC at age 23. I needed you to hold me accountable as I fumbled with words and when I spoke too soon or too little or not well. I did the same for you. Talking across gender, class, race, disability, illness was not always easy, but we hung in there. We found ground with each other to strengthen our web and assist with our collective safety when we were vulnerable out in the broader world.

OUT! DC, you laid in the street with me, so I could trust you with my vulnerable places of unlearning, re-configuring and loving differently. When we were locked to a building, or locked in a building, we took the time to plot, scheme, and dream together. We were predominantly white, middle-class, and educated queer activists in my affinity group. We saw the limits of this web we created. We also believed in the possibility of change and how these changes could lead to lives being saved.

OUT! DC, we may have only had a brief burst of years together. But in each other we found sparks for many of us to commit to life-long efforts toward social justice. We took risks in the street so we could then take risks with our hearts. We saw ourselves reflected in each other and felt our kinship network grow. Meeting activists from other towns as we traveled felt like coming home once more. Our web of connection grew and we saw the whole response to the AIDS epidemic change. We demanded and dreamt of a world where healthcare could be a right for all people. We saw growing vibrant communities where we lived freely because we had agency over our own sexy bodies, our own freaky lives, and our own queer loves.

OUT! DC, you taught me that I could continue to live, process and love fiercely in many other affinity groups in the past 25 years since you happened. I have found other affinity groups who helped me and held me. You taught me how to show up, talk through our differences, and still find a way to pull off an event. I think of our mutual learning as I have collaborated in groups fighting for lesbian health, groping for sexual liberation, clamoring for transgender survival, and envisioning an end to the capitalist white-supremacist patriarchy.

OUT! DC, words cannot thank you enough for the passion you ignited in me. To my beloved OUT! affinity group: Robin, Scott, Tracey, Phil, Linda, Sue, Brian, Rea, Michael, Eve, Mark, Mary, Gerry, Tammy, Monte, Liz, Dewey, Jarmila, Joanne, Kristen, Anne, Wendy, Tom, Urvashi, Robert, Cheryl—I bow deeply with gratitude and with my fist up high in the air for you, my comrades.

rwethereyet
A Conversation

AJAMU, JANE STANDING AND MARAI LARASI

'rwethereyet' is the title of a 235-mile, 20-day fundraising walk undertaken by Ajamu and Jane Standing in 2012. They set out from the development site of the Black Cultural Archives, Brixton, London, on Monday, 27 August 2012, and reached their destination, Hudawi Caribbean Centre, Huddersfield, on Saturday, 15 September 2012, for a celebration with Valerie Cockburn, Ajamu's mother, both their families and friends, and a wonderful meal together. Five different teams of people moved Daisy, the campervan, from London to Huddersfield, from one campsite to another, night after night; erected tents, shopped, prepared meals and provided moral support to the two walkers, who were friends, colleagues and directors of small, but remarkable NGOs at the time.

The project drew upon a long tradition of black and minority ethnic groups, women, queer and working-class people walking for causes, and organizing landmark events to raise social and cultural concerns which placed the body at the heart of practical politics;[1] in the words of Bayard Rustin: 'our bodies are the only weapons we have'. The idea emerged from endless conversations between Ajamu and Jane on early-morning walks in Brockwell Park, Brixton, near where they both live. The project was about voluntary and community organizing and the importance of innovation in identity-based activism. It was about overriding the complex frustrations that can trip you up if you try for the aspirational, the celebratory, or the ordinary route in this field that favours attention to the discriminatory and the oppressive.

The walk was made possible by the intricate workings of many supportive relationships and a 'thing' between two people. In January 2015, the wonderful Marai Larasi[2] spoke to Ajamu and Jane in London, to get closer to what the 'thing' might be. Excerpts from this conversation are reproduced here.

AJAMU. On an early-morning walk in the park, a regular routine, I said to Jane, 'If the Guildhall Art Gallery accepts my "Fierce" photographic exhibition,[3] I will walk to Huddersfield to give my mum her invitation.' When Jane said, 'We can do that.' I knew then, that very moment, that my instinctive desire to connect the celebration with Mum would become a reality—we could do it.

JANE. Ajamu and I have this joke about a rugby ball. One of us throws out an idea—sometimes we throw it straight back, sometimes we hold it for a bit and sometimes we just run with it. That day, that idea, felt instinctively right. Those walks in the park, those talks, really helped me through the last five years that I worked at Centred.[4] I can see why causes lead to walks; it is partly about going somewhere, but also about discharging something that is built up and pent up. It requires a physical movement, not just a verbal response—especially when it feels like the arguments don't work any more.

MARAI. You have this 'thing', you have those relationships in life—not like there is no hard work involved, in fact there's a lot—but it just works for both of you.

AJAMU. We have a thing, honey—there is the northernness[5]—that's a thing. Sometimes that's a bridge that gets us through other things, just the ways we communicate. People miss that because our primary relationships tend to be formed around race and gender. The northernness is the primary bond—and I think that's more so the connection, out of all our identities. I also couldn't imagine anyone else that I would walk with. That's something because in terms of this area of work, LGBT work, this doesn't happen—this kind of relationship doesn't happen. People cannot work us out— Jane Standing, white woman, bald head. Ajamu, beard, Muslim-looking. Why would they connect? The sector doesn't seem to allow us to connect because it is in silos on one level. Many of the relationships are built around the work and this was built around the work and something else.

JANE. It felt natural that it would be us walking. It felt instinctive that we couldn't complicate it any more from where it started. We needed everybody else we knew to make it practically possible. It took a lot, getting the group of people to help all along the route— and that was all we could do. People went out of their comfort zones to make it happen—and that's to do with the relationships that had existed before.

MARAI. There's also the whole thing quite literally of going home to Mum—handing her this thing—you two together. I am quite interested in this idea. You had the idea Ajamu in your head, then Jane took it up, and this is the person that you walked with. How you both created this, the infrastructure it took, and the relationship.

———

FIGURE 4.1 rwethereyet promotional poster, 2012.

AJAMU. There was one day, maybe three quarters of the way, we had walked about 180 miles and I had a major wobble. I was shattered, and had to say to myself that today I just have to walk for myself, Ajamu. Until that day the walk was about Fierce, about Centred, about raising the issues. If I had got to a point and decided I wasn't gonna walk any further, I would have let myself down, first and foremost. Then there was my sense of self and all these other things going on around the process. But then the wobble had to happen too. I was just done. I re-adjusted—just Ajamu being Ajamu.

JANE. There was a wobble moment for me earlier, maybe in May—when I thought I just couldn't do it—the amount of planning and work in it. It was at the moment of booking Daisy, the campervan. I remember the conversation—I was digging for where you were with it. There was no sign of an ounce of doubt in you, and I knew that I just needed to do it. It was like a leg up—'Come on, we can do it.' I was thinking about our difference just now—listening to you about what made it happen, I feel like I was practically capable of doing rwethereyet, and you were emotionally capable.

––––––––

JANE. I did the map reading.[6] We had a whole, humour thing around that—stereotypes shouldn't really be repeated here—but the day before the last day of the walk, we got lost. I had been saying that for about an hour, looking for markers. It was getting dark, we still had about 7 miles to go. I was explaining all the options, how we got there—my confusions. This look came over Ajamu's face, a kind of 'what are you even telling me all this stuff for'. I knew you were nervous because I was, and we had already been on some terrain that day—it was difficult, not the usual, quite off the path, but what came out of his mouth was, 'I trust you, I trust your process.' So I went back to planning the route ahead, looked for the options and alternative as I understood them—because me laying out the options was more of an under-confidence thing—because we hadn't navigated by negotiation before. At that point, it was really serious and I said: Well, I think we should go this way, and all Ajamu said was OK. Basically saying, 'I will walk with you, I trust your process', and not 'Are you sure? Let's talk it through.' We did about 5 more miles, on the road, in the dark, but we did it.

MARAI. I am interested in trust as the foundation of this. It feels like the whole theme—you know, you say this thing, and Jane goes 'OK,' it's the random nature of it. Even the random nature of how the thing travels feels like it is rooted in trust. Symbolically, if I think about the two of you on that journey, everything from biology and gender, body, identity—you a white woman, you a black man, you know just all of these things . . . I want to hear more about trust.

AJAMU. I think the trust thing is about when you feel out of your comfort zone and you have somebody saying, 'Actually you can do this thing.' I think with lots of the work around LGBT, you do need people to say, 'Yes you can do it'—affirming, because for some of the ways we engage, I would argue there are very fixed ways about how things could and should work.

MARAI. I get it, there is something intimate there . . . that thing you describe, like 'I can't do this'—that day—or like on the moors, getting lost, and saying to Jane 'I trust you' . . . there was a huge amount of intimacy. And that day: 'Today I'm gonna walk for myself.'

AJAMU. Yes, and some kind of ability to let go because in that moment, it is about letting go of my own ideas around masculinity and gender as well, while part of my work is about challenging it. In that moment it was also about letting go of more of that stuff . . . Actually, I think politics should be intimate.

MARAI. There needed to be huge intimacy to allow you to have that vulnerability and accept it. There are other things you said, and you just nodded—the thing around learnt masculinity. There's acceptance of non-conformity, that's one thing, but then another thing of saying, 'I'm not going to do that'—this is another way of having the conversation that is really about how gender should play out. This is a very elevated involved space, and there is always another level of excavation going on. These things speak to me, without going, you know, let's have a conversation about race and gender. That idea of going 'I trust your process,' so, 'I am socialized as a man, and although my very existence says that's fine, I still have residual access to the normative performance of masculinity, I still have to deal with myself.' As a reader, the potential for that to travel, that one message, around a gender narrative, is really powerful.

———

JANE. I was going to talk about Grim's Dyke too because the first night of the walk we stayed in a hotel in one twin-room, which we had never done before. We didn't have Daisy until the second night. My niece and sister picked it up, drove it down from the lakes, 350 miles, picked up all our stuff in Brixton, and then drove to the first campsite for Night Two. So that first day we walked across London with all our stuff. We got a posh hotel really cheap—and shared a room. We'd never done that before but it just didn't feel like an issue.

MARAI. You know you two—only you two!

JANE. I said to Ajamu: Look you know we have no budget, so it's one room. We worked out campsites, food, petrol, for the whole thing, we funded it all ourselves and everybody who supported the route—if they had money they spent on us, if they didn't we spent on them—we didn't think we could make any charitable ask for the trip itself, because we needed to save the asking for the walk. In some ways, I felt the walk was as much for me as for Centred so I didn't feel the organization should commit anything.

MARAI. So you decided to move in together for the night—you two are hilarious! (*Laughs*)

JANE. And I don't think we really thought that through. (*Laughs*)

AJAMU. No! (*Laughs*)

JANE. Anyway, we said we wouldn't do it again, didn't we?

AJAMU. Ha ha . . . yes.

MARAI. So within the context of intimacy: was that a . . . step too far? Sharing rooms?

JANE. No, I think the interesting thing is that in terms of intimacy it didn't feel it was a step too far—it felt right. It's just that Ajamu snores.

———

AJAMU. We have been on a very long journey, so this is an extension of that dialogue that we have been having for years around our work, our differences, our practices, and we don't fall out.

FIGURE 4.2 Jane and Ajamu, rwethereyet 2012

JANE. Well, Ajamu doesn't fall out, I fall out on my own—not very often. One time, something came up for me about what we posted online. We had the 'rwethereyet' Tumblr site and every morning we both recorded a little snippet for it. You know that phrase 'one, one coco full basket',[7] well some donations had been coming in, and Ajamu put that phrase on his own Twitter feed. I wanted to put it on the rwethereyet site and feed, which was a joint feed, and he didn't want to. I felt excluded, I wanted to feel part of something, and felt I was on the outside. It doesn't sound like much now, but I was seething because I didn't understand. I understood later—a few hours walking and seething later—that it was about appropriation. At the time, I just wanted it . . . He was really clear he didn't want to use it on the site.

AJAMU. I don't remember that at all.

MARAI. Meanwhile Ajamu's like, 'I've moved on,'—he's thinking, 'That's your business, because guess what, honey? That's not mine.'

FIGURE 4.3 Ajamu and Jane with Teya, 2012.

MARAI. Just that thing about the batting back and forth of the idea, you know, the ball getting thrown—picked up—that requires a degree of synergy and trust. Then the thing you said about you being practically able to do the thing, and Ajamu being emotionally able to do the thing, and when and how you had your wobbles, all of those things. You can't step away from who you both are symbolically in that space—it would be a bit like doing queer studies and not talking about race.

AJAMU. Really, I think for me part of it is about how do you create, how does your politic work in action—what else is going on?

MARAI. Yes, you mean what other excavation is required of me in that moment, that dynamic? In that moment, it can be about who I am, and how that can show up, and be present in the politics—can I live and work it?

————————

MARAI. There are so many dimensions to this story—I love the ideas you mention about trust and the strength of the friendship, and how that held conflicts that came up on the walk. Like the thing about 'one, one coco full basket', and the 'trusting your process'. You could write a whole paper just on what you saw of humanity on that trip.

JANE. Yes, there was plenty of humanity—the good, bad and ugly, racism, heterosexism, and the random acts of kindness, though these were mostly from friends and family! It was really obvious that when we told people on the route what we were fundraising for, they just didn't get it and we weren't immediately welcome in many spaces. Local press would have picked it up a lot more if we were walking for a more mainstream cause. One local LGBT paper picked up the lead, despite all local press along the route being contacted. To be fair, the company that hired out Daisy gave a good discount, and even a couple of campsites, if you said the walk was 'for charity'. But when you said what, a grey confused look would come over peoples' faces. Brands like Paul Smith and Barbour have no idea what Ajamu could do for their business . . . we approached them all!

AJAMU. And Muji! We were on a deserted path one day and saw these guys with a van—they were just staring, quite threatening. When we got a bit further away I made Jane laugh, which resulted in a brief video recording: 'So we just passed these two whites, just staring at us, so I says to them, "What's up, have you never seen a Muji raincoat before?"' (*Laughs*) Humour is important in making the connection.

JANE. We walked into this pub one day—Ajamu was in front of me— what do you go into a pub for?—A drink. The manager walked fast straight over to the door and said 'Can I help you?'—'Well, this is a pub, I am after an orange juice.'

AJAMU. Yes, we went somewhere else. Often we just walked on, hungry —like that bikers' rally we came across. I mean, I like leather, but not that kind. It was scary: bikes, Confederate flags, people just staring. We only wanted to charge our phones and have a bite to eat.

JANE. And the Help the Heroes convention in Northampton with Ingrid.[8] Combats, massive super trucks, dogs, all white (not the dogs)—that was surreal too.

––––––––

MARAI. I have to say this to both of you: we still have those rwethereyet postcards at work. They sit on that pane of glass in the meeting room, and there is still one on the wall when you come in the building, and it's really interesting having it there and keeping it there because it gives a symbolic importance to it. You two were there doing this thing—your random thing, and it was all about funding, sector, race, sexuality and one of the things is how that can then travel in different ways—what your amazing act then provided as an emotional and psychic place of connection. You know something around how in this country black people have no physical monuments, where you can go, and in lots of ways that's also true across LGBTQI—I know both of you value the importance of archiving—just having the postcard there in that place, for me, that does it. A monument, in a space where, in a difficult conversation, it is this very gentle, loaded thing. You know this postcard is funny and quirky and easy and accessible—but containing really tough stuff—I wanted to just say that. I look at it every single time I enter the building, which is really interesting, so you two are there, up in Imkaan[9]—you in this women-only space, and you with a white face. Honestly, both of you, getting in there, sitting up there in Imkaan, hilarious.

AJAMU. That's how we roll, honey . . .

JANE. One of the things we do—not just on the walk but all the time: I'll be doing a thing, looking at a gender thing as I see it, then you'll take it and do a thing, where you say, 'Yes, but this is a race thing.' Sometimes the other way around, then there's a gay thing we both are trying to do but also both aren't the same—then we'll say, 'Yes, but we neither of us is a Black Lesbian are we? So, we don't know do we?' Imkaan is a strong reference point for us, how personally, organizationally you think about things.

MARAI. I guess as one of the people who was there kind of doing the 'yayyyy', about this walk, it meant something. Symbolically something happened for us—the fact that it was this random thing, and the fact that you did say that you would give your mother the invitation. Then standing over here; to actually know that that journey would happen—and in the way that it did. There are a whole lot of words I might use for both of you, but you bring such integrity—and for many of us, but speaking for myself, political integrity, as in the everyday living of your politics. That's what that journey felt like it meant to me, that random; and it was hilarious and playful too, with people saying 'Hey?', but then the thing about it making perfect sense at the same time.

JANE. Centred's infrastructure allowed an awful lot of it to happen too, with the postcard, David's[10] amazing creativity, the technology, everything, doing the work while we prepared for and did the walk, we couldn't have done it without that: Tim[11] updating the map—every night—every night loading photographs and messages, mapping our route on the site.

MARAI. He's a star. And talking about fan base, there was this moment when I was talking to Tim on the phone, during the walk. He said, 'Diana King's following us,' and he was just like—(laughs)— 'Ahhhhhhhhhhhh!!!!' We were both so excited. It was indeed a great place of making connections. Who he is, who I am? And Diana King? We had this whole different fan base—retweets going out to loads of people.

AJAMU. I think there is really something about bringing different sets of people together, who otherwise might never connect with each other—so creating these other kinds of spaces where people crisscross. Like Antoine and Hakeem coming for three days,[12] and me watching Blaxploitation films with them on a day off, in Daisy. I just needed that. I hadn't connected with Hakeem in that way before.

JANE. Antoine singing 'Wading in the Water' at Thong . . . tha . . . thong . . . thong Thongbridge; Anjum and Dipti trying to squeeze a blow-up mattress the size of a house into a small tent, with Teya shouting, 'Catty, be careful with Catty'.[13]

AJAMU. Lisa[14] driving Daisy when she hadn't driven for ages, and definitely not a van, all through Leicester town centre on her own. Ingrid being Ingrid and the three of us staying at my niece, Nicole's house.[15]

JANE. David, behind us all the way, coming to meet us at the end, giving so much time.

AJAMU. Joan[16] and Tim coming to meet us half-way across London on the first day, your sister Lyn and Emily[17] cooking spaghetti, and David and Lisa seeing us off in Brixton! Every single day we knew somebody would be making us a warm meal at some random unknown campsite. And the random phone calls—people just cheering us on. Your guest post on the website, Marai—amazing!

MARAI. There is also something about the claiming or constant claiming? So doing that journey at a time when you have social media, when you connect a whole set of people into that conversation, at speed, internationally, who might not otherwise engage in that conversation. Why are they doing this? Who are these people? A daily

FIGURE 4.4 The welcome party, rwethereyet 2012.

conversation. Why does this matter? What is this conversation about equality? It was beautiful in terms of being able to observe. Social media built an inclusion or place of connection that couldn't have happened in the same way just 10 or 15 years ago. That creates a whole other thing about who family is as well, who gets invested in the journey.

JANE. One day we were looking across and down the valley at Antoine, miles away in the campsite. It was the morning we talked about jetsetting round the world at conferences talking about the walk and the issues, the process, complexities, the daily challenges. Like running away from cows and you with the killer-sheep fantasies. We talked about how we would write papers, present at conferences and share videos (*laughs*). We had a big megalomania moment on that hillside. Now I think it just mirrored the magnanimity of the experience inside. Those were the days when we would think: for this view alone it has been worth the work and effort.

MARAI. We've reached the top of the mountain. Mad as shad!

AJAMU. Mad as shad. What's 'shad' by the way?

MARAI. A fish with really small bones, like herring. There was a period when it was common, mostly in brine, really lovely, with ackee, but really bony. Two shad tied round your head—you very mad people—love you.

AJAMU. I have never known what it is—except from mad as shad.

MARAI. Quirky and zany, mad as shad—you see it and work with it.

AJAMU. That's the energy.

MARAI. Listen to me, if you think about anything else—no walking across Jamaica.

AJAMU. That would be awesome, wouldn't it? You remember working out a 240-mile route across Jamaica, Jane?

MARAI. That would be a whole other thing, #justsaying. You could take coastal roads for some of it. There are the mountain ranges, you would have a fair bit of main road, like that stretch to Negril.

AJAMU. That would be awesome.

JANE. Yes, it would.

AJAMU. I know, Jane—I have the ball—anyway, universe . . .

MARAI. rwethereyet?

Notes

1   'Practical politics' alludes to activism, engaging in politics in an applied way. For the authors, this has been about working in organizations that by their very existence challenge infrastructure that has otherwise been established to facilitate voluntary action.

2   Marai Larasi is director of leading UK-based black feminist organization Imkaan which is dedicated to ending violence against women and girls. She was asked to facilitate a conversation because of her extensive academic, activist and political credentials; she is also a great and supportive friend to Ajamu and Jane Standing.

3   Fierce' is a body of photographic work by Ajamu featuring young Black LGBTQ people which opened at the Guildhall Art Gallery in February 2013.

4   Centred is a community-based organization in London, run entirely by and for diverse lesbian, gay, bisexual, trans and queer people

5   Ajamu belongs to Huddersfield and Jane is from Chester, the north of England.

6   'Map reading' entailed daily route planning, months in advance before we set off (with the help of Ingrid Pollard); repeated revised route planning in the weeks before, to link the walk directly to campsites and projects; nightly route planning for each subsequent day during the walk; and orienteering each day. Other than the first 8 miles, neither of us had walked any of the route before and we largely stayed off roads, following public footpaths through open fields, woods and along canals and rivers.

7   Refers to a Jamaican proverb meaning, 'success is not achieved overnight.'

8   Ingrid Pollard, artist, photographer and a friend of Ajamu and Jane.

9   A UK-based black feminist organization: www.imkaan.org.uk

10   David Spence is the current CEO of Centred, he was the innovations director at the time of the walk.

11   Tim Aldcroft is the programme and volunteer manager at Centred.

12   Dr Antoine Rogers is the co-chair of Centred, academic and great friend. Hakeem Kazeem is a writer, cultural producer, great friend.

13   Dipti, Anjum and Teya Ruby Mouj are a family, two mums and their daughter, and great friends; Catty is a cuddly toy.

14   Lisa Lynch is Jane's partner.

15   Nicole Coby, Ajamu's niece, who is a great host.

16   Joan Neary, ex-staff member at Centred and a dear friend.

17   Lyn Standing and Emily Hewitt, Jane's sister and niece, both of them supported Ajamu and Jane through the journey.

CHAPTER FIVE

Kinship, Friendship and Researching Queer Digital Media in India

ROHIT K. DASGUPTA

In this short chapter I reflect on the various ways through which friendship and kinship became useful methodological tools for doing research on the queer community in eastern India.[1] Gordon Brent Ingram, Anne-Marie Bouthillette and Yolanda Retter have defined a queer community as a 'full collection or select subset of queer networks for a particular territory, with relatively stable relationships that enhance interdependence, mutual support and protection' (Ingram, Bouthillette and Retter 1997: 449). This interdependence and support is predicated on the interaction, solidarity and affirmation of queer men and women who position themselves and their presence within an allied commonality. As I have argued elsewhere (Dasgupta 2014), this community is far more stratified, concealing certain tensions that provide an illusory perception of an 'imagined' community. Scholars such as Paul Boyce (2014), working on subaltern sexual categories in India, have often commented that the queer community (mostly gay and male) excludes trans, female and bisexual people.

The engagement of queer men in India using the Internet displays a remarkable shift in the ways in which one understands social expression within the public and private spheres. The Internet, as I have explained elsewhere (Dasgupta 2015), is used by queer men for purposes of intimacy, support and social networking as well as offering new opportunities for political and social actions. The Indian queer community has only recently started to mediate their lives through the digital fora, unlike the West. However, the history of digital networking and development in India almost parallels the growth of new queer media. From the use of the early listservs to the proliferation of mobile apps such as Grindr is a long story of the 'virtual' lives of queer men in India. While contemporary Indian society continues to normalize and privilege heteronormativity/heteropatriarchy, there have been subtle changes both on the social and political levels which have led to improvements in civil rights of the LGBT people. The historic judgement of 2 July 2009 when the Delhi High Court proudly struck off the antiquated Section 377, thus decriminalizing homosexuality, remains a milestone in the narrative of queer India. While legal and social recognition are entirely different, it cannot be discounted that the 2009 judgement had an impact on the ways in which gay/queer men in India have renegotiated their lifestyle. The growth of queer parties and social spaces (such as Pink Kolkata Party) as well as the burgeoning queer representation in Indian cinema and television (Datta, Bakshi and Dasgupta 2015) are cases in point. Of course, most recently in 2013, the Supreme Court has overturned the High Court's historic judgement leading to the backtracking of queer recognition and rights.

A simplistic linear explanation of the birth of the cyberqueer in India, borrowing Nina Wakeford's term, would be to attribute it to globalization and economic liberalization in the 90s followed by media representations of queer people, leading to queer consciousness and backlash, then queer activism; and finally the move to the digital sphere. While this might seem the most logical explanation, it does not succinctly capture the nuances and circumstances which led to its mass proliferation. When the Internet emerged in India, the first few people to sign up were educated, of certain economic means and English-speaking. This ready constituency of gay/queer men were the first to make the leap into the digital sphere. Spurred on by the creation of transnational/diasporic web pages and listservs, for South Asian queers living abroad, it also found a ready home among the queer people back home. This potential of digital culture was noted early on by the activists and community organizations and led to the creation of a series of activist and organizational listservs and, of course, the now-famous *Gay Bombay* (2008). There was also a thriving queer/gay populace in the major metropolitan cities: New Delhi, Mumbai and Calcutta. There was thus a considerably significant (even if small) community of queer people in these cities who were ready to make use of the Internet for meeting other queer people, disseminating information and advocacy.

The role of the English media despite its class bias played an important role in enabling the queer to emerge out of the closet, even though over the last few years there has been a remarkable growth in regional-media reporting on queer issues. The virtual lives of Indian queer men are not so much to do with their negotiation with digital technologies but, rather, the ways in which they have managed to negotiate their lives and identities, and forged their existence within a largely heterosexual/patriarchal mainstream society. As Sara Ahmed writes, inhabiting and leading queer lives is a matter of everyday negotiation:

This is not about the romance of being offline or the joy of radical politics (though it can be), but rather the everyday work of dealing with the perception of others, with the 'straightening devices' and the violence that might follow when such perceptions congeal into social forms (Ahmed 2004: 107).

The public visibility of the queer community in India has grown exponentially in the last decade with queer prides in almost all the major metropolises (Bangalore, New Delhi, Mumbai and Calcutta) and smaller cities such as Bhubaneswar and Madurai. This however should not be seen as some form of tacit endorsement/acceptance. We must also remember that queer struggles in India are far from being intersectional. Issues such as class and caste are especially compelling within the 'Indian context'. As Arvind Narrain and Gautam Bhan remarked in their landmark anthology *Because I Have a Voice*:

Perhaps the most relentless construct which assaults queer people is the conceptualisation of their lives as the preoccupations of a small, Western educated, and elite minority, whose understanding of sexuality is thus aped from the West (Narrain and Bhan 2005: 15).

While the West undoubtedly informs certain aspects of the discourses on sexuality, being queer in India is also constituted within local discourses that go beyond the Western framework of identity —kothi, hijra, launda and other. During the course of this fieldwork, I was also introduced to several other examples that have gained currency within digital and local contexts (terms such as 'gayboy', 'rituparno', etc.).

When I started my research on queer digital cultures in India, I was extremely optimistic about the non-exclusionary politics that queer spaces online would afford its users but was far from surprised to see that the same hierarchies and exclusionary mechanisms had been carried over from their physical counterpart. Kate O'Riordan has criticized this essentialist account of the disembodied figure of the cyberqueer, arguing instead that it is a destructive force that potentially evacuates power from accounts of identity (2007). Queer spaces in India suffer from several biases and segregation politics which reflect the gendered and classed nature of Indian society. Kothis are largely missing from the Internet discourse both because of language constraints, and the urban and class biases, that underscore these spaces.

The various examples of queer digital cultures that my research explored are the responses from the community. Whether they are queering mainstream spaces (through active presence and participation) like Facebook, establishing user profiles on Planet Romeo, accessing Grindr from their family room, or using these spaces to mobilize people for protests—they are taking part in the process of visibility and representational politics.[2] An issue that undergirds all of this is kinship. Kinship refers to a form of lived relationality extending from the heterosexual family to their children. As Elizabeth Freeman has argued, kinship also matters to non-heterosexual people who might not fit the dyadic model of family structures so prevalent within heteronormative societies whose emotional, financial and domestic patterns exceed the patterns dictated by marriage and reproduction (2007). In a gay/queer digital culture that is so preoccupied with sex, kinship might seem slightly out of place, especially following Leo Bersani's line of argument that sex defamiliarizes and estranges and, ultimately, does not lead to any form of meaningful exchange between the two subjects (1988).

This line of argument that sex negates any social value and that erotic activity (not necessarily the physical act of sex) does not provide a form of community and kinship is incorrect. This was something that most of my research participants critiqued and instead explained how intimate encounters[3] opened up a larger kinship and friendship network. Kinship according to my participants is almost synonymous with friendship but seen as a more intimate gesture, one that is inscribed within relationality. This relationality can be read as a reworking and revision of the social organization of friendship, sexual contacts, and community to produce non-state-centred forms of support and alliance (Butler 2002).

One of the posts which first spurred me to start thinking about virtual intimacies (McGlotten 2013) was on the 'Queer Campus' Facebook group about a friend's coming out, which I observed and participated in.

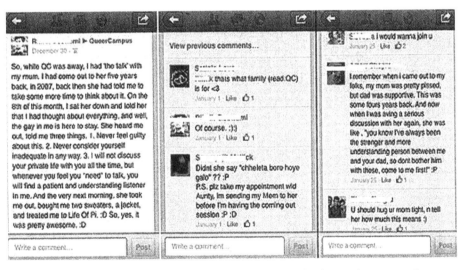

FIGURE 5.1 Rik's coming out story on Queer Campus Facebook page (last accessed on 20 December 2013).

Queer Campus (QC) is a Facebook group that was set up in 2010, specifically as a student and youth collective and is active in New Delhi, Bangalore and Pune. When I read the coming-out post on QC, I decided to interview Rik. And he had written:

So, while QC was away, I had 'the talk' with my mum. I had come out to her five years back, in 2007, back then she had told me to take some more time to think about it. On the 8th of this month, I sat her down and told her that I had thought about everything, and well, the gay in me is here to stay. She heard me out, told me three things. (1) Never feel guilty about this. (2) Never consider yourself inadequate in any way. (3) I will not discuss your private life with you all the time, but whenever you feel you *need* to talk, you will find a patient and understanding listener in me. And the very next morning, she took me out, bought me two sweaters, a jacket, and treated me to *Life Of Pi* :D So, yes, it was pretty awesome :D (30 December 2012).

All the comments were congratulatory and Rik thanked everyone on the forum for supporting him through this. Rik's coming out to his mother which he described on the group's page was eventful and a way for him to celebrate his acceptance from his family. He was using the forum to share the experience with them. In doing so, he was participating in a friendship–kinship and acknowledging the role they played in his decision and was now using his experience to support and urge others to do the same. As two other members replied:

- Thats what family [QC] is for <3 (1 January 2013).

- Didnt she say "chheleta boro hoye galo" [literally, 'my son has grown up']?? :P P.S. plz take my appointment wid Aunty, im sending my Mom to her before I'm having the coming out session (1 January 2013).

Rik's story encouraged other members to also talk about their own coming-out experience and share their concerns and insecurities over it. Another user replied:

I remember when I came out to my folks, my mom was pretty pissed, but dad was supportive. This was some four years back. And now when I was having a serious discussion with her again, she was like, "you know I've always been the stronger and more understanding person between me and your dad, so dont bother him with these, come to me first! (25 January 2013).

This allowed a larger discussion to take place around support that the group could give to each other through this process. These responses are symptomatic of the intimate nature of the queer spaces and the ways in which digital media can help create virtual webs of friendship and companionship. After all, as Adi Kunstman has pointed out: 'digital culture in itself can be a site of investment of feelings' (2012: 6). The investment of feelings allow for the formation of intimate chains of words, emoticons, screen-body interactions as the members of QC exemplify.

Friendship has a very rich affective life within the Indian imaginary. From Hindi films espousing the role of *dosti* or *dostana* (friendship), an important trope in Bollywood narratives even at the expense of heterosexual love, to the Bengali concept of *adda*. *Adda* is literally the practice of friends gathering together on a recurrent basis, for extended informal conversations (Chakrabarty 1999). The concept of *adda* exists within other Indian cultures, but it is an indispensable and essential characteristic of the Bengali male. Although *adda* in itself does not have a gendered connotation, Dipesh Chakrabarty notes that even as recently as 1960 it was uncommon to see women participating in *adda* with men and this remains so.

As a Bengali male, friendship was thus an effective point of entry into the lives of my research participants. Through the interpellation of my Bengaliness as well as queerness, this friendship was substantialized through a queer kinship. It would also not be wrong to acknowledge that my own class position as well as the marker of having an English education and studying abroad may have facilitated my entry into the lives of some of my research participants. Through this kinship, by virtue of belonging to the same linguistic and class background I was recognized as 'one of them'. Many of these kinships resulted in me being invited for house parties, informal get together(s) and *adda* sessions. Indeed by being plugged into these different social networks by virtue of a shared kinship I was able to gain insights and examine areas I had not envisioned.

In one sense, these kinds of kinship networks challenge the hierarchies of heterosexual kinships, but they are also entrenched in a very segregated and exclusionary politics (Butler 2002). In fact I had to constantly move between the different registers of kinship recognition when I worked with participants I had recruited through contacts in NGOs and those who I had met through friends and digital sites. I was aware of my metropolitan location in terms of class, linguistic and economic privilege, and I cannot discount that this might have also been a deterrent for other potential respondents. *Adda* was essentially a non-documented form of my research, and some of the most interesting information and insights I gained was through informal *adda* sessions with my research participants and their friends. How do we think about using such data as researchers, considering the fact that much of this information was revealed to me by virtue of friendship and not necessarily as an ethnographer. Some of them remain as research notes but have played an important role in shifting my own thought process. This has been a constant thought even as I began ideating and writing about queer digital cultures in India.

These practices of friendship through kinship networks and *adda* complicate the research process. While the bonds of kinship that were created between myself and my research participants serve to seal a sense of community, the asymmetries of some of these bonds between myself and the research participants also challenges the notion of reciprocity. I was well aware that most of these interactions and interviews would eventually become a part of my research output. However, it was also apparent that our bonds of kinship interrupted the interview data with the emotional entanglement of a neutral participant-observer and a friend who was a part of the *adda*. The virtual queer populace as I have outlined is quite homogenous in terms of class, economic background, gendered identity and politics, but there is also a growing number of spaces that have opened up to those in the 'margins of the margin', as one participant described. My institutional location and academic privilege made it possible for me to seamlessly chat and interview people from most varied backgrounds.

I do not want to suggest that friendship and kinship is debilitating for 'good' research and neither do I want to suggest that the asymmetric bonds formed help gain some unknown knowledge. Rather, I want to think about the politics of knowledge production within academia that being seeped in digital queer culture brings about. This politics is also dependent on ethical dilemmas: should I be using the data that was provided during an *adda* session or should I have to discard some important data because it was revealed due to our kinship bonds? As activist and community-based researchers such as Aniruddha Dutta have argued, it is imperative to communicate this ethically created knowledge back to the community in ways in which they can understand and not leave them to be consumed within institutional silos (2015).

My attempt in writing this article is to register some of these issues that have been at the core of my thinking process during my ethnography and the questions that were posed to me by my research participants. Rik, for example, questioned me: What good will this research do for the community? Are you going to come up with a set of recommendations or a toolkit?

Unlike other social science projects which come with a toolkit and a set of recommendations for users (such as Mowlabocus et al. 2015), my research can make no such legitimate claims. Through engaging with issues of social significance and within the academic production of knowledge as capital, all I have tried to do within my institutional limitations is provide a narrative of a community and space that I have been a part of and that is an integral part of my life that has informed my subjectivity. I would also like to take this opportunity to not self-aggrandize community-based research as the only legitimate form of ethical research. In fact this sense of continuity is often dangerous from the position of the *native* academic as the *genuine* informant (Spivak 1999). However, collaborative community-based research also means that it offers the opportunity for critique of one's methods. As Frank Schaap writes, in contemporary times, the ethnographer's 'journey is not just about getting to know a strange land and understanding the Other, it is also, and maybe more importantly, a way to better understand the Self . . . ' (2002: 1). Thus despite our shared kinship and being able to stand in critical solidarity (Chari and Donner 2010) with my friends both online and offline and those working in the 'field', I can also question practices and have my own methods and modes scrutinized. Though the location of most of my research participants have been the urban metropolitan cities of New Delhi and Calcutta, I am conscious of similar work that needs to be done in other peri-urban locations. Queer digital culture is located within the urban space with peripheral influence in the suburban locations. While there has been some work done on the use of mobile phones within trans communities (Ganesh 2010), these have been health focused. Framing the discourse of LGBT identities in India through health and sexual interventions is an institutional necessity at times, constrained by funding politics (Boyce 2014).

Queer kinships have helped me create a family outside my biological one. These friendships have sustained through transnational alliances, critical arguments, *adda* and political solidarity. Through a reflexive approach that demanded awareness of and appropriate responses to my relationship with my research participants who were also my friends and kin also demanded accountability. Friendship as a research method is not the same as ethnography or participant observation. As Tillman-Healy (2001) reminds u,s it is being able to study social life at the natural pace of friendship. For me these meant turning off the recorder and going out for a meal together and being more invested in the lives of my participants who became my friends. We might have been brought together through what was once a doctoral project but some of the investments we have made in each other's lives and social well-being go far beyond the few years of writing the thesis.

Notes

1   I am immensely thankful to Aniruddha Dutta whose thought-provoking paper, 'Ethnography as a Politics of Friendship' presented at the American Anthropology Association Meeting in 2015, spurred some of the ideas in this chapter.

2   Processes of visibility and representational politics also reproduce mainstream norms, so it might be more rational to then say these spaces are 'partially queered'.

3   In this chapter, I have used three terms: sex, erotic activity and intimate encounters, all of which have been used by my research participants at various points. All three terms indicate different forms of sexual and/or erotic intimacies.

Works Cited

AHMED, Sara. 2004. *The Cultural Politics of Emotion*. Durham: Duke University Press.

BERSANI, Leo. 1988. 'Is the Rectum a Grave?' in D. Crimp (ed.), *Aids: Cultural Analysis, Cultural Activism*. Cambridge: MIT Press, pp. 197–222.

BOYCE, Paul. 2014. 'Desirable Rights: Same-sex Sexual Subjectivities, Socio-economic Transformations, Global Flows and Boundaries in India and Beyond'. *Culture, Health and Sexuality: An International Journal for Research, Intervention and Care* 16(10): 1201–15.

BUTLER, Judith. 2002. 'Is Kinship Always Already Heterosexual?' *Differences* 13(1): 14–44

CHAKRABARTY, Dipesh. 1999. 'Adda, Calcutta: Dwelling in Modernity'. *Public Culture* 11(1): 109–45

CHARI, Sharad, and Henrike. Donner. 2010. 'Ethnographies of Activism: A Critical Introduction'. *Cultural Dynamics* 22(2): 75–85.

DASGUPTA, Rohit K. 2014. '"Parties, Advocacy and Activism: Interrogating Community and Class in Digital Queer India" in Christopher Pullen (ed.), *Queer Youth and Media*. Basingstoke: Palgrave Macmillan, pp. 265–77.

————. 2015. 'Articulating Dissident Citizenship, Belonging and Queerness on Cyberspace'. *South Asian Review* 35(3): 203–23.

DATTA, Sangeeta, Kaustav Bakshi and Rohit K. Dasgupta. 2015. 'The World of Rituparno Ghosh: Texts, Contexts and Transgressions'. *South Asian History and Culture* 6(2): 223–37

DUTTA, Aniruddha. 2015. 'Ethnography As a Politics of Friendship: Participant Observation Among Gender Variant Communities and the Space-Time of Academia'. Unpublished paper presented at the American Anthropological Association Annual Meeting, Denver, CO, 18 November.

FREEMAN, Elizabeth. 2007. 'Queer Belongings: Kinship Theory and Queer Theory' in G. Haggerty and M.McGarry (eds), *A Companion to Lesbian, Gay, Bisexual, and Transgender Studies*. Malden: Blackwell, pp. 295–314.

GANESH, M. 2010. 'Mobile Love Videos Make me Feel Healthy: rethinking ICT's for Development', *IDS Working Papers* 352: 1–43.

INGRAM, Gordon Brent, Anne-Marie Bouthillette and Yolanda Retter. 1997. Conclusion in Gordon Brent Ingram, Anne-Marie Bouthillette and Yolanda Retter (eds), *Queers in Space*. Washington: Bay Press, pp. 447–58.

KUNTSMAN, Adi. 2012. 'Introduction: Affective Fabrics of Digital Culture' in Athina Karatzogianni and Adi Kuntsman (eds). *Digital Cultures and the Politics of Emotions.* Basingstoke: Palgrave Macmillan, pp. 1–19.

MOWLABOCUS, Sharif, Justin Harbottle, Ben Tooke, Craig Haslop and Rohit K. Dasgupta. 2015. '"Because Even the Placement of a Comma Might Be Important": Expertise, Embodiment and Social Capital in Online Sexual Health Promotion'. *Convergence: The International Journal of Research into New Media Technologies* 21(3): 375–87.

NARRAIN, Arvind and Gautam Bhan. 2005. Introduction in Arvind Narrain and Gautam Bhan (eds), *Because I Have a Voice: Queer Politics in India.* New Delhi: Yoda Press, pp. 1–30.

O'RIORDAN, Kate. 2007. 'Queer Theories and Cybersubjects: Intersecting Figures' in Kate O'Riordan and D. Philips (eds), *Queer Online: Media, Technology and Sexuality.* Oxford: Peter Lang, pp. 13–30.

SCHAAP, Frank. 2002. *The Words That Took Us There: Ethnography in a Virtual Reality.* Amsterdam: Aksant Academic Publishers.

SHAHANI, P. 2008. *Gaybombay.* New Delhi: Sage.

SPIVAK, Gayatri Chakravorty. 1999. *A Critique of Postcolonial Reason.* Cambridge: Harvard University Press.

TILLMANN-HEALY, Lisa M. 2001. *Between Gay and Straight: Understanding Friendship across Sexual Orientation.* Walnut Creek: AltaMira Press.

WAKEFORD, Nina. 1997. 'Cyberqueer' in Sally Munt and Andy Medhurst (eds), *Lesbian and Gay Studies: A Critical Introduction.* London: Cassell.

CHAPTER SIX

Global Day of Rage in London
Reflecting on Queer Activisms, New Media and Friendship

ROHIT K. DASGUPTA, SUNIL GUPTA and RAHUL RAO

On 11 December 2013, the Supreme Court of India decided to rein-state Section 377.[1] The activists were quick to respond and within hours of the judgement, Twitter and Facebook were weighed down by the outrage expressed by scores of people. In an attempt to organize a collective global action, a Global Day of Rage (GDR) was announced for 15 December 2013 which would be observed around the world.

The official press release condemning the judgement articulated the following points:

WE ARE OUTRAGED . . .

- That the Supreme Court of India on December 11, 2013 set aside the July 2009 Delhi High Court judgment which decriminalized consensual sex between adults in private, effectively re-criminalizing all lesbian, gay, bisexual, transgender and queer Indians and reduced them to the status of 'unapprehended felons'.

- That the Supreme Court has betrayed its own progressive history of extending rights for all by taking away rights from Indian citizens with this judgment.

- That the Supreme Court has failed to live up to its role as the protector of rights for all citizens without discrimi-nation, as guaranteed by one of the world's most progres-sive texts—the Indian Constitution.

- That the Supreme Court has thus betrayed the fundamental constitutional promise that the dignity of all citizens would be recognized and that equal treatment is a non-negotiable element of the world's largest democracy, thereby shredding the very principles it has sworn itself to uphold.

- That the Supreme Court has criminalized all consensual sexual acts that do not involve penile–vaginal penetration. This applies to all people, irrespective of their gender identity or sexual orientation, including heterosexual people and not just LGBT Indians.

- That the Supreme Court has empowered blackmailers, bullies and homophobes who will now find easy victims in LGBT people whose rights have been denied.

- That the Supreme Court has encouraged corporations and companies to discriminate against their LGBT staff and discouraged those few companies which moved after the Delhi High Court judgment to ensure non-discrimination against LGBT staff within their organizations.

- That the Supreme Court can use the phrase 'miniscule minorities' to dismiss the rights of LGBT people, thus ignoring the spirit of inclusiveness which is at the heart of the Indian Constitution. The size of a minority is irrelevant, what matters is that every member of it, every Indian citizen has an equal right to protection granted by our Fundamental Rights and it is the SC's duty to enforce this, not throw it away.

- This Global Day of Rage is being organized by queer Indians, the queer India diaspora, queer people of all countries, our supporters, relatives and friends. All are coming out on the streets of cities across the world on Sunday December 15, to together raise our voices against this travesty of justice.

The Global Day of Rage was entirely planned and executed using social networking sites such as Facebook and Twitter—the first email proposing the event was sent on 12 December 2013. Initially the idea was to hold a protest across cities in India and around the world. Wherever there were 5 participants available, volunteer-coordinators were asked to organize the protest in their cities. By the end of the day, volunteers from almost 32 cities across the world had signed up to take part in the protest. Within a single day there was a logo, a press release and Twitter hashtags to document the event and keep the pressure on the Indian government.

A conversation that took place between volunteers Sunil Gupta, Rahul Rao and Rohit K Dasgupta—who along with Sneha Krishnan, Charan Singh and Ash Kotak[2] helped organize the Global Day of Rage in London[3]—meanders through reflections on queer politics in London, building alliances and friendship and has been transcribed here:

ROHIT. I have recently been thinking about friendship among queer men. I think the ways in which friendship is represented within Indian media and, more broadly, within the public discourse is inherently quite masculine and heterosexual. So my first question would be: How do you conceive friendship among queer men? Also, does being a man and being queer differently affect the ways in which you think about friendship?

RAHUL. I'm going to take the liberty of answering this question more specifically with reference to my friendship with you and Sunil which really got me into helping to organize the Global Day of Rage protests. Actually, I didn't know Sunil very well at the time, but I have a funny story about how I first encountered his work. I was at a conference in San Francisco in 2013 and spent some of my downtime hanging out in Castro, as one does. I did the Harvey Milk-tourist stuff, and remember feeling rather emotional about it all—these are my ancestors too, etc. Then, browsing in a bookshop, I happened to pick up one of Sunil's books and had a slightly jaw-dropping moment when I saw my friends Gautam and Anokhi resplendently nude (or semi-nude in G's case) in a series of photographs called 'The New Pre-Raphaelites'. 'Fuck Harvey

Milk,' I thought, 'these are my people!' So that's how I encountered Sunil! I met you in multiple ways—through Shamira [Meghani] and Devina [Sivagurunathan].[4]

Friendship, how one knows people, is important to me, particularly in the context of queer activist organizing in diaspora. It seems as if so much of our energy recently has been taken up with pushing back against ill-informed homonationalist, white-Western activism, that knowing and trusting the people with whom I engage in public advocacy feels really important.

SUNIL. I think friendship among queer men is totally unique—it is familial on the one hand, and truly global on the other. It also cuts across class and occupational lines much more readily. I grew up gay and proud and deliberately looked outside the biological family to make close friendships. A handful of my long-term friendships have arisen from former live-in or love relationships. I've rarely found this phenomenon outside of the queer world. I think gay social relations are very coloured by the possibility of sexual flirtation—something that's lacking in our heterosexual counterparts. So the notion of 'friend' can easily extend into the 'lover'. In fact, 'friend' has been a euphemism for lover ever since I've been around. This is even more so in India where the emotional bonding suggested by *dosti* far exceeds what 'friend' connotes in English, meaning someone quite like family but not a part of the extended family. When I was frequenting the South London gay scene in the 1980s, there was a familial atmosphere even tho', on the face of it, people were just trying to get off. It was because you began to recognize these same people night after night and realize that they were local in a very comforting way. Hence, we never went to the West End or to North London because they seemed full of strangers.

ROHIT. Thank you both for your responses. I am very interested in what Sunil said about queer friendship cutting across class and occupational lines, something I have to disagree with—based on my own experiences, I have felt the kind of friendships I have made were very stratified. This was very acute especially when I worked in the NGO sector. I remember, for instance, at a conference in Jadavpur University organized by Sappho for Equality, most of the delegates stuck to their own social groups (kothis, the academic gay men and so on). I don't know if this is unique to my own experience. In fact, this kind of class shaming is so common within online spaces too, like Planet Romeo, where I frequently come across profiles saying 'Vernaculars stay away' or 'Speak in proper English'—very symptomatic of the classed nature of our kinship/friendship 'communities'. I am also intrigued by the aspect of 'friend' as 'lover'. I would hope to get back to both these points through this conversation . . . maybe Rahul can pick up on these. But I want to now ask a little bit about the Global Day of Rage and how you became part of the movement and what role you feel queer kinship and friendship networks played in making it such a success. On my part, I would like to reflect on the role of new media since the entire movement was championed through the Internet: from the 'We are Outraged Statement' to organizing this even which happened over the listservs created for this purpose. I remember that after Sunil requested I be added to the conversation, there were as many as 50 emails in two hours. Quite a remarkable feat! But what about you two?

RAHUL. I think my experience of queer networks is closer to Rohit's, both in India and here in the UK. Which is to say, I find social queer spaces in India—as opposed to self-consciously activist ones—to be quite class segregated, not a remarkable observation in itself, and of a piece with the rest of life. Ditto in London, where I seem to circulate almost exclusively in networks and spaces of university-educated middle-class people.

Additionally, race seems to mark space in London, perhaps even more sharply online: witness the number of profiles on gay social networking media that declare racial fetish or antipathy. (I wonder if there are generational issues to consider in parsing the differences between our respective responses.)

On the question of new media and the organization of protest, of course Facebook was enormously helpful in allowing us to connect and reach out to a wider public, really indispensable in making the GDR happen. But it also provided a platform for quite a few problematic initiatives. You may remember one of the other protests in London, soon after the judgement passed by the Supreme Court of India. It was called by two individuals whom none of us diasporic queer South Asians had heard of and whose protest page featured all sorts of problematic memes and tropes (pictures of a baboon as stand-in for an Indian homophobe). A reminder of the not-always-helpful anarchism of new media. On this occasion, rather than challenging positionality ('Who are you to speak for', etc.) which can come across like a turf war, I found it more useful to make a ridiculous joke (I named the baboon Thomas Babington Macaulay, whom we can credit for Section 377).

SUNIL. Uff . . . you guys have lived sheltered lives behind the Internet . . . :-) In Delhi, we braved the wilds of Delhi-NCR to go to the disco with all and sundry. There is only that much one can take of middle-class college-educated types. By the way, my husband is also from Delhi and crosses class lines on a regular basis. And in London: I lived in South London bars for two decades which were pretty mixed class-wise, my whole circle was mixed. And I dated a guy who sold shoes and had never been to college but he had a body to die for!

ROHIT. Thanks for those responses. I think this gives us some fascinating insights into how we have experienced queerness. But while we are still on the topic of the Global Day of Rage, Rahul did you have something to ask?

RAHUL. What do we make of the use of Soho as a space for protest? Why did we go there? How did the protest 'work' in that space?

ROHIT. In reply to Rahul's question. I think Soho was an excellent location for having the protest. I know there were a lot of discussions among us about finalizing an appropriate location, and the Indian High Commission had rejected our permit early on for it being scheduled for a weekend. I think it was more than just being a symbolic protest—it was also about challenging and engaging those around us. Soho as a (supposed) centre of queer London was a great choice. However, Soho, as we know, has also gone through changes over time—I am sure Sunil would have more to say about this!—and coming to this space for the first time from India, it felt quite white/hostile and mainstream. The GDR protest kind of helped shake it up and queer the space a bit. It was amazing to see so many brown, black and allies making their way on a rainy day, shouting slogans and politicizing the mainstream.

Did that space work for us? I think it did. We had no plans to actually march through Soho and Carnaby Street. It was meant to be in the Soho Square. I don't know if you guys remember, but there was another protest organized by Wendyl who is from one of the trade unions; also on the same day at the High Commission. It took quite a bit of convincing from my side to get them to agree on Soho, though I must say, unlike the 2 individuals whom Rahul mentioned, they were more than happy to let us take the lead on this. I think they felt Soho would not work, there was no 'politics' here; there was nothing 'symbolic' for us (as in no history to India or Article 377) but for many of us, migrants, Soho was both a space where we enter mainstream queer culture and a space which reminds us of the racialized nature of it in London.

SUNIL. Regarding Soho as the place for protest, I agree with Rohit in that the two obvious choices—the Indian High Commission and the Nehru Centre—were inappropriate on a weekend as they were shut and even the neighbourhoods tend to be deserted. Yes, Soho has gone though many changes, but remains at the core of a visible queer life in London as it has since at least the Victorian times. To think of Nash, one of whose stated objectives in building Regent Street, as Walkowitz notes, was to provide a 'complete separation between the Streets occupied by the Nobility and Gentry, and the narrower streets and meaner houses occupied by mechanics and the trading part of the community.' It worked: Cockney inhabitants were pushed to the East, making room for the immigrant populations that rapidly took their place, and then created business and entertainments that were frequented by the rich, despite—and because of—their proximity to the edgy, 'vicious' spaces of Soho . . . the social transformations created by 'men and women of many walks of life: rich and poor, unschooled émigrés and Bloomsbury literati, moral purity campaigners and libertarian anarchists, undercover police and dance hostesses, fascists and anti-fascists, queers and heterosexuals.[5] Therefore, it seems to me we couldn't have thought of a better neighbourhood to hold the protest, given its history. And even in our own more gay, liberated times, as the Pride marchers headed off to commercial extravaganzas in parks, Soho turned itself into a free people's festival.

We also went there because of the more expedient fact that it is centrally located. We have to acknowledge that we live in a metropolitan city and we could seek out target South Asian neighbourhoods but then it would become impossibly far for some of us. I almost never leave South London, so I'm not used to not seeing black people, but brown people are rare. We might not have got the gay boys from Wembley if we had held the protest in, say, Vauxhall, for example.

I think it worked, the march, as Rohit described. Though unplanned, it gave a boost to the event and the rally made sense. And, once more, yes, the location of being at the heart of a global metropolis worked since the collective 'Day of Rage' message was meant to be global and to make that point across to the Indian government.

RAHUL. I too think Soho worked really well. I think of Soho and Vauxhall as London's two major queer enclaves, although there's now a Shoreditch–Hackney–East London circuit taking in the George and Dragon, Joiner's Arms [not for much longer :(] , Dalston Superstore, Bethnal Green Working Men's Club, etc. I've always thought of Vauxhall as bigger, edgier, more impersonal, saturated with the possibility of dirty urban anonymous encounters, and Soho as smaller, kinder, more familiar—but also increasingly more boring because it's been colonized by restaurant chains, which seem to mock its rich history that Sunil alluded to earlier, memorialized in its many blue plaques and in the conversation of old timers who frequent the more long-running establishments. So one of the really wonderful things about the GDR protest for me was that it seemed to reintroduce politics into a space that usually feels emptied of politics by the twin forces of decriminalization and gentrification, at least for a brief moment. It was also affirming to see a train of mostly brown queer people claiming space, like a weird kindred spirit of the (much whiter) Hare Krishna crew who can be seen more frequently doing pretty much what we did, with an entirely different cosmological agenda of course. And there is much to be said for marching along unplanned routes at high speed: we felt much bigger than we were.

I suppose my second question would be something along the lines of the impact we might have had: Were we able to convey a message to India? Did the event do something for us as the queer diasporic South Asian, regardless of the effects it may or may not have had in India? And where do we go from here? Should we operate primarily in reactive mode, or are there more proactive things we could be doing? I realize, of course, that there are lots of diasporic desi[6] queer organizations that do great work. But in asking this question, I'm thinking more specifically of the informal network that crystallized around this protest.

ROHIT. I must admit that this was a difficult one. I am not sure of what effects it had back home. I am not sure if it would be possible to even track any direct changes. The single most important message that I think it sent out was affirming the importance of collective voice. Thinking intersectionally, I guess—I'm glad we managed to gather together such a disparate range of voices, from the diasporic desi queers to the trade union supporters and organizations such as Southall Black Sisters who walked with us in support. Thirty-two cities across the world collectively voicing their disapproval of this ruling and the widespread media coverage would not have gone totally unnoticed. I think there is quite a lot that we can do from here as diasporic queer activists. It is important that we keep voicing our disapproval and keep the pressure on. While I am wary of recent petitions like 'Obama Save the LGBT's in India', I do think there is a need for international voices to show their support without taking over the movement or appropriating it.

As a media scholar, I do want to stress on the role of new media. I think for me GDR was a very good example of how social media facilitates collective action that Paulo Gerbaudo[7] recently called 'choreography of assembly', a way by which public space is symbolically constructed and provides a site for activists to 'gather'. The GDR hashtag triggered a response from the worldwide queer community (in a similar way that Jadavpur University used #hokkolorob for student dissent in 2014) and helped sustain it across a transnational scale. I think the informal networks that have created the need to be sustained. I am slightly critical of desi queer organizations, I must admit. Having volunteered for over a year in one and being involved with another, I was shocked at how little political engagement they have initiated. There also seems to be a move towards 'visibility politics', with certain desi queer 'faces' of the community making it an essential part of their politics, but maybe that's another question.

SUNIL. Regarding the impact in India: I think we have been able to influence and mobilize people, so it was well worth it from that point of view. It might have been brief and sharp but we did effectively communicate that we care. Also, the Indian media is obsessed with goings on in London and other global cities and that might, in some way, reflect on India. So even a fleeting congregation would have had some kind of impact. Plus, it reflected back on the local Indian organizers' ability to reach out to a global network and mobilize actual physical protests from distant shores. A feat in itself! I did it in response to a call to arms that came from people I care about in Delhi. As far as us here in London, I think it brought a number of people together and established an informal network that wasn't there earlier. Now it's up to us as to take it from here, and this is always difficult in Western metropolises where individuals have very complicated work and home arrangements. Somehow in India it always seems easier, maybe because they have domestic help . . . :-)

When Rahul says 'operate in reactive mode', I'm assuming he means reacting to events in India, but I'm wondering if that is enough to sustain a network over here. I think being proactive is more likely to be workable in the long term, but then we have to think about our position as a migrant minority ethnic group in Europe. Otherwise we will be a useful but limited reactive 'rent a crowd' for events in India.

I would like to ask if the legacy of the GDR in London will be the formation of a more proactive South Asian Queer Network in London and, given the background and interests of all of the organizers (born in India, academic/cultural workers), what would its goals be? And how will it even formulate goals without accommodating the local British-born South Asian non-academic queer experience?

RAHUL. I'm going to address both of Sunil's questions since they seem to be interconnected. I think any new organizational initiative would have to take into account the fact that it is entering a crowded field. By this I mean that we would have to acknowledge ongoing work by queer South Asian organizations (Imaan, Safra project, etc.) and their allies (Who might these be? Southall Black Sisters? Women Against Fundamentalism?) and figure out how we might complement what they are doing. This addresses Sunil's question about accommodating local experience, except that we might find that experiences are so different that accommodation can be difficult or perhaps not the main priority.

I've had many conversations with diasporic South Asians in which they've expressed surprise at developments in India—in law, media, campus politics, etc.—and contrasted this with their own experiences growing up in South Asian communities in Britain (I'm sure we've all had these sorts of conversations). The contrasts run in both progressive and conservative directions, so in making this observation I don't want to suggest a progressive homeland–regressive diaspora dichotomy here, or vice versa. But the contrasts are real, which leads me to wonder if perhaps our role as 'born in India, academic/cultural workers' as Sunil so aptly describes us, and particularly as people who are able to travel back and forth between India and Britain fairly regularly, gives us an opportunity to function not so much as a separate group with a distinct representational function but to operate as translators, conduits of information, connections between here and there. Perhaps our role is to leverage our dispersed contacts, to make use of the fact that we have feet in both places, to promote a greater understanding of what is going on there over here, and vice versa. I'm going to leave that intentionally vague because networks are like that. Perhaps the virtue of operating in reactive mode is that it leaves us flexible and able to adapt to shifting exigencies. Whatever we may say and want in our more utopian moments, politics never really ends. I'm sure we'll need to mobilize our rage on other occasions, in solidarity with other groups. And hopefully, there will always be much to celebrate too.

ROHIT. Thanks for the questions, Sunil and your response Rahul. My response mirrors much of the sentiments that Rahul has expressed. I think it is extremely important to pay attention and work with South Asians here and their local experience. Like Rahul, I do not want to essentialize the homeland as progressive vis a vis the regressive diaspora. It is also important to acknowledge that the resonance of the Article 377 ruling and the subsequent protest has had a direct and indirect impact on the South Asian queer populace here. For example, right after the protest I met with Mohit (pseudonym) who was born and is living in Essex. He said that when he came out to some of his friends and family, they blamed it on the 'Western influence' of London, claiming that this would not have happened if they were still living in India, going so far as to say: 'This country has cost us our children.' Now there is already a prevailing idea within the diaspora who still want to see the homeland as 'unsullied' and 'pure', and with the 2009 ruling I think many woke up to the 'progressive' politics of the Homeland. Closer still, people like Sunil Babu Pant in Nepal rued how the Supreme Court ruling would be a setback to the Global South, many of whom were charged up after the 2009 ruling. So I think it is important that we work with allies and organizations here but also South Asians in other parts of the world. Their concerns might be different from the ones we have back home but there are several points of intersection to consider.

I like how Rahul describes us as 'translators and conduits of information'. I think that could indeed be one way to think of our role as academic and cultural workers. I am deeply concerned, though, I must say, that South Asian gay politics (at least in London) seems to be largely centred around 'visibilizing the invisible', and over here I am talking about Asif (Asifa Lahore) and their constant call for South Asians to come out. But on the other hand, I am also aware of groups such as DOST organizing family days where parents and family of gay/queer South Asian men are invited to come together in a 'culturally sensitive space' to talk about issues such as homophobia and community support. I think it would be useful to enter these dialogues as well.

SUNIL. Thanks for your responses. I think the gaps I was seeing in the 1980s are still with us from what I have experienced in the last couple of years of being 'back' in London. It might be that 'we' who grew up in India didn't have to struggle with a racialized and vilified national identity—'Paki bastard'. On the other hand, the gay liberation experience in the larger society here has led to great gains and recognitions of rights. That can't be said of South Asia. I detect an imbalance of a peculiar kind: we can mobilize a Day of Rage in support of India for example, but there's an equal lack of interest on the other side, that is to say, the problems of South Asian queers in the diaspora. Perhaps because they are seen to be cushioned by a liberal society and, therefore, not worthy of much support. I have also seen the 'Black' moment of the GLC's 1980s where black did not represent colour, but something wider and more postcolonial which has now increasingly come to represent only people of African descent. Therefore, I feel that South Asian queers, in the UK at least, have fewer avenues open for support and friendship networks, being as they are from archly conservative households. In that sense, I support Asifa Lahore's call to 'come out', it's a bit strange sitting in Soho at a DOST meeting listening to stories of forced marriages in this country. Finally, I think as we are here, we have to engage with and expand our networks and empower queer people of South Asian descent because none of the other communities are going to do it for us.

Notes

1   See Arvind Narrain and Gautam Bhan (eds), *Because I Have a Voice* (New Delhi: Yoda Press, 2005); and Niharika Banerjea and Debanuj Dasgupta, 'States of Desire', *Sanhati* (2013). Available at: http://sanhati.com/articles/7185/ (last accessed on 11 July 2017).

2   Sneha Krishnan is an academic working on gender and sexuality, Charan Singh is a photographer and Ash Kotak is a playwright and community organizer.

3   See Svati P. Shah, 'Queering Critiques of Neoliberalism in India: Urbanism and Inequality in the Era of Transnational "LGBTQ" Rights', *Antipode* 47(3): 635–51. A visual documentation of the day is available in a short film by Ash Kotak which features still images by Charan Singh. Available at: https://goo.gl/DjdtHQ (last accessed on 11 July 2017).

4   Shamira Meghani is an academic and a contributor to this volume. Devina Sivagurunathan worked at SOAS, University of London.

5   Judith R Walkowitz, *Nights Out: Life in Cosmopolitan London* (London: Yale University Press, 2012).

6   *Desi* is a colloquial term used for people, culture and products from South Asia, more specifically, those from the Indian sub-continent.

7   Paulo Gerbaudo, *Tweets and the Streets: Social Media and Contemporary Activism* (London: Pluto Press, 2012).

CHAPTER SEVEN

In Terms of 'The Excess'

AKANKSHA AND SUMITA BEETHI

Akanksha Speaks

At around eight o'clock in the night, the Sexuality Resource Centre 'Chetana' at Sappho for Equality, Calcutta, was closing for the day. Along with 8 members of our team, we were coming out of the office. All on a sudden we were attacked by them, with weapons in their hands. The weapons were nothing but the fragrant dye, *abeer*, used for playing Holi, the popular spring festival of love, friendship, frolic and colours celebrated in India as well as Indian diaspora across the world. After all it was the eve of Holi. With the huge almost-full moon in the sky we were sprinkling colours on each other's faces and hair for the next half an hour in the tiny front garden of Chetana (literally, 'the consciousness'). They spent almost one and a half hours to fetch *abeer* of six specific colours—violet, blue, green, yellow, orange and red— symbolizing our very own queer rainbow. I played Holi after many years. Smudged with colours, I was walking down the road, holding the hand of my friend-comrade-partner with whom I have shared the last twenty-two years of my life. Back home, while washing the colours off my face and hair, I was traversing the time trajectory, reminiscing about the monochromatic days of my life.

I was lonely, docile and the only girl-child of an orthodox family, quite happy with my books and study, abiding by all set rules around, until my father died of cancer. Looking after my father in those fifteen terminal days I matured into an 'adult' at the age of 24! By that time, I could manage a seemingly good job and started sharing a major por-tion of the financial burden of my family, as I was the eldest of my siblings. As usual, according to the 'norm', proposals were coming from men and I too, in my plight, to explore the 'quasi-dark' zone of erotic desires entered into a few consecutive unsuccessful relationships with them. But surprisingly, I was completely unaware of the need for friendship. And then I met my soulmate, my woman of life! The synergic effect of romance, love, sex, bonding, trust and friendship metamorphosed me. Spontaneously, I became a new me. With my companion on this journey, I started the new episode, in search of a different meaning of life. She expressed: There must be others like us in this city—let's look for them. An eager me thought: Will it be really possible? We found two more couples! She suggested: Let's give an interview when we are approached by a journalist of a leading news daily. A scared me fell into a dilemma: What will happen if people come to know about our relationship? The interview got published with no damage done, though about 30 like-minded women contacted us through the postbox number published in that interview. She took the daring step: Let's form a group. An arguing me fought: Why form a group, we are so happy with our newly found friends, isn't that enough? Is it the right time for organizing? She encouraged: Come on, we are not alone, we have more than 30 people now, and together we can make a difference. An assured me created the logo for Sappho, the first support group for lesbians and bisexual women in eastern India in 1999 under the leadership of three same-sex couples. And thus, under the policing eyes of the society, an underground activism sprouted out of non-normative love and friendship.

The commonalities of oppressions in forms of violations and violence in family, workplace and larger society, formed a strong bonding among us with the promise of a long journey together. That we all were suffering from similar atrocities based on our sexual orientations made us recognize the root cause—homophobia. We have to fight in unison, and the battle will only be won if we act in solidarity. The bond of friendship transformed into that of solidarity. Instinctive feminist consciousness of being in a lesbian relationship traced the linkage between homophobia and patriarchy, the sole pillar of domination, and thus led us to the unanimous decision that we should reach out to the local women's groups involved in the larger feminist movements. Our lived experiences showed us that solidarity should not only be based on the pre-given condition of same-sex orientation as in our case but should also be seen from the point of view of an integrated subjugation associated with womanhood in general, that is to say, we are doubly discriminated as women. Sexual and domestic violence were the most common issues addressed by the women's movement in West Bengal until recently. We began to introduce the idea of considering sexuality as the second lens through which discriminations based on gender may be explored further.

During the course of our journey it became obvious that a major part of the oppression is perpetrated by the non-queer section of society, including the family. This was the stark reality at the time,[1] which was reinforced through a nationwide qualitative research on violence against LBT (lesbian, bisexual woman and female-to-male transgender) and much later during 2009 and 2011.[2] Until and unless we affirm our presence there, within the so-called mainstream, the crusade for claiming the right to a dignified life for sexually-marginalized women is going to be only partially successful. The autonomous social, legal and political space will never be ensured if we stick together in the ghetto of a community-based support group. Reasoning with shared information, reversible understanding (as heterophobia is equally threatening) and the master key of friendship can build the bridge leading to a trustworthy coexistence of the queer and non-queer. We started to interact with the public through different open-house seminars and meetings; we received positive responses from quite a number of individuals who wanted to join hands in our struggle and support our cause. It was then, in 2003, that Sappho for Equality emerged as an extension of Sappho. Creating the political platform for anyone and everyone, irrespective of gender and sexual orientation, and for those who dare to question and challenge the cooperative establishment of homophobia, compulsory heterosexism and heteronormativity. Today, Sappho for Equality is leading the sexuality rights movement in eastern India. A meaningful and barely felt agency and autonomy stems from inclusivity and friendship with the so-called enemy, although our enmity was never with the heterosexual people. Our target is the ivory tower of patriarchy which offers the heteronormative world a false sense of superiority. The seed of personal friendships that were sowed then, is now a full-grown tree, under which we recharge ourselves politically for the next course of action towards fulfilling our mission.

Going back to the political understanding of womanhood, we will now look into the discourse of 'realness' of a woman as Sappho for Equality fights for the rights of transmen (persons assigned female gender at birth) and talk over the issues of transwomen (persons assigned male gender at birth). Though truth for lesbians, bisexual women and transmen are not similar to that of transwomen, we can still locate points of conjunction in different cross-cutting issues. We have become politically matured enough to recognize the common enemy, patriarchy. Based on this differential consciousness, the essence of solidarity is now shifting from commonality of oppression towards having a common enemy, and also that of our standpoint, from identity-based politics to issue-based politics. Here I cannot help quoting Saskia Wieringa as she writes, 'Thinking about feminist and sexual politics on the basis of affinity opens the ground for the building of rainbow coalitions, built on shifting political practices. According to the political project at hand a coalition is built around that project, of people and organizations who from whatever position they stand on, agree to collaborate.'[3] The affinity bonding thus produced, neutralizes 'us' and 'them' segregation, transferring the onus of the issue-based coalition on a consensus—'we', an inclusive yet pluralistic subjectivity. It is, therefore, the call of the day to identify points of congruence with various marginalized groups and mainstream bodies to form issue-based alliance, because we strongly believe that it is possible to create an unbiased world for and within non-normative gender–sexual communities through political kinship.

Sumita Beethi Speaks

Friendship is personal and activism is political, right? That was how I used to approach these notions. In fact, I never thought much about friendship or activism consciously for a good part of my life. Friendship came as casual friends or classmates or *para* (community) pals. I guess some people forge lifelong bonds, or at least long-term relationships, with their classmates or *para* pals—I could not. I just lived, while some 'friends' came, stayed and left without much ado. It pained, but I accepted.

Till I reached the stage of political consciousness and activism. Yes, I have a 'pre' and 'post' life marked by activism where the main indicator was 'consciousness'. And as I grew conscious of my activities/thoughts/reactions, generally my living, I realized that friend/s and friendship are two different terms. The idea of having friend/s is not friendship and my lack of friends does not necessarily mean my incapability of appreciating and utilizing friendship for more than personal reasons. I am consciously using the term 'utilizing' vis-a-vis friendship.

In 2002, I was introduced to a bunch of women, aged between 20 and 40 (now I know the eldest was not exactly 40 at the time, but she looked 40-ish), coming from varied backgrounds, identifying as lesbians and bisexual women. It was an un-registered, emotional support group for such persons who have had hardly or no space to express themselves, celebrate their sexual/erotic/emotional exhilarations and, most importantly, no one to share the grief, violence and violation of an 'unspeakable desire'.

What struck me at that moment was not so much the cause (that would come later)—I was fascinated to see friends holding each other's hands in the most difficult journey called life, or life against the tide. That was Sappho, born in 1999, the first collective of lesbian and bisexual women in eastern India.

Why did this bunch of oddly similar women fascinate me so much? I tried to look into the matter. Friendship as I understood till then was an important social relationship between peers and like-minded individuals. People need friends even if they have families and other close relations. Friendship is built upon mutual trust, support, care and love and also has a distinct element of fun in it. The Sappho bunch were all this and more, and that 'more' was intriguing.

As I started getting to know the group, I could see individuals connected through a bond of similar desire (unspeakable, therefore threatening), creating a tapestry of mutual support, dependence, care, love and celebration—like in friendship. And then this rich tapestry of friendship and warmth (missed out this word earlier, I'm going to make good use of it now) was used to: (a) provide emotional support, (b) share the burden of violence/rejection/human rights violation experienced by the members and, most importantly, (c) take significant steps, unify and resist.

'Warmth'—the word I missed out in the beginning—played a very important part in my association with Sappho. I was the slightly awkward introvert who tried to hide her loneliness and melancholy behind a mask of self-assurance. I was rather unsure in 2002, with my short career in advertising (which I had left with much bitterness), and a 'very late awakening' to difficult desires and challenges. I felt calm, warm and satiated, sitting (rhetorically on the fence, actually on a couch perhaps) and watching friendship and activism unfold in front of me. My 'girlfriend' (none of us could exactly be called a 'girl', we were well past 40) asked me to join the group formally, but I felt no reason for it and the group also never insisted.

Sappho for Equality began in October 2003. By then my association with the group had considerably increased. My 'girlfriend' and I had separated, and at that time of personal crisis, I had reached out to Sappho (who else?), which perhaps helped me finally to decide and become a part of the group.

From 1999 to 2003, Sappho functioned as a support group initially for lesbian and bisexual women and later, in 2001 or 2002, for the transmen. They also interacted with many people who were open, sensitive, thoughtful and supportive, who were not from the LGBTQ community but responded to the cause as part of a greater rights–justice framework. Friends of Sappho, they were called. In October 2003, when Sappho for Equality was registered as the forum open to all genders and sexualities, for activism against sexuality-based discrimination, directly working towards rights and social justice of LBT persons, friendship played an important part. Many friends of Sappho became members of Sappho for Equality, actively participating in the movement against hetero-patriarchy.

I was one of the founder members of Sappho for Equality along with a handful of other non-Sappho members like Dr Ranjita Biswas, Dr Amit Ranjan Basu and four out of six co-founders of Sappho: Malobika, Akanksha, Nupur and Mallika. I also remember

Dr Ratnabali Chatterjee, Rajasri Mukherjee and many more faces around me, around us, who celebrated the birth of Sappho for Equality as it secured a space for itself within Sappho.

This crucial and critical combination of multiple spaces within and without also provided another significant meaning to friendship. We talked about sharing, caring, supporting and protecting a friend and in the same breath talked about fighting for rights and justice, 'coming out', raising voice and visiblizing the invisible; we reminded ourselves many a times of the fine balance between these two objectives. One cannot overpower the other. Sappho thus coexists with Sappho for Equality as the community-based safe space, while the latter opens out to interact with the rest of the world.

My personal journey with the organization is that of a long and winding uphill route that began almost spontaneously, not clearly knowing where it would lead me. My entry into social activism came from a vague idea of righteousness (?!) and the slight overdose of a semi-radical leftist past: all lofty, high-sounding, ideological pursuits; or political correctness, in today's term! The group of women who called themselves Sappho were in opposition to that cultured distance.

I am not going to talk about feminism and what it taught us (either we know or never will), but politicizing the personal was the first alphabet I started practising and till date it seems imperfect. It was a moment of realization that I had nonetheless, because for a long time, I had resisted friendly intimacy and created a 'pure political parameter' of activism, but was automatically drawn towards the friendly warmth of a collective that was unabashedly founded on friendship. How personal! How threatening!

From 2002 to 2015, I had learnt to accept myself as an emotional being, my need for friends (intimate and personal) and my need for comrades (still intimate and even more personal). In Sappho I had seen friendship; in Sappho for Equality, I experienced camaraderie. My political motivation and personal needs came together, though not always in harmony. I let some of my comrades hug me, and sometimes even tried to initiate the hug. In-between, I learnt how to work alongside my ex-lover, how to step out of a suffocating friendship when the moment arrived and how to negotiate the personal–professional dictum with my present partner and biological daughter (all three of us are part of a research programme and share an intense emotional space). And I survived!

These days I am travelling a lot to different parts of West Bengal, north-eastern India and Bangladesh with our Sappho for Equality team. It's a programme called Beyond Boundaries, where we are trying to step out of the comfortable boundaries of our work zone and venture into the new and unknown. It was designed to serve two objectives: as a campaign programme for raising awareness about non-normative gender-sexual expressions and practices in the rural areas of West Bengal, and as a facilitating programme for collectivizing LBT identifying persons in north-eastern India and Bangladesh. As a trainer/facilitator for both the programmes I utilized friendship to connect with people. Also with rural women through similar experiences as persons assigned female gender at birth, where our stories of shattered dreams/dreamlessness or stealing forbidden moments of dreams brought us together. By asking the simplest or, rather, the most complicated question: how is life, we entered into the courtyard of a house with many windows and no door. And after a while, rural and urban, homo and hetero, normative and not (so called), melted into a fierce embrace of helplessness. With LBT persons in geographically marginalized north-east and religiously distant Bangladesh through our similar experiences of unspeakable desires, unattainable choices and indomitable zeal to make life, we made connections to work forward, facilitating the process of collectivization and activism. We shared, cared, progressed and even regressed together to find ways to express and to hold back emotions at the same time.

I realized I was making friends, forging bonds with people I may or may not meet ever again, and yet this is friendship. I realized my personal is inching towards political . . .

They Speak

—. As I was reading your piece, I realized that neither of us actively sought friendship— that's something common between us. So did we look for activism instead?

—. I don't think I actively looked for activism. Rather, I wanted to live my life on my terms. The way I see it, Sappho was born to help me live the way I want to—the way I am. Later, if we think about Sappho for Equality, when I met you, just before Sappho for Equality was formed, I wasn't sure if you were from the community, I knew you as an empathetic person, as someone supporting our cause. Not only you, Ranjita Biswas, Amit Ranjan Basu, Banani Ghatak, they were also there. At that time, Malobika and I thought support from non-queer persons was important for us,

—. Don't you think people came to support Sappho, in friendship?

—. I don't think we sought friendship. We—you and me or Ranjita and me—did not begin our journey as friends. We hardly knew each other in those days, in 2003. While Sappho for Equality was not yet formed, we had built a community within Sappho. However, you joined us later and so could not be a part of that experience, that history. But none of us were looking for friendship then, or to form Sappho for Equality.

—. Did you look for friendship when you formed Sappho?

—. Yes. And that is interesting. Our lives at that time were more individualistic, more personal, than organizational. Sappho was providing a common platform to us, but that was less formal and more heartfelt. I am trying to understand the driving force behind Sappho for Equality . . . What do you think it was?

—. I think it was different for each one of us. However, there was a common thread indeed. I think all of us took note of the widespread human rights violations, and that some people remained deprived of justice. We felt connected with these people, and especially to this issue of same-sex love among women. Why this issue, I do not know. Is it because I am part of this community, or my own same-sex desire? I don't really know. Rather, I would say, I was looking for some kind of meaning of life, and later realized that unless I go beyond myself, beyond the personal, I cannot attain it. What I find interesting is that Sappho began with a quest to seek friends, like-minded people, and worked towards a larger platform of activism. And Sappho for Equality began with a common platform for activism with persons of various interest, expertise, experiences—nothing was common, not even their biological gender (we have male members in Sappho for Equality)—our lives were different as chalk and cheese! But we took this journey together since 2003. From then till 2015, today, as we sit here and discuss friendship and social activism: Who are we? Are we just colleagues?

—. I will simply say, Sappho began with a quest for friendship and progressed towards activism and Sappho for Equality began with activism and is moving forward towards friendship . . .

—. This is precisely the point that I wanted to make! Today, we are not just colleagues, or friends who grew up together, went to the same school or college, etc. We are more than friends, more than colleagues; it is a curious 'excess' that makes this relationship interesting and intense—a bond that is inexplicable otherwise.

—. What bond is this, I wonder! My relationship with you, I call it a 'relationship' not using any other adjective because as you said there is this element of 'excess' in it, more than something—it is different from many experiences.

—. Imagine, 13 years ago, when two persons one named Akanksha, the other Sumita met each other, what did they bring into that moment? Akanksha was looking for a non-community ally, and Sumita was looking for a space to grow her self-worth. This began rather simply, but today they are talking about a complex 'relationship', created through an 'excess'!

—. You know, there can be many interpretations of chemistry between people. Ours is a mysterious chemistry, you can say! We had some kind of attraction for each other, not necessarily erotic, but attraction nonetheless, which gave meaning to this complex yet fulfilling relationship.

—. Therefore, to reach a certain intensity, you may need to bond with your fellow traveller with some kind of extra passion, with a special 'excess'. That passion can be a combination of many elements—some known, some not. But it exceeds over marches, meetings and mass campaigning.

—. I see two levels of movements here: movement of our personal moving towards our political. And at another level, your personal/political moving towards my personal/political . . .

—. With an equally passionate intensity! This is perhaps how that 'excess' is created in a relationship . . .

—. Yes, through resonance—giving and receiving with similar frequency. And imagine, we have never fought with each other in the last 13 years, have we?

—. We have argued most bitterly, disagreed over almost everything, been each other's worst critic, but, yes, we've never had a serious fight—ideological or political disharmony. I say this also to highlight that political harmony is very important for our relationship since our personal is so politicized that it influences our bond to a great extent.

—. Do you think then our relationship is political friendship or political alliance?

—. No, I don't mean that. But the friendship is politicized, as the persons involved in this relationship are conscious of their politics. I cannot be apolitically friendly with anyone. I cannot even have a cup of tea at the roadside shack with someone who does not have a political self. The vision can be different, but the person has to be political.

—. That's exactly how I feel about myself.

—. And moving back to the fact that we did not have a serious political disharmony, I also want to point to the fact that Sappho for Equality's leadership, or the steering committee, also did not have serious political disharmony. Sometimes there were disagreements—yes, but disharmony—never. In a de-centralized leadership situation like ours, when all the members of the steering committee have qualities and competence in their own fields, they could have fought for power over others. Instead they created a unique bond through that 'excess'—I see something very special in this. I have learnt to accept that there is something—call it organization, call it ideal, call it political conviction that is beyond me, larger than me. I have learnt humility in this process.

—. I have learnt to appreciate you and others working with me. I may not agree to what you say, or x or y says, but still can appreciate your thought—a process of constructive confrontation. I have learnt to respect you. This is our bond, 'the excess', I think.

—. Perhaps we are extending the meaning of friendship in this manner. Friendship may begin with playing with your *chaddi buddy* (childhood friend), but it may go beyond; it may arrive at a point where you can appreciate and respect your comrade even with all the disagreements between you . . . perhaps this is who we are, bonding over an extended and complex meaning of friendship . . .

—. Camaraderie?

—. Why not?

—. Long live revolution and longer live friendship!!!

Epilogue

We wanted this to be a joint article because we were not just making a philosophical point on friendship and its connection with social activism. Akanksha and Sumita are friends, colleagues, comrades and more. Two individuals, two different backgrounds, two different entry points, two different sets of agendas coming together for something as tangible and as esoteric as friendship. And the activism needed their individual voices, in tune and sometimes off. We, therefore, spoke separately at the beginning while tracing the history to accommodate two coexisting points of view in a subjective approach.

The last section was a conversational piece but we did not want to put individual names to indicate the speaker so as to maintain a pluralistic inclusivity. As we transcribed the conversation, we could clearly see that while the two of them are speaking to each other, their dialogue is a process of togetherness, an engagement with each other only to create something more than Akanksha or Sumita, or both. It was, and still is, in terms of excess.

Notes

1   See Akanksha and Malobika, 'Sappho: A Journey Through Fire' in Brinda Bose and Subhabrata Bhattacharya (eds), *The Phobic and the Erotic: The Politics of Sexualities in Contemporary India* (London: Seagull Books, 2007), pp. 363–68; Subhagata Ghosh, 'Honour Through Freedom: A Non-Heteronormative Take' in Manisha Gupte, Ramesh Awasthi and Shraddha Chickerur (eds), *'Honour' and Women's Rights: South Asian Perspectives* (Pune: Mausam Publications, 2012), pp. 445–70.

2   See Subhagata Ghosh, Sumita Basu Bandyopadhyay and Ranjita Biswas, *Vio-Map: Documenting and Mapping Violence and Rights Violation Taking Place in Lives of Sexually Marginalized Women to Chart Out Effective Advocacy Strategies* (Calcutta: Sappho for Equality, 2011).

3   Saskia Wieringa, 'From Sisterhood and Feminist Solidarity to Affinity', *Swakanthey* [In Our Own Voice], (January 2009): 9.

CHAPTER EIGHT

'Baar Baar Sakhi'
In Search of the Queer Temporalities of Sakhya

TORSA GHOSAL AND KAUSTAVI SARKAR

A group of college students and amateur performers fall like a stack of cards on the gathered audience to the accompaniment of poems being recited. The performance employs spoken word, improvised movements, and stipulates that the audience and the performers transgress the boundaries separating the pedestrian from the aesthetic. Such productions underscore the potential for embodied understanding through audience participation which has been the cornerstone of contemporary activist theatre groups and movements including the Third Theater in Calcutta as well as Open Theater and Living Theater in New York City, among others. Similar participatory politics can be discerned in the productions of Ananya Dance Theater (ADT). ADT's performances deconstruct yoga, Odissi, and Chhau[1] in order to call the audience to act and ensure social justice for women of color. Imbued with lived experiences of participating in such performances, we decided to combine our trainings in dance and literature to make explicit the implicit connections among bodies, patterns of movements, and specific histories. In order to do so, we bring in the concept of Sakhya[2]—which has a layered history and multiple connotations, as explained in this article—and open it up as a framework that can be productively used to activate collective becoming.

Sakhya is simultaneously elusive and omnipresent in our memory and imagination. In his nineteenth-century text, *Brahmanism and Hinduism* (1883), Sir Monier-Williams, explains Sakhya as one of the five phases of worshipping the Hindu god, Krishna. Votaries start with the calm contemplation of the godhead (*santi*), followed by active servitude (*dasya*), a feeling of personal friendship (*sakhya*), a feeling of filial attachment (*vatsalya*), and tender affection resembling a young girl's love for her lover (*madhurya*). So according to this nineteenth-century Oriental reading of Vaishnavism,[3] Sakhya comes somewhere in-between—when the devotee shares camaraderie with Krishna but has not yet reached the state or desire necessary for heterosexual consummation. However, *sakhya* is also one of the seven tenets that undergirds the traditional Hindu marriage. The priest chants 'Om sakhi jaradastayahga/attramshe sakshino vadet pade'[4] while the bride and the groom take their seventh and final step, completing the *saptapadi* rite of the Hindu wedding ceremony. Through this vow the groom hails the bride as his 'sakhi' or friend. Thus, Sakhya is replete with religious connotations. It is perhaps no surprise then that the notion figures prominently in Jayadeva's twelfth-century Sanskrit poem, *Gitagovinda* which celebrates the cult of Krishna.

However, Jayadeva's *Gitagovinda* also promotes Sakhya as a notion that is certainly more complicated than the traditional Hindu interpretations. Sakhya is the eternal conglomeration of bodies and souls that underlies Jayadeva's text. It is the erotic drive toward the 'other' across the porous ontological boundaries which distinguish the divine Lord Krishna from the mythical figure, Radha, and the actual poet, Jayadeva. Sakhya also stipulates that the poet—despite the conspicuous erotic invitations—yields the narrative voice to Radha in the end. Radha's 'loins . . . take the thrusts of love' but she, in turn, asks Krishna to heed 'Jayadeva's splendid speech' (Jayadeva 1977: 124-5). So while reading *Gitagovinda* in search of a theoretical framework for Sakhya, we note the queer ontological and temporal tendencies inherent in the concept.

As a fictional-mythical text,[5] *Gitagovinda* presents us with multiple embedded storyworlds. The framing narrative suggests that the poet figure, Jayadeva, is speaking to an audience whom he urges to repeat the songs after him so as to praise Lord Krishna. Jayadeva is the chosen poet figure because his soul is in perfect tune with that of Krishna. At the level of framed narratives, we have the tales of Radha and Krishna. However, the framing and the framed narratives are not separated as the poet figure not only has access to the characters in the framed world—which could be explained because the characters are his constructions—but the constructed characters also have access to the poet figure. Thus, Sakhya in *Gitagovinda* stipulates the transgression of ontological boundaries resulting in a version of 'metalepsis' —a paradoxical transgression of ontological boundaries in narrative texts, in this case the author-narrator directly interacts with the characters and participates in his composition as opposed to being the omniscient or invisible narrator. Jayadeva might have borrowed this metaleptic structure from the traditions prevalent in classical Sanskrit drama.[6] The resulting ontological fluidity prompted by the overall narrative structure configures Sakhya and, in turn, brings this fluidity into the re-imagined and interpretive re-creations of the ur-text, *Gitagovinda*. It subverts the linear experience of time. In the popular culture of twentieth- and twenty-first century Bengal, prominent artists with divergent sensibilities from Rabindranath Tagore to Rituparno Ghosh continue to return to this ur-text and the notion of Sakhya.

As dancers, we also interpret Sakhya through our performative projects that use multiple modalities such as gestures, music and poetry. Our understanding of Sakhya draws upon our shared experience of Indian classical dances' pedagogic practices. As we were being trained in classical dance forms (Sarkar in Odissi; Ghosal in Kathak), we came into close physical contact with several male and female bodies—of friends and strangers—and forged physical connections with them on stage and during rehearsals. *Gitagovinda* remains an oft-performed text in the repertoire of both Kathak and Odissi. Owing to our mutual interest in Indian classical dance vocabulary and South Asian aesthetics, we embarked on a collaborative project, Herstories in 2013.[7] This project juxtaposes movements of Kathak and Odissi with the meters of an eponymous English poem[8] in order to trace the figure of the Devadasi, or the temple dancer.[9] Historically, the Devadasi enacted the lyrics of *Gitagovinda* in front of the male Hindu deity Jagannath in the temples of Odisha. In these performances, they simultaneously inhabited the multiple subjectivities of the characters from *Gitagovinda*, including Krishna, Radha, sakhis—Radha's female friends—and the poet Jayadeva. Through *Herstories*, we symbolically re-enact the multiple proximities developed in *Gitagovinda* by alluding to the iconography of Radha and Krishna. The iconic postures of Radha and Krishna are transposed onto the bodies of the female dancers, whereby the 'madhurya rasa' (or heterosexual love) reincarnates as Sakhya—a choreographed intimacy or companionship among female bodies—on stage.

In the process, Sakhya emerges as a 'queer' bond not only because it fosters relationships encompassing multiple sexual identities and orientations but also because it forges a sense of omnitemporality where the mythical, the historical and experiences of the present become coterminous. Thus, the notion defies historical emplotment, recalling Eve Sedgwick's metaphor, 'this rack of temporalities' (Barber and Clark 2002: 1). Barber and Clark observe that Sedgwick's theories deal with a 'problem about temporality'—even as Sedgwick designates the time frame in which she writes as a 'queer moment,' she also relegates this moment to the past by saying, 'It *was* a QUEER moment' (ibid.: 2). The queering of time for Sedgwick relates to the experiences of gay men dying due to the AIDS epidemic. At the same time, Sedgwick traces the word queer through its Indo-European roots to mean 'twisting' (Sedgwick 1993: *xii*). Consequently, Jane Gallop reads Sedgwick's metaphor as a simultaneous affirmation of the 'twisted' temporalities that constitute a queer phenomenology and also a scene of torture as it amplifies the awareness of life's and time's transience (Gallop 2001: 47–53). Gallop's interpretation of Sedgwick's 'queer time' emphasizes concurrence and overlap among various irreconcilable temporal experiences: 'Temporality here is so tortuous that terrifying speed can be, at the same time, hauntingly slow' (ibid.: 51). In this reading, Gallop further observes that Sedgwick rejected the notion of 'friendship' in favor of love to characterize her 'fairly strange' relation with the art critic and gay activist, Craig Owens in 'Memorial for Craig Owens' (Sedgwick 1993: 123; Gallop 2001: 53–4). Sedgwick discards the notion of friendship as euphemism because it denies the perverse 'desire' that her portrait of Owens, after his death, wants to exalt. In her reading of Owens' texts and in writing his obituary, Sedgwick performs her 'queer desire' that challenges the legitimacy of death as a means to thwart bodily relations. Queer desire, then, potentiates impossible temporal experiences. While we draw upon the notion of queer time from Sedgwick and Gallop to explain the intertextual and inter-authorial relations among Jayadeva, Tagore and Ghosh, through our choreographic performances we also claim Sakhya as a distinct mode of friendship that does not elide twisted sexual experiences but necessitates it.

Thus, in this essay, we conduct a comparative, intertextual and queer (un)historical reading of *Gitagovinda*, Tagore's *Bhanusimha Thakurer Padabali* (1884) and Rituparno Ghosh's cinematic compositions (both film-texts and lyrics penned by him) to highlight the manner in which they employ Sakhya as a framework for envisioning collective subjectivity. We undermine genealogical relation among texts while focusing on their morphological connections. Further, we illustrate the manner in which we use Sakhya in our choreographic practices, wherein we synthesize as well as transform these received notions. Our textual reading and choreographic interpretation is, to use Valerie Traub's phrase, 'strategically anachronistic' (2002). Using this tactic, we implicate ourselves within the network of connections, across temporal boundaries. This enables us to 'keep open the question of the relationship of present identities to past cultural formations— assuming neither that we will find in the past a mirror image of ourselves nor that the past is so utterly alien that we will find nothing usable in its fragmentary traces' (Traub 2002: 32). As Sedgwick's metaphor, 'rack of temporalities,' highlights multiple temporal experiences are coterminous and, in fact, inherent within one another. Our article is structured around the four conceptual images informing *Herstories*: Bandhani, Nimilita, Pranata and Vishara.[10] Drawing upon these four concepts, we analyze our choreography in relation to the other texts.

1. Bandhani

Unlike the cloudy skies that evoke an erotic mood in the expository verses of the *Gitagovinda*, *Herstories* begins in the heat of a tropical afternoon. Five female dancers dressed in black shirts and orange skirts line up haphazardly to perform the opening lines. One of the dancers is equipped with a microphone. She recites the poem while dancing and the others perform to the rhythmicity and phrasing. Our movements are choreographed according to the aesthetics of Odissi

FIGURE 8.1 Dancers performing the expository verses of 'Herstories'. Ohio Union, The Ohio State University, 2014. *Photograph courtesy Vineet Jitendra Bailur.*

and Kathak. We attempt to create a choreographic solidarity for the Devadasi. As Jayadeva remained a narrator throughout his text, our *sutradhar* (dancer-narrator) continues to prompt our movements through her spoken word performance.

> *Dha Dhin Dhin Dha*
> *Dha Dhin Dhin Dha*
> *Na Tin Tin Na*
> *Tete Dhin Dhin Dha*

Marking time on Teental, all the dancers walk in a circle. As they complete one cycle, consisting of sixteen beats, each dancer introduces a lag. Soon each of the five voices refer to a different section of the rhythm cycle, voicing divergent temporal measures that are concurrent but do not converge. Meanwhile, the circles are not completed on the same plane. The stage has three steps and completing a circle entails traversal of all of these three parallel planes. Thus, from the very outset, both aurally and visuospatially, the performance enforces a 'rack of temporalities'.

In the following movement, the dancers represent the quintessen-
tial moment of the Devadasi's consecration by tying the ghungroo,
anklet, through mimetic gestural language. In addition, Karkata
Samyukta Hastamudra[11] is used here as a visual metaphor to further
establish the idea of tying, or bandhani. The dance itself inflects the
narration as the sutradhar's own ghungroo, vibrating to the choreographed rhythms, intersperses her verbal performance. Though a performative synchronization occurs between Jayadeva as narrator of
Gitagovinda and our sutradhar, her performance also modifies the nar-
ratorial situation as she partakes in the subjectivity of the Devadasi
herself.

The tying of the bells associated with the Devadasi's initiation is
not only a moment to be understood within the context of the historical narrative but also as one replete with formal repercussions for
bringing poetry and dance together. In the first part of *Gitagovinda*,
Jayadeva claims to harness spoken language—with the blessings of the
goddess of speech—into a lyrical poem. Subsequently, he introduces
himself as a character within the text, on the same plane of the page
as the mythical lovers, Radha and Krishna. Further, he encourages his
narratees to join this amorous game when he writes, 'If remembering
Hari enriches your heart, / If his arts of seduction arouse you, / Listen
to Jayadeva's speech / In these sweet soft lyrical songs' (Jayadeva 1997:
69). This invitation conflates devotion and seduction. At the same
time, it equates Hari's art of seduction that arrests Radha and the other
gopis, cow-herding girls, with Jayadeva's art of telling, that binds language in and as poems to entrance the narratees. In this double bind,
the poet enacts his desire of being one with the god he attempts to
eulogize. Yet, in *Gitagovinda*, this oneness is not of the metonymic sort
where the poet as a character represents in part, the whole that is
Krishna, although a religious reading might attempt to interpret the
text as such. The poet figure does not crave Radha, in the vein that
Krishna does. On the other hand, the poet figure craves Krishna and
his Sakhya. In the final stanza of the invocatory poem, for example,
Jayadeva pictures Krishna in Radha's embrace. The first couple of lines
describe Radha's breast under Krishna's sweating chest, whereas the
final couple of lines address the narratee with the deictic 'you,' asking
them to partake the pleasures of Krishna's bodily intimacy: 'May his

broad chest bring you pleasure too!' (ibid.: 73). This rapid switch among the various ontological planes performs the 'tumultuousness' that the poet envisions to be the essence of the queer camaraderie around Krishna. The various songs in *Gitagovinda* from within the confines of strict metrical patterns celebrate the possibility of blurring and blending of boundaries that distinguish bodies. This quasi-erotic, quasi-divine metalepsis epitomizes the notion of Sakhya. Yet, strictly speaking, Jayadeva's poet figure never dissolves his distinctive subjectivity completely within Krishna, Radha or the sakhis.

Sakhya returns in Rabindranath Tagore's rendition of the tales that make up *Gitagovinda*. Tagore's *Bhanusimha Thakurer Padabali* even more explicitly than *Gitagovinda* projects Sakhya as the pivot for lyrical musings. In the poems and songs, Tagore merely alludes to Krishna and Radha's heterosexual and adulterous relationship. The poems primarily narrativize Radha's desire and ability to communicate with her sakhis as she pines for Krishna. Through the routine tasks with sakhis and friendly banter, Radha finds a means to make sense of her desire for Krishna. The macro-narrative of *Bhanusimha Thakurer Padabali* is dilatory. While Jayadeva rapidly puts Hari–Sri (another name for Krishna–Radha) in each other's embrace to urge his narratees to embrace Hari as does Sri, Tagore's poems keep Radha waiting. Yet, during this wait, we find Radha confiding in her sakhis, '*Sokhi lo, sokhi lo, boltoh sakhi lo / jato dukh pawol Radha / nithur Shyam kiye aapon monome / paaol tuchcho kachu aadha . . .*' (Friend, tell me, does Shyam suffer half as much as Radha?). Sakhis remain literally and metaphorically at the very centre of Tagore's text ensuring Radha's sustenance.

It is important to note here that Tagore's text is not a direct translation or even transcreation of *Gitagovinda*. The poems of the fifteenth-century poet, Vidyapati and seventeenth-century poet, Govindadas that narrate the tales of Radha and Krishna also serve as inspiration. It is as if Tagore has managed to lift these poets from their historically distinct contexts and bring them together as a coterie to which his poet-character Bhanusimha also desires to belong. Thus, Bhanusimha exists only in relation to the other poet-narrators: along with forging a historically impossible friendship with Jayadeva, Vidyapati and Govindadas, Bhanusimha also takes a cue from them to enter the textual world. In this textual world, he befriends Radha. Through the song, 'Aaju sakhi muhu muhu', Tagore evokes a tender, celebratory and fragile mood in which the body or bodies of unidentified characters seem to quiver and wander. Readers familiar with the renditions of Radha–Krishna's affair would recognize Radha among the unspecified characters but the only body that the poem identifies by name is 'Bhanu'. In the final line, the poem says, 'Bhanu is dying,' implying the wasting away of his suffering body. Thus, this song prompts us to understand Bhanu's suffering with reference to the sufferings of his sakhi, Radha. What remains ambiguous, however, is whether he is suffering because Radha suffers or he is suffering, like Radha, for the lover, Krishna.

The simultaneous pain and pleasure resulting from this dissolution of ontological and historical boundaries mark Tagore's reading of *Gitagovinda* and of his queer camaraderie with Jayadeva and the other poets. In an even more contemporary context, filmmaker and actor Rituparno Ghosh revisits the same repertoire of Radha–Krishna stories via Tagore. Rituparno Ghosh's own visibility as a queer artist and projection of a distinctive queer identity as a director as well as an actor is inextricably tied to his intertextual relation with Radha–Krishna and Tagore. In his first film as an actor, Kaushik Ganguly's *Aarekti Premer Golpo* (2010), Rituparno Ghosh plays a gay filmmaker who reads Gourango (the devotee of Radha and Krishna) as an androgynous historical figure and expresses himself through Tagore's songs.[12] In another film, *Abohoman* (2010), Ghosh as writer-director depicts an attempt to film the song 'Gahan Kusum Kunje' from Tagore's *Bhanusimha Thakurer Padabali*. Ghosh's later films more often than not had a self-reflexive element in them: the framing narratives would depict the making of other performances or films (*Abohoman*, *Chitrangada: The Crowing Wish* in 2012); while the framed storyworlds transcreated Tagore's texts. Ghosh, briefly before his death, made a documentary on Tagore, *Jeeban Smriti* in 2013, and videos about its 'making' featuring him in place of Tagore's sister-in-law, Kadambari Debi. These are scenes where the director is merely showing an actor, Raima Sen, how to play Kadambari Debi's character but this directorial project is in itself a performance and a means to inhabit the space occupied by Kadambari Debi—Tagore's sister-in-law, friend, and speculated lover. Notably, Tagore had dedicated

Bhanusimha Thakurer Padabali to Kadambari Debi. Tagore's relation with Kadambari Debi was the subject of a film entitled *Chirosokha He* (2007). The film's title refers to the opening line of Tagore's poem and literally translates to 'hail eternal friend'. In the song, the narrator asks the eternal friend, or Chirosokha, not to forsake him or the mortal world. The video showing the making of *Jeeban Smriti* resonates with these subtexts as Ghosh performs Sakhya with his idea of Tagore.[13] This performance evidently recalls Tagore's own similar endeavour to forge bonds across impossible temporal frames with the poets like Jayadeva. Our sutradhar, however, engages more closely with the subjectivities of *Gitagovinda*'s performers, that is, the Devadasis, rather than the coterie of poet figures following Jayadeva.

2. Nimilita

Looking down at the *tribhangi*, a position in Odissi, of one of the dancers, another brings in the notion of the demure Devadasi expressing her desire for Radha's feet. With her hands tied into a knot in front, she almost wishes to be tied to the feet of the other woman whose tribhangi references the iconic posture of Krishna, also known as 'Tribhanga Murari'. Literally, tribhangi implies three distinct angular deflections of the body, a series of corporeal twists (Donaldson 1987: 389). Our sutradhar recites:

> *Tribhanga*, my stance, bends one
> my neck, two my waist,
>
> three my knee. Don't waste
> me a deity; I am no Lord Krishna's gopi, out
> for divine grace.

Thus this moment, even while citing Krishna's gesture, retains the distinct subjectivity of the Devadasi who refuses to be subsumed within his divine grace. The emergent Sakhya harmonizes these multiple subject positions and shifts the emphasis on the network of relations instead of treating Krishna as the singular centre of the textual world. The choreography also subverts the 'economy of repetition and reproduction' of Indian classical dance by re-organizing the performative act around Sakhya rather than around Krishna. Our performance,

FIGURE 8.2 Devadasi expressing her desire for Radha's feet. Ohio Union, The Ohio State University, 2014. *Photograph courtesy Vineet Jitendra Bailur.*

therefore, critically reflects on those acts of *Gitagovinda* where Krishna's body operates as a bridge for sakhis to connect with one another.

Sakhis in Jayadeva's text consolidate their corporeal bond by collectively making love with Krishna. Radha, who desires his exclusive attention, is envious of the other gopis. Yet, she continues to confide in her sakhi. In the fifth song of *Gitagovinda*, Radha tells her sakhi about the way she feels when Krishna kisses and caresses other gopis: 'My heart recalls Hari here in his love dance, / Playing seductively, laughing, mocking me' (Jayadeva 1997: 78). A notable feature of this song is the cohesion of bodies: using collective nouns, Radha as narrator conjoins the subjectivities of the other women. She mentions the 'mouths of round-hipped cowherd girls' that Krishna kisses, the 'thousand cowherdesses' (ibid.: 78–9) with who he interlocks his arms. Despite her aforementioned envy, Radha retains her empathy and performs Sakhya when she notes that Krishna's 'cruel heart is a hard door bruising circles of swelling breasts'. Here too the breasts of the gopis are collectively imagined but this is a picture of shared suffering. It is the collectiveness of this suffering that unites the sakhis as much as their mutual love and longing for Krishna. In an earlier song, Radha, the narrator, while watching Krishna 'dance with young women' mentioned that it is a 'cruel time for deserted lovers' (ibid.: 74). Even when referring to her own suffering, Radha situates herself among the plurality of 'deserted lovers'.

The collective suffering of bodies in cohesion enables Radha to share her narrative with sakhis. Tagore's interpretation of the Radha–Krishna tale foregrounds the collective cohesion of sakhis, while Krishna's body remains a marginal presence in the macro-structure of *Bhanusimha Thakurer Padabali*. Songs begin with Radha as the narrator asking rhetorical questions such as '*Sakhi re peerit bujhbe ke?*'— 'Friend, who will understand love?' but the fact that the narrator continues to enumerate her sufferings implies that the sakhis understand and empathize with her. This empathy is prompted by their collective experience of pain and separation (*biraha*) from one another and Krishna.

Years after publishing *Bhanusimha Thakurer Padabali*, Tagore continued to explore the motifs of separation and cohesion through his songs in *Prem* and *Puja Parjay*. In *Arekti Premer Golpo*, Ghosh while playing a celebrated male jatra actor Chapal Bhaduri, who impersonated female characters on stage for the popular folk-theatre form in Bengal, dances to Tagore's *Puja Parjaay* song, 'Praano bhoriye trisha horiye'. Within the film's narrative, this act performs Sakhya as Chapal entertains Gopa, the wife of his *nagor* (lover), Kumar. Both Gopa and Chapal have been abandoned by Kumar, even as Gopa remains confined to her bed in Kumar's house due to ill-health. Earlier in the film, it is shown that Chapal and Gopa crave for Kumar's love and companionship. However, at this point Chapal holds Gopa enabling her to stand on her feet and dance to the rhythms of Tagore's song. Kumar remains outside the threshold of Gopa's room and watches this performance of Sakhya from behind the curtains. His gaze and presence are neither desired nor acknowledged by the sakhis— Chapal and Gopa.

3. Pranata

This movement requires the dancers to adopt multiple subjectivities and navigate between surrender and transgression. The custom of consecrating the Devadasi entailed locating female desire within the male gaze. Yet, limiting the discussions of this mythical and historical figure to patriarchal exploitation refuses recognition of potential rupture. The temple dancer is known as the fallen woman and, due to caste politics, confined to the bottom most rung of the society. Traditionally, they were 'married' to the deity but were not allowed to enter the inner sanctum of the temple because they were considered to be 'impure' or 'fallen'. *Natyamandapa*, the dancing hall, would always have a threshold separating the ostensibly polluted Devadasis from their divine consort. She used to be a ritual specialist whose services were needed but who was not respected for her work as such. Her performance of surrender before Jagannath was a crucial aspect of the worship as it symbolized the deity's sexual appeasement. As a Devadasi and Jagannath's consort, our sutradhar asks,

> . . . How to speak
> a tongue of warm
> devotion through a marriage, eternal and quiet?

As the dancers line up diagonally along the stairs while performing *Herstories*, each shows the imagined potential of the temple-dancer. While the one at the bottom of the stairs has her head down delineating the idea of the fallen or the surrendering woman, the dancer next in line dons an Ubhayakartari, a double-handed gesture depicting the act of kissing according to the Odissi vocabulary. Two other dancers have their heads and hands held high as if pointing to a higher plane, desirous of ethereal or spiritual elevation. The metaphor of fall comes up again and again in this particular moment as the dancers navigate between succumbing to patriarchal mores and transgressing cultural boundaries through performance.

The desire for transgression originating in the Pranata's suffering is articulated in the folk song used in the opening sequence of *Arekti Premer Golpo*. The non-diegetic soundtrack plays '*Bonomali tumi parojonome hoeo Radha*,' which means that the narrator wishes Radha

FIGURE 8.3 Surrender. Ohio Union, The Ohio State University, 2014. *Photograph courtesy Vineet Jitendra Bailur.*

to be reborn as Krishna and vice versa, so that Krishna pines away for Radha the way she does for him in this birth. However, the use of first- and second-person deictic pronouns (I and you) in the song reposi- tions the characters such that the singer seems to channel Radha's desires and become her voice. It is as though the singer is one of the sakhis in whom Radha confided her sorrows. Ghosh also penned songs emulating Jayadeva's and Tagore's styles for films such as *Raincoat* (2004) and *Memories in March* (2010). In one such song, enti- tled 'Bahu Manaratha,' the narrator, Radha, announces to her sakhi that she is dressing up for her journey to see Krishna. Though we do not hear her sakhi's response in the song, Radha's monologue cues us into understanding that her sakhi is skeptical of this undertaking. Radha also confesses that she is 'chira-abhagini,' eternally unfortunate, and in previous occasions she has spent entire nights waiting for Krishna who did not arrive but still she hopes to undertake the jour- ney. The song shifts from hope to hopelessness but Radha continues to believe that both extreme happiness and pain are epitomized in her relation with Krishna. Ghosh here might be taking his cue from Tagore's song, 'Baar Baar Sakhi,' where a sakhi warns Radha about the futility of her journey to Mathura to see Krishna. The visual, aural, and literal repetition in the phrase 'baar baar' highlights the cyclical nature of Radha's journey and her oscillation between hope and hope-lessness. The phrase also stresses the fact that this conversation among Radha and her sakhis has occurred several times in the past and might again repeat with little variation in the future. Thus, Sakhya in these texts is both a practice in authority and helplessness. Sakhis have the authority to chide one another, advise one another, but ultimately, they also helplessly watch one of them (Radha) suffer and partake in that suffering. However, this collective suffering also becomes a mode of survival and potentiates queer union among the sakhis.

4. Vishara

The flaying of arms through space to bare the chest enacts Vishara. Historically the Devadasi performed bare-chested in front of Jagannath for his sexual pacification. *Herstories* intervenes in this custom by simultaneously citing and subverting it. While the Devadasis arms would be contracted in Utsanga to partly cover her breasts enacting coyness, *Herstories* prompts the dancers to thrust their breasts outward accompanying the expansive movement of the arms. Yet this moment of contrasting body movements is more complicated: baring the chest for Devadasis entailed dancing without any drapery covering their chest and this was prompted by the custom; in our per-formance, the baring of chest is a metaphoric as well as mimetic, accompanied by the choreographic choice of retaining the sartorial covering. Sakhya happens on a number of levels in Vishara. The tem-poral lag introduced in the first act of *Herstories* continues through the divergent movements among dancers in the rest of the acts, but in Vishara, all the dancers perform the same movement, at the same time, articulating the phrase, 'Shout out'. Thus, the final note in *Herstories* is also its loudest as it is voiced and performed collectively.

The final act of *Gitagovinda* depicts Radha's lovemaking with Krishna once her sakhis have left. The sakhis brought Radha to the *kunj* (forest) but did not cross the threshold. They urged Radha to enter Krishna's 'intimate world' (Jayadeva 1997: 118). The twenty-first song of *Gitagovinda* presents the scene where Radha and her sakhis stop at the threshold of Krishna's world. The song itself blends the voice of the poet with that of the sakhis and the collective voices urge Radha on. However, during the final act, the sakhis are no longer physically present, though Jayadeva remains. It is here that Radha, as narrator, after making love with Krishna urges him and the narratees to sympathize with 'Jayadeva's splendid speech' (ibid.: 125).

FIGURE 8.4 Expanding Beyond the Horizon into the Unknown. Ohio Union, The Ohio State University, 2014. *Photograph courtesy Vineet Jitendra Bailur.*

Despite Jayadeva's presence, the concluding movement of *Gita-govinda* undermines Sakhya as Radha's and Krishna's Madhurya takes over. There is no direct counterpart of this moment in Tagore's *Padabali*. In performances of the recital often Govindadas's 'Sundari Radhe Aawe Bani' is used as the concluding piece. This song describes Radha's physical beauty. The narrator in this song is the poet figure and often, a chorus sings this piece, reinforcing the collectiveness of the narrative voice that describes Radha.

While Jayadeva's and Tagore's texts do not emphasize the transgressive potential of Sakhya because the sakhis finally cede centrestage to Radha, Ghosh's films also do not highlight the transgressive potential of the collective as they conclude on a note of singulative action.

Chitrangada's final scene shows Rudra undergoing a sex-change operation. The film ends with the surgeon telling Rudra that Partho, his lover, sent the message, 'Be what you wish to be'. This sequence is edited in a manner such that the message comes from the surgeon rather than Partho. Visually in the two cross-cut sequences Partho and Rudra seem to go on their own distinct ways. In *Arekti Premer Golpo*, Roop not only moves away from Kumar but also recognizes his inability to connect with Chapal, whose life had become a means for his self-exploration. When Chapal resists being subsumed within Roop's narrative, Roop reacts with hostility. Ghosh's films, thus, draw to a close through their emphasis on the singulative in place of the collective, seemingly betraying a distrust of sakhya.

However, through *Herstories* and this article we stress the collective potential inherent in Sakhya. It unifies five non-uniform body types and disparate dance trainings. The moment becomes infinite in its shared possibilities. This endeavour challenges a Brahmanical Sanskritized definition of the concept within a religious context which resists intercaste collectivity and intimacy. Vishara announces the diffusion of multiple identities, sexual orientations and temporalities. The anachronistic and morphological reading of various texts through our performance gives us an opportunity to revel in Sakhya. It provides a temporal space of revelling in and rebelling in each moment, conjuring what Anurima Banerji calls 'paratopic time': 'the time of paratopia stretches across past, present, and future, to create a zone of coeval time / shared time a duration that stretches across each of these partitioned temporal structures to create an encounter with the contemporary' (2009: 355). Each historical moment becomes concurrent and simultaneous in our reading. The moment becomes infinite and transient.

Sakhya introduces a twist to the archetypal narrative of desire by revealing and concealing, expanding and constricting, stretching and contracting at the same time. Karmen MacKendrick finds a similar moment while comparing dance and writing as she observes that 'For words and bodies alike in motion, it is the love of the moment that demands the moment in all its irreplaceable, indeed its unplaceable, singularity. It is the impossible recognition of every moment as infinitely lost already, the infinite longing for the moment that as lost is always yet to come' (MacKendrick 2004: 146). So, *Herstories* not only engages with the past but also projects a future through the moment of Vishara.

Herstories opens the possibility for synthesizing various modes of research and interpretations. Presented as an ongoing research exercise between poetry and movement, *Herstories* activates several temporalities. It shares time with the twelfth-century *Gitagovinda*, the nineteenth-century *Bhanusimha Thakurer Padabali* and the twentieth- and twenty-first century films. Our reading primarily critiques the search for the soul in Sakhya prevalent in the Brahmanical legacy by bringing bodies into the discussion. While this allows us to investigate queer temporal possibilities of the Devadasi's performance, we as dancers continue to stand in and for actual Devadasi bodies. Davesh Soneji critiques Indian classical dance pedagogy's practice of supplanting the actual Devadasi bodies. Following his encounter with Saraswati, a contemporary Devadasi, he observes, 'Even though Saraswati lives in the same city as India's most successful Bharatnatyam dancers, she must assume a different temporal position; as a non-Brahmin woman from a Devadasi background, she remains suspended in a vestigial, twentieth-century modernity and cannot integrate into the present economies of South Indian culture' (2012: 226). Notably, in Soneji's ethnographic reading the figure of the Devadasi continues to queer time and in *Herstories*, we emphasize such twisted temporalities. While our project is not without its limitations, it also attempts to re-imagine the figure of the Devadasi through collective becoming epitomized in the notion of Sakhya.

Notes

1 Chhau is a tribal dance form popular in the Indian states of West Bengal, Odisha, and Jharkhand. It employs elements of martial arts, acrobatics

and athletics and is usually based on religious or festive themes and folk tales.

2   In Hindu religious understanding, Sakhya is the devotional friendship to Krishna and the reciprocal love between dear and intimate friends. In this article, we critique this dominant denotation of the term. For an application of the dominant meaning of *Sakhya,* see Chattopadhyay 1995 and Bryant and Ekstrand 2004.

3   Vaishnavism is a major branch of Hinduism involving the worshipping of Vishnu and his avatars. Krishna is said to be an avatar of Vishnu.

4   Literal translation: Now you have become mine and I offer my life to you/ We will be truthful to each other and love each other.

5   *Gitagovinda*'s form eludes strict categorization. The ashtapadis (stanzas gathered in groups of eight) oscillate between narrative and lyrical moments. Each ashtapadi is preceded by a shorter verse that establishes the setting for the action to follow.

6   Brian Richardson observes that classical Sanskrit drama's multiple framing devices potentiated metalepsis. Dramas such as Kalidasa's *Shankuntala* would start with an invocation, followed by a miniature drama set in the theatre that would serve as prologue to the play (2015).

7   The gestures in *Herstories* are adopted from the lexicon of the Indian classical dance in general and from Odissi and Kathak in particular. Odissi is the Indian classical dance form from the eastern Indian state of Odisha while Kathak originated primarily in three northern Indian cities, Jaipur, Lucknow and Varanasi.

8   The poem 'Herstories' was written by Torsa Ghosal. It has two sections: the first section breaks the fixed verse form, Sestina. Sestina is a twelfth-century European verse form where the end words of each of the lines in the first stanza repeat in the subsequent stanzas in a particular pattern. The end word of the first line of the first stanza becomes the end word of the second line of the second stanza, third line of the third stanza, and so on. The pattern follows a bottom-up cycle. Typically, sestinas have six stanzas and a tercet. Ghosal does away with the sixth stanza and the tercet while introducing a second section to the poem that continues to shuffle end words in three quatrains and a tercet.

9   *Devadasi* is used to refer to women dedicated to deities in Hindu temples. Allen (1997), Chatterjee (1945), Gaston (1992), Jordan (2003), Kersenboom (1998), Meduri (1996), O'Shea (2007), Parker (1998), Prasad (1991), S. Anandhi (1991), Srinivasan (1985), Thieleman (2002) and Vijaisri (2004) have extensively discussed the social, political, anthropological and economic dimensions of lives of Hindu temple dancers.

10 Bandhani is a feet posture in which the top of the foot rests in the back of the knee. Nimilita is an eye gesture in which the eyeballs point directly below. Pranata references the image of the fallen or the surrendered. Vishara refers to diffusion and spreading out. See *The Odissi Dance Path Finder* (Bhubaneswar: Odissi Research Centre, 1988) and Kapila Vatsayan, *Classical Indian Dance in Literature and the Arts* (New Delhi: Sangeet Natak Akademi, 1968) for more details.

11 Karkata Samyukta Hastamudra is a double-handed gesture in which the fingers are interlocked with each other; see *The Odissi Dance Path Finder* (1988).

12 Though Kaushik Ganguly was both the writer and director of *Aarekti Premer Golpo*, Ghosh was identified as the production designer and creative director of the film; the music of the film was composed by Debojyoti Misra who has collaborated with Ghosh in most of the projects we mention here—*Raincoat* (2004), *Memories in March* (2010), *Ganer Opare* (2010–11), and *Chitrangada* (2012).

13 See Dasgupta, Bakshi and Datta (2012) for an alternate analysis of Rituparno Ghosh's Rabindrik sensibilities.

Works Cited

ALLEN, M. H. 1997. 'Rewriting the Script for South Indian Dance'. *TDR* 41(1): 63–98.

BANERJI, Anurima. 2009. 'Paratopias of Performance: the Choreo-graphic Practices of Chandralekha' in Andre Lepecki and Jenn Joy (eds), *Planes of Composition: Dance, Theory, and the Global*. London: Seagull Books, pp. 346–71.

BARBER, Stephen M, and David L. Clark (eds). 2002. *Regarding Sedgwick: Essays on Queer Culture and Critical Theory*. London: Routledge.

BRYANT, Edwin, and Maria Ekstrand. 2004. *The Hare Krishna Movement: The Postcharismatic Fate of a Religious Transplant*. New York: Columbia University Press.

CHATTERJEE, Santosh Kumar. *Devadasi Temple Dancer*. Calcutta: Book House, 1945.

CHATTOPADHYAY, Maya. 1995. *Devotional Friendship (Sakhya) in the Vaiṣṇavism of the Early Caitanya Tradition*. Dissertation. Montreal: Concordia University.

DASGUPTA, Rohit, Sangeeta Datta, and Kaustav Bakshi. 2014. 'The World of Rituparno Ghosh: Texts, Contexts, Transgressions'. *South Asian History and Culture* 2: 223–37

DONALDSON, Thomas E. 1987. *Kamadeva's Pleasure Garden, Orissa*. Delhi: B. R. Publishing Corporation.

GALLOP, Jane. 2011. 'Sedgwick's Twisted Temporalities "Or Even Just Reading and Writing"' in E. L. McCallum and Mikko Tuhkanen (eds), *Queer Times, Queer Becomings*. New York: State University of New York.

GASTON, Anne-Marie. 1991. 'Dance and the Hindu Woman: Bharatanatyam Reritualized' in Julia Leslie (ed.), *Roles and Rituals for Hindu Women*. Rutherford: Fairleigh Dickinson University Press.

GHOSAL, Torsa. 2015. 'Herstories', *Muse India* 60 (March–April). Available at: https://goo.gl/Xq5Ld5 (last accessed on 11 July 2017).

―――. 2014a. *Herstories*. A performance choreographed by Kaustavi Sarkar. Ohio State University, Columbus (January 31).

―――. 2014b. A performance of 'Herstories'. Ohio State University, Columbus: US Bank Theater (March 7).

JAYADEVA. 1977. *Love Song of the Dark Lord: Jayadeva's Gitagovinda* (Barbara S. Miller ed.). New York: Columbia University Press.

JORDAN, Kay K. 2003. *From Sacred Servant to Profane Prostitute: A Study of the Changing Legal Status of the Devadasis, 1857–1947*. New Delhi: Manohar.

KERSENBOOM, Saskia. 1987. *Nityasumangali: Devadasi Tradition in South India*. Delhi: Motilal Banarsidas.

MACKENDRICK, Karmen. 2004. 'Embodying Transgression' in André Lepecki (ed.), *Of the Presence of the Body: Essays on Dance and Performance Theory*. Middletown, CT: Wesleyan University Press.

MEDURI, A. 1996. *Nation, Woman, Representation: The Sutured History of the Devadasi and Her Dance*. Dissertation. New York University.

MITRA, Royona. 2009. 'Dancing Embodiment, Theorizing Space: Exploring the 'Third Space' in Akram Khan's *zero degrees*' in Andre Lepecki and Jenn Joy (eds), *Planes of Composition: Dance, Theory, and the Global*. London: Seagull Books, pp. 40–63.

MONIER-WILLIAMS, Monier. 1974. *Religious Thought and Life in India: Vedism, Brahmanism, and Hinduism*. New Delhi: Oriental Books.

The Odissi Dance Path Finder, VOLS 1 and 2. 1988. Bhubaneswar: Odissi Research Centre.

ORR, Leslie C. 2000. *Donors, Devotees, and Daughters of God: Temple Women in Medieval Tamil Nadu*. New York: Oxford University Press.

O'SHEA, J. 2007. *At Home in the World*. Middletown, CT: Wesleyan University Press.

PARKER, K. 1998. ''A Corporation of Superior Prostitutes': Anglo-Indian Legal Conceptions of Temple Dancing Girls, 1800–1914'. *Modern Asian Studies* 32(3): 559–633.

RICHARDSON, Brian. 2015. 'Towards a History of Unnatural Narratives' in *Unnatural Narrative: Theory, Practice, History*. Columbus: Ohio State University Press, pp. 91–120.

SEDGWICK, Eve Kosofsky. 1993. *Tendencies*. Durham: Duke University Press.

SONEJI, Davesh. 2012. *Unfinished Gestures: Devadāsīs, Memory, and Modernity in South India*. Chicago: University of Chicago Press.

THIELEMANN, S. 2002. *Divine Service and the Performing Arts in India*. New Delhi: A. P. H. Publishing.

TRAUB, Valerie. 2002. *The Renaissance of Lesbianism in Early Modern England*. Cambridge: Cambridge University Press.

VATSAYAN, Kapila. 1968. *Classical Indian Dance in Literature and the Arts*. New Delhi: Sangeet Natak Akademi.

VIJAISRI, P. 2004. *Recasting the Devadasi: Patterns of Sacred Prostitution in Colonial South India*. New Delhi: Kanishka Publishers.

CHAPTER NINE

the circle of friends

AULIC

the circle of friends
moves from house to house

scattered and driven out
no city would have us.

we shift and turn with
spinning heads, twinkling eyes

to stop at nothing but shame
guilt or anything like it.

what we lose we gain
staying far breathing close

where do we go but here
air earth water and the sun

feed us with a melancholy
deeper than sorrow

lighter than pleasure
wider than the sky in its bluest hour.

the circle of friends changes
its face, or the many coloured mask,
receives pain with delights
or joy with its thorny belts.

what good is the proximity of a friend
if it won't break us open?

what good are our words
if they keep us from a necessary shout?

———

A Note on the Poem

There was a time when friends lived in the same city. There was a time when we knocked on each other's doors around midnight. To laugh, to cry, to kiss. To throw stones at the barricades that walled up against our dreams. We fought against state violence, patriarchy, homophobia and a long list of discriminatory habits of the societies to which our destinies were tied to. Then we left. Each to her own carved migratory patterns. To the west, north and south. A few got lost on the way. Even fewer returned. This poem is a tribute to the migratory fellow fighters, the beautiful passionate courageous women I had met and befriended in South Asia. I, too, am a migrant now. A nomad looking for another 'circle of friends'. To embrace, to love, to desire and to fight together. East or West, South or North, Asia or Europe. The time to die and to live is not over.

Aulic
19 March 2015

CHAPTER TEN

The Unruly Grammar of Friendship

DEBANUJ DASGUPTA

Dear WD, loving is amorphous. Never hold on to the person you care for. Attachment is painful. Loving presence is joyous. We fly into each other's lives; we fly with each other as birds in the sky; difference marks us intimately and yet our intimate formations fulfill us. I will never forget your exuberant smiles, corky sense of humor, and that butch voice of yours, which saw me through the first year of my recovery.

Dear HLL, traveling with you around India on long train rides has been a joyous as well as a learning experience. I felt vulnerable while discussing my parents' financial issues with you. I was crying as we watched Ganga Aarti on Dashashwamedha Ghat in Banaras. It was unbelievable that I had been addicted to substance for the past 13 years. And, today here we were standing next to each other on a boat, undergoing an intense spiritual experience. We are different, coming from distant lands, and intimate friends.

We come to this fellowship brutalized, devastated with addiction, and with legal consequences. My body was tired, spirit dead, rife with chemically conditioned emotions. I remember walking into my first meeting shaking with fear. I felt bare, and afraid of finally acknowledging my addiction. As I looked around the room I looked for difference. I did not know what my next day would look like. I needed to save myself. A tall white guy with long curly hair looking like Jesus walked up to me. "Hey man! This is my phone number, please call me anytime." He gave me a hug and a smile. This was my first lesson in the fellowship. I called him from the bus. "I can give you a ride to a meeting tomorrow." I said,

"Yes." Good god since then my life has opened up to one of the most loving and spirited journeys in my life. I came to quit drugs, and today, I am learning to practice love and friendship across corporeal differences.

One Brown / One White

You and I are differently placed in society.
White like New England Yacht Club
Brown like smelly Indian food
Your eyes give me hope
Junkie
Whore
Diva
Fear, anger, resentment
Entropic white blood cells
Regenerative medications

"We keep coming back Debanuj"
"I am scared WD!"
Phone calls
Text to Text
Captain Kirk, Dr. Spock, and the Starship Enterprise
We fly
We land
"Debanuj, recovery means step work. Faith, keep faith Debanuj"
"Happy anniversary, crazy Indian"
As you walked me through my first year of quitting drugs, I learnt to trust another gay man of my age. Once again! Once again WD!

Trust that does not ask for proof
Yet the dis-ease asks for proof
Anger
Jealousy
Disbelief
Anger, Jealousy, Disbelief keeps me wrapped up in negativity
Learning to get out of self-obsession vital for my recovery

Recovery is about relationships
Relationships are like shifting lines in the sand
I cannot struggle across differences anymore
I need a friend, someone who shows excitement in my life
"I am scared of your anger"
Righteous indignation
"You cannot hoard love, Bubba. We pass it on. We share that which
is shared with us so freely"

I gave away my one-year coin to FW
We keep what we have by giving it away
To whom must one submit?
One must submit to the one who loves
Love that is pure and perverse
Love between an older and younger man
Love between a brown, black, white, and yellow addict

We were dying singularly
We learn to live collectively

In this essay, I (re)member my experiences with learning to live without drugs. Friendship is vital to recovery. Learning to stop using drugs, and living a new way of life requires forging friendships with other recovering addicts. Many addicts come into recovery through courts, jails, and after surviving long-term health consequences. Our bodies and pleasures are intensely regulated through routine drug tests, court appearances, probation officers, child-services departments, and intense medical regimens. Friendships in the time of recovery create a vital network that helps many of us endure within intense zones of discipline and regulation. I present the fellowship forged through recovery as a form of coalitional ecstasy shared between addicts. Coalitional ecstasy is a carnal experience, one that is forged through sharing openly and honestly about trauma, addiction, and bodily sensations. Sharing corporeal differences in the recovery period helps forge bonds between bodies situated across striated spaces, bringing us together, and driving us toward spiritually fulfilling journeys.

The essay is written in a form of a queer epistolary exchange, a love letter for all of my friends. The central argument being: *friendships across differences hold potentials for cutting through biopolitical regulation of bodies marked as diseased addicts.* Following Michel Foucault, I argue that drug- and disease-related regulations are a biopolitical apparatus that massify people into population categories such as felons, pathological addicts, delinquents, and criminals. The criminalization of addiction through drug-related offenses exclude recovering addicts from the gates of the polis. Such exclusions range from barring felons from voting, pursuing jobs in different fields, or taking away licenses for the practice of nursing or pharmacy. Regulation of addict bodies through probation officers, rehabilitation centers, and clinical procedures bears similarities with the Foucauldian analysis of disciplining madness. Utilizing Foucault's ideas about friendship as a way of life, I present my friendships within a 12-step recovery program as a kind of vitality that holds potentials for cutting biopolitical regulations of life and death. The essay and several sentences do not follow any specific grammatical or academic form. Part-letter, part-reflection, this essay takes extracts from my 12-step work, conversations, theoretical journeys, in the hope of registering intimacies between diseased, perverse, criminal bodies. The reader is welcome to make her own meaning of this diverse discursive horizon.

A Mosaic of Flesh and Words.

In the first section of the essay, I will elaborate Michel Foucault's ideas about biopower and friendship. Drawing upon Socratic ideas of friendship and love, Foucault had begun to enumerate an ethics of the self as a form of political resistance (Foucault 1988; Roach 2012; DasGupta 2014). According to Foucault, friendship consists of reflection, friends writing letters to each other, taking an inventory of their daily activities. In this way everyday relations forged through friendship have the potential for desubjectivation. I bring Foucault's ideas about friendship in conversation with my experiences with a 12-step recovery program.

In the second section, I will sketch sensations traveling through my body in order to draw the force relations forged within my friend-

ship networks. I attend to the everyday entanglements of my relationships within a 12-step program in order to locate dense points within
which power is transferred between our bodies. Power is conceived as
a kind of vitality generated through this program between bodies
which are otherwise relegated to regulation, and ultimately death.

In the final part, I will attempt to delineate contentious intimacies
forged across differences between strangers within the 12-step program that create potential for a new form of life. Such life, I argue, does
not culminate in a miraculous counter-public (Povinelli 2012) but
rather operates as a form of enduring vitality shaping the economies
of shared favors within the otherwise delinquent bodies.

Biopower and Addiction

Michel Foucault enumerates that after the anatomic discoveries of the
human body and its codification in Biology, there emerges the perception of "man as species" (2003: 242). Man as species is the classifi-
cation of bodies where individuals are situated within a larger
population ("global mass"), which is affected by "overall processes of
birth, death, production, illness and so on" (ibid.: 243). Power therefore
becomes interested in seizing populations rather than individuals.
Technologies of power are therefore not simply limited to drilling discipline into individual bodies but, rather, interested in managing, controlling masses. This according to Foucault is the biopolitics of the
human race. The domain of biopolitics encompasses illnesses that
sapped the productive capacity of different population categories, such
as senility, infirmity, accidents, and anomalies. These accidents, anomalies, long-term illnesses neutralized individuals and put them out of
the economic circuit. These illnesses or conditions could not be erad-
icated but needed to be managed, to defray the costs on the society,
economy, and the government. Biopolitics therefore gets interested in
problems of birth rate, fertility rate, mortality rate, in- and out-migra-
tion. All of which are pertinent factors in establishing power over populations. Following Foucault, I will argue that those dealing with
addiction are categorized as dangerous delinquent bodies. Addiction-
related criminal procedures intersect with the racist nature of the
prison industrial complex in order to create categories of bodies

marked as "dangerous threats to society" (Chin 2001; Gilmore 2007). In the US, drug convictions have been freighted with the most severe collateral consequences. Offenders may lose out on student loans and other educational benefits, drivers' licenses, professional affiliations, access to public housing, food stamps, and other benefit providing necessities of life (Chin 2011). Most drugs-related offenders are white; however, most people imprisoned for drug offenses are not (ibid.). This paradox aptly represents the long history of drug-related racialized criminalization in the US. In the early twentieth century, drug ingestion in the US became a criminal act based upon fear of the dangerous foreigner and internal racial minority (Chin 2011; Musto 1999). According to the historian David Musto, white Americans feared that "Negros" using cocaine could survive bullet injuries or engage in sexual battery. Similarly opium use in Chinatown was feared—since smoking opium could break down sexual inhibitions (Musto 1999). The addict in this way is always a racialized Other, sexual predator, dangerous and a mad figure. Containment and regulation of the mad addict figure becomes a vital pre-occupation of drug-related criminal procedures. In recent times, the "War on Drugs" initiative started by President Ronald Reagan intensified the efforts to criminalize addiction by heightening the collateral consequences (Chin 2011). Regulation of the addict is geared toward violently disciplining the mad body and at times excluding the body from opportunities of participating in productive folds of the society. In other words, addicts are criminals relegated to die in shame, biomedically regulated through rehabilitation centers and drug counselors.

Let me shift my writing style. The previous paragraph feels dense. I feel cold. My gut is cramping. I am taking a break. I turn on Facebook to change my cover picture. I see TJ, CJ, and LJ's smiling faces in this picture. We are dressed in our best suits for CJ's wedding. We are smiling. You really cannot say who has what kind of collateral damages. We are standing shoulder to shoulder loving each other.

We were dying singularly. Together we are smiling.

Dear FJ, I cannot take your collateral consequences away. Arrested at the age of 22, convicted as a felon, you are now unable to take student loans. Neither can you pursue several professions, or find meaningful employment. Remember the time we were siting at my kitchen table? I was warming up the leftover *khichdi* and eggs. We are brothers, close friends, sipping coffee. You are heterosexual and I am homosexual. We both talked about being angry, our sexual fantasies, and fears. You looked up and said, "But you are pursuing a good career, man. I do not resent you or others any more. I am accepting my consequences, bro." A few years ago "acceptance" would sound like defeat to me. I would ask of myself, "How can you accept the consequences of an unjust criminal justice system? Isn't this about becoming a docile body? We need to resist and fight."

And then we walk to a meeting together.

My home group.

SM has set up the chairs in a circle. He leaves a gap between the rows for people to move around, get coffee, and get to the restroom.

MS is making coffee. She is struggling to stay clean right now

Crazy Fredric is announcing all the local recovery events. Some say he lost a part of his brain in a car crash. Since, then he rambles and is erratic.

I look around the room

Erratic bodies

Smiling faces

Balding queers

Cancer survivors

Veterans surviving PTSD

Young addicts speaking about falling in love

MS is talking about losing her child to addiction

Eye close my eyes

There is no difference

White upon white upon brown upon black upon crazy upon the wretched.

"Surrender, Debanuj! The first step is about surrender."

"WTF!! I don't like surrender. That sounds defeatist. I have never surrendered to racism, sexism, homophobia and cis-genderism."

"Acceptance, Debanuj. Learn to accept your past. Making amends helps in forgiving yourself. Forgive yourself and those who have harmed you."

Step 9 is about making amends.

I call Suzette. I tell her about the times I was absent from her life, taking advantage of our friendship. I am learning to remain account-able in conversation with my sponsor RM. I wrote an email to RM after making amends with BRR in New York City this summer. This was my first time clean in New York City. Visceral presence. Each street, each corner, each park rife with memories, scenes of friendship, loss, yearning . . .

Scenes of Accountability

Dear MRR, I have no words. A bundle of sensations. All I want to do is to turn off the lights and get lost in dreams. At 48th and 8th we held each other and said goodbyes.

"BR, I am leaving a piece of my heart and life with you."

"Me too D, I am leaving a piece of my heart with you."

Yearning for the days when we spent the night with each other, shaved each other's back. My friendship with BR is my sense of home, my innermost sense of security, belonging, loving and being loved. One of my biggest resentments has been losing his friendship, well-being in physical proximity with him. Why? Why did I use, make it difficult for him? And, for me . . .

"D, I was worried you were going to die, I was going to loose you." I decided to keep quiet and listen to his fear, confusion, and how he is dealing with his boyfriend's depression now. I acknowledged that I had taken advantage, lied, acted from resentments, jealousy, and fear. I told him I will never do this to a friend again.

We looked into each other's eyes.

I wish I did not have to say goodbye to him. I wish we were neighbors, sleeping in each other's arms. We are best buddies, and seeing him bid goodbye while sobbing in the middle of maddening Times Square hurts. I want us to get on the same train . . . like we used to in our late 20s. I wish time would stop, or as BR put it, "Can you take a job here and come back? Please, I miss you."

Today I will sleep being grateful that I am experiencing this moment and being in NYC clean.

Tender

Bitter

Sweet

Heart Cracked Wide Open . . .

Absence.

Presence.

Tears

Feelings

Remorse

What can you do when you feel the pain of a friend?

Acceptance

Care of the Self and the Other: One Day at a Time

At the end of each day during my first year of recovery I would call WD (my first sponsor), like clockwork at 10 p.m. Our conversations ranged from my fear of the future, learning to accept my past, learning to feel and live with feelings, to an inventory of each other's day.

"Did you have any resentments today?"

"Did you lie?"

"What could I have done better today?

My love for WD, and now for RM, is a tender bond. I respect their journeys in recovery. My nightly conversations with RM (my present sponsor) are not as frequent these days. We speak about twice a week.

I email him my nightly inventory and gratitude list. The relationship between a sponsor and a sponsee is a special bond. Both my sponsors hold a dear space in my heart. Our flesh and being are entangled through nightly inventories, Step work, and loving guidance. WD and RM have their own sponsors. They were newcomers at some point. Over a period of time, and finishing all of the 12 steps, they are now sponsors for newly recovering addicts. I now have the opportunity of sponsoring two newly recovering addicts. Our journeys speak to what Foucault had pointed out as "care of the self," an everyday practice carried out by the Stoics (1988: 34). The writing of letters, a detailed inventory of everyday life, and the insistence of learning to practice ethical principles in everyday life bears similarities with the 12-step process—one that requires detailed examination of oneself, learning to take an inventory of one's entire day, and promptly making amends when one falls short of acting ethically. In this everyday exchange, the subjectivation of "addicts" as delinquents is potentially cut through. Friends sharing with each other across age, race, class, sexuality differences operate as a technology for desubjectivation.

I do not know who I am. I only know what we are becoming . . .

"The truth will set you free."

Freedom in recovery is not a freedom from regulation in society. Rather, it is everyday act of love and accountability. Working on my daily inventory, promptly admitting my wrongs. Realizing, fear is the cheapest room in my house, while sharing with friends is perhaps the window that brings in fresh air.

In this now there is no answer, no formula for a brilliant future, no plots to overthrow the criminal system. Just learning to practice friendship. Being challenged by my sponsor to practice the ethics of accountability, not holding resentment, being there for each other.

Life–serenity–endurance–living.

An unruly quotidian grammar. Inversion. Friendship. Struggling through difference. Friendship, an ethics of discomfort, a challenge to live differently. Just for today.

Works Cited

CHIN, Gabriel J. 2002. "Race, the War on Drugs, and the Collateral Consequences of Criminal Conviction." *Journal of Gender, Race, and Justice* 6: 253.

FOUCAULT, Michel. 1988. *Technologies of Self: A Seminar with Michel Foucault.* Amherst, MA: University of Massachusetts Press.

———. 2003. *Society Must Be Defended: Lectures at College De France 1975-1976.* New York: Picador.

MUSTO, David F. 1999. *The American Disease: Origins of Narcotic Control.* Oxford: Oxford University Press.

POVINELLI, Elizabeth. 2011. *Economies of Abandonment: Social Belonging and Endurance in Late Liberalism.* Durham, NC: Duke University Press.

ROACH, Tom. 2012. *Friendship as a Way of Life: Foucault, AIDS, and the Politics of Shared Estrangement.* Albany: State University of New York.

CHAPTER ELEVEN

Life-Making

NIHARIKA BANERJEA

I have selected the following lines from a larger narrative around life-making that I have written over the past two and a half years around myself and a friend, a lover, a collaborator, an interlocutor, a partner. These are reflections about work and workspaces, desire, pleasure, politics, love, recognition, mourning, loss, the everyday themes that are lived but also unshareable. I hope we can connect through these unshareable lines and perhaps mutate together into something else— even if momentarily.

1

I do not wish to render intelligible the magic,
the spectral desires and hauntings;
our bodies and words appear
in the cracks of regulatory regimes—
where dreams are made and lives lived.

2

Tantalizing ecologies,
affective voices and blind silences
obligate us not to predict but inhabit and work through
our generative intimacies.

3

Let's make some life in these queer times—
Let make our matured bodies move—
with some music, words and places . . .
Perhaps we will always calibrate through undesirable temporalities
But when did we ever have a fixed referent?

4

White, brown and orange
Dancing with the dark sea and dark eyes . . .
Your tentative moves filling up the entire screen
Interspersed with tales of violence and a lost child in-between

5

Precarious relationalities—
Active and unhinged through fraught histories;
A chance nevertheless—
Prompted by an elsewhere . . .
Where the 'I' is beside itself . . .

6

If loss is meant to be
Let it be with you,
Amidst the tea, rocks and dust
I am
Holding on to the last moments of a fading day . . .
Old footprints staring at me
As I strain to make new ones in the sand.

7

As one morning sculpts itself on the other
Through sounds, colours, smells and faces
That participates inadvertently

In conversations, bodily pleasures, and south to east taxi travels,
I sort, sift and rupture with you—
Producing myself over and again
In this everyday aesthetics of existence.

8

As we work the theatre
Of overflowing bodies, words and interim streets,
The scorching sun makes me wonder
if it's a late-winter afternoon
And what the early summer will bring
With you . . .

9

Standing naked with you
I play with intimacy and distance.
The togetherness somewhere in-between
At times lived, at other times to be desired.
With nothing to govern,
Except for the minutiae of living
In the here and now.

10

Let's live tomorrow evening around differential precarities
With the glossy hoardings and garish posters.
The taut and marked skins—
So wretched
So alive
Will be our template and our memorial.

11

(Ser)
Playful translation,
Meticulous pedagogies,

Molecular erotics,
Is *to be* at ease with the world
With her.

12

It was a different public space.
On the floating road
Escaping the mechanical eye
Breathing the rock art
We were together . . .

13

When my fingers met
The striated underbelly of the Himalayas
The etched stones spoke through her leathery lips.

14

A place for kinship—
That secretes through the cracks of hypernormative regimes;

A place for pleasure—
The resides amidst unintelligible faces;

A place for friendship—
That undoes us over and over again.

15

I know the boxes are gathering dust,
I know the translations are inadequate,
I know the texts are framed in another life,
Yet—
In an ordinary afternoon
I am calmed
By an opaque music from the future.

16

Perhaps Cuba will never be . . .
But Juanica's sand sifter
Will sadden her
On such unbearable afternoons.

17

Lost afternoons are mostly melancholic . . .
But were they always so irremediable?

18

She exceeds my reductions
And I live
Enfolded by her death.

19

Another afternoon turns
With—
wild flowers,
lived words,
despondent messages
And—
the madness of your carnal embrace.

20

The act of reaching a place
Is not the goal.
So she never arrives
But travels . . .
Alone
And
With me.

21

A certain non-knowledge
Is necessary for change.
But being undone in knowledge—
Is perhaps also
The act of mourning.

22

The singular moment—
Lost, imminent, non-present.
She—
Inhabiting the moment
As it is . . .
Non-representable, not of a property
Singular.

23

That elusive tranquility—
Is scattered within her objects.
I converse with each fragment
About the perils of desiring the prosaic
And
The promises of a different ordinary life.

24

Pain stabilizing the timeworn bodies
And forming new stimuli
For the upcoming days . . .

25

Flash points—
Places
Bodies merging

Narratives being written
To make bearable
The insipid times.

26

The dot on my screen—
Green and yellow
Yellow and green
Tingles my skin.
She—
My precious interlocutor.

27

Obstreperous contradictions
Pointing the limits of reality and
A life, elsewhere . . .

28

Moving parts never inhabit.
And so, continues—
The heaviness of accruing knowledge.

29

Vicissitudes of my inheritance—
Madness and death.

30

Perhaps this is a zero hour
And thus—
No coping,
No despair.
I die
So I can live.

CHAPTER TWELVE

'I Get By with a Little Help from My Friends'
Ending Domestic Violence One Friendship at a Time

SHANNON PEREZ-DARBY

In the first generation of our modern domestic violence movement we've had many successes: we've dramatically changed the public's idea about domestic violence, transformed narratives around victim blaming; built economic infrastructures of support for survivors. But what we haven't done is significantly reduce the overall rates of domestic violence.

Survivors of domestic violence are not a monolith; there's so much diversity in experience, severity of violence and paths to healing but there are important similarities. In my 10 years of working as a domestic violence advocate, the one thing that has united all the survivors I've worked with is the experience of isolation. Numerous studies cite the impact of isolation on survivors: from the power and control wheel to domestic violence 101, it is common knowledge that the isolation experienced by survivors is a powerful and effective tactic of control.

When we understand domestic violence as a pattern of power and control that limits survivors' agency (ability to make choices), it doesn't take long to see how effective isolation is in trying to control another human being. If you're trying to control someone, if you want them to do what you want, or what you say to them, and be in-service to your choices and goals instead of theirs—it's a very effective strategy to keep that person isolated from their friends and family, the people who might be able intervene.

Domestic violence needs isolation, it needs us all to be separate, it feeds on romantic myths about how 'love is all you need' and 'if we love each other enough, we can make it work'. These stories help us justify the moments we choose to ignore our friend's text in favour of cuddling up with our sweeties and tell us that we should value our romantic relationships over our friendships. These stories make it possible for batterers to isolate survivors.

Survivors reach out to their friends and family long before they ever access formal domestic violence services. Survivors have a complex set of needs that can never be replaced by social services agencies. They need the same things we all need, support to live the lives we envision for ourselves.

Survivors often find that their friends and family, although eager, don't know how to provide the care and support they need. It's easy to see why: often survivors go back to their abusive partners many times over. This isn't because survivors are stupid or weak but because domestic violence is powerful and effective and feeds on the social stigma associated with the victim. The path out of an abusive relationship is often long and non-linear. Friends and family may feel overburdened or overwhelmed (like the survivors) with all the back and forth and eventually find it easier to pull away than engage.

What if we took all of the support people in the survivor's life and equipped them with the skills to offer help? What if these same skills could also address the underlying cause of domestic violence?

A Ten-Step Guide to Supporting Survivors While Not Losing Yourself

Hold on to your friends! Don't let it be acceptable when your friends drift away just because they are 'in love'. It can be hard to hold on to friends who are in abusive relationships—do your best. Try and be flexible and creative in your support.

Trust your instincts. Domestic violence functions by being hidden: abusive gestures are often hidden within innocuous everyday interactions which rely on misconceptions of romance and love. People often think that if there's violence in a relationship, they'll know. The truth is, by the time you see signs of violence the abuse is usually quite escalated. Trust your gut, don't ignore the signs: if something doesn't seem right, talk to your friend and listen to your instincts as to the best way to move forward.

Don't do it alone. Support people also need support. As someone who is trying to support a loved one, you're going to be at your best if you have support from the people you trust. But what about privacy? This doesn't mean you have to share intimate details of another person's life, rather a simple 'I'm supporting someone in my life who is having a hard time and could really use help in my own self-care' could suffice.

Support Survivor Self-Determination. While domestic violence is a pattern of power and control that limits survivors' choices, sharing each other's stories and anecdotes support survivors in self-determination, encouraging them to live their vision of their lives (not yours). It's tempting to want to tell survivors what to do, especially in the interest of their safety. Safety without self-determination and independence is moot because while important, safety alone does not make for a life worth living.

Talk directly to people, face them. Find yourself always texting and messaging but never actually speaking directly to each other about what's going on in your lives? Make sure you prioritize time to speak directly to the important people in your life. Haven't heard from someone in your inner circle in a while? Reach out!

Third Time's a Charm. When I find myself talking about someone behind their back, I get 3 opportunities to vent, get it off my chest and complain; and if I find myself still talking about this person after the third time, I have to talk directly to them about my concerns. This keeps me accountable to my values of open communication and not gossip, helps to counter the conflict avoidance I am often prone to. Domestic violence thrives on indirect communication and isolation. Focusing on loving and direct communication helps me to make sure that I share concerns with my loved ones.

Don't be a nag. Finding the line between sharing concern and nagging can be difficult. I believe that it's important, even essential, to share my concerns about my loved one's actions and choices. But I also believe that once I've shared my concerns, it's important to shut my mouth and listen. It's my job to speak up when something doesn't sit right with me but I'm not responsible for other's actions and choices.

Make a pact with your bestie (sister, mother, auntie, mentor, sponsor, co-worker or any other important person in your life) that you'll continue to value your friendships no matter what the status of your romantic relationship. Make your values known and enlist your friends and family to help you stay accountable to those values.

Make Time. I find it very helpful to have regular hangout times with my closest people. This helps to anchor our relationship and make it much more obvious if one of us is struggling or pulling away. This might mean a regular TV or dinner date or could be like monthly Skype dates with far away friends and family.

Take Care of Yourself. Just because you're trying to support someone who is in an abusive relationship doesn't mean you have to give yourself to them entirely. In fact, keeping healthy boundaries is an awesome opportunity for those around you to see that you can support others without compromising your health, wellness or fundamental elements of who you are.

Easier Said Than Done

Every day at work, I talk to survivors, work on safety plans with them, hear about their struggles and successes and I support them to build and live fabulous lives. What I don't understand is why it is so much harder to support my friends in their abusive relationships. Being a domestic violence advocate is a different task than being a friend. As an advocate my task is clear, as a friend the water is murkier.

It's scary to tell the ones we love that we're worried about them. It's not a skill many of us are encouraged to cultivate. The risk of telling my friends exactly what I think about their relationships is something they won't want to hear it. That's the irony of the whole exercise—to achieve the connection I sometimes find myself at odds with my closest people. Several times I have tried to talk with friends about concern I have for their relationships and instead of bringing us closer it has created a divide.

Many years ago, I was in a relationship that was not working out me. I was in my early 20s, unemployed, freshly out of college and just starting to find my queer communities when I started a flirtation with another queer I'd known for a while. He was recently out of a long-term relationship and the path forward was littered with red flags. At first, I proceeded cautiously but after a month I was knee deep in a whole heap of drama.

My mom sat me down for a heart to heart. She told me she was concerned about what she was seeing and that if the relationship kept heading in this direction it would probably end badly. I heard her concerns and I told her, 'Mom, you're right, but I'm going to do it anyway, I have to try.' She said, 'OK, honey, just remember that we had this conversation and that you made a choice.'

That moment was very powerful for me, not so much for what happened next but for what happened years later. I did move towards that relationship and it was bad. It had many dramatic ups and downs and the end it found me at a personal low. My mother's support could not have been more appropriate; she shared her concerns but also let me figure it out for myself. When we kept breaking up and getting back together she set boundaries, many of which felt hard for me. It hurt my feelings when she didn't want to talk to me about my relationship or when my partner/ex wasn't allowed in her house. In hindsight, I understand that this was the most loving care she could offer me—she was not willing to allow unacceptable things. Her rejection of the melodrama and dysfunctionality in my life wasn't a rejection of me. In the end, she loved me with a kind of consistent fierceness which I work each and every day to cultivate in my own relationships.

The Way Forward

Engagement is an act of love and deep respect. These conversations take a toll and I wouldn't do it unless I believed that it's an essential part of changing the conditions that allows domestic violence to exist. Domestic violence thrives in silence, grows in isolation, and demands our compliance.

We have to hold on to each other and be willing to have hard conversations. We have to support survivors to live full fabulous lives and we have to do it together. This work demands us to be fierce as well as kind and we have to take care of ourselves in the process.

Domestic violence hurts every member of our community, it erodes our connections and eats away at our ability to support each other. We have to hold on the world we are building, one where each of us has a part in creating the condition to support loving equitable relationships. We have to know what we're moving not just that we are ending. It's our responsibility to not let our friends slip away, it's our responsibility to nurture our relationships and do the work our dreams demand of us; and it's our responsibility to figure out how to wake up every day and put these things into practice, one day at a time.

CHAPTER THIRTEEN

Seven Is a Prime Number

SUMITA BEETHI

যখনই নিজের জন্য কোনো নাম ঠিক করতে চাই, নামেরা বেদম ঠকিয়ে দেয়। আমারই নামে গাদা গুচ্ছের লোক আমার জামা পরে ঘুরে বেড়ায়, আমার বিছানায় শুয়ে ঘুমায়ে, এর মধ্যে কোনটা আদত আমি তা ঠাহর করা হয়না। হয়তো বা আদতে আমি বলে কিছু হয়ই না, যা হয় তা সবই মায়া। তবুও নাম চাই, পরিচয় চাই, কারো ঘরে ঠাঁই চাই। তাই লিখি, আর খুঁজি এর মধ্যেই কিছু দাগছোপ আছে কি না, তার মধ্যে দিয়ে কোনও নকশা ফুটে উঠছে কিনা, বা ছবি বদলাচ্ছে কিনা। এগুলো সেই খুঁজে বেড়ানো। এরা বলছে আমি বদলে যাওয়ার চেষ্টা করছি, একটু একটু দায়িত্ব নিচ্ছি বদলে দেবারও, যুক্ত হতে চাইছি/করতে চাইছি বদলের নানান পথ ও পন্থা, চলে যেতে যেতেও ফিরে আসি বদলের অংশীদার হব বলে . . . আমি অচলায়তনে ফাটল ধরাতে চাইছি!

১
কুড়িয়ে খেয়েছি চিরকাল
এইবার কেড়ে খাব মুখের আড়াল

২
পুব থেকে পশ্চিম তুমি
আমি দক্ষিণ থেকে উত্তর
এভাবেও যোগ চিহ্ন হয়

৩

এক মাঠ পলাশ আর মজাপুকুরের তলায়
ঠিক আমার মুখের মাপে একটুকরো আয়না
কেউ ফেলে গেছে
নাকি রেখে গেছে যত্ন করে

৪

প্রত্যেকবারের পর আরও কিছু খুদকুঁড়ো জোটে
ভাঙা ইঁটে উনুন সাজায়
টগবগ ভাত-ফুল ফোটে

৫

যাবার কারণ ছিল
সচরাচর যেমন থাকেই যাবার কারণ
যাত্রাপথ তন্নতন্ন করে ফিরে আসা খুঁজেই চলেছি

৬

ঠোঁটের কপাট খোলো
জিভেজিভে জানাজানি হবে
রক্তপাত হবে ও
কিছু সমাপতনের ইতিহাস

৭

হাওয়া চললে সমুদ্র
হাওয়া থামলে পাহাড়
পিঠে জনপথ আর বুকে জঙ্গল
এখানে থমকেছে
ঠিক হোক অতঃপর
জল তবে কোথায় গড়াবে

Every time I think of naming myself, names delude me. There are so many people, all wearing my clothes, sleeping on my bed, I can almost never find the real I. Perhaps it means there is no 'real I', the whole business is unreal. But the demand to name, to identify, to belong, remains—so I write and look for signs that would help me recognize a pattern or changes in patterns. These are such attempts. They say I am working for a change, I am taking some responsibilities to make the change, I am trying to communicate/connect to facilitate change, I am coming back from wherever I am to take part in change . . . I am actively seeking change of the existing order!

1

I've scoured for food for ever
but now I'll devour the veil that hides the face

2

you stretch from east to west
I go north to south
this is also how a plus symbol may appear

3

underneath a field of *palaash* and a dry pond
a broken mirror just the size of my face
seems to have been left behind by someone
or maybe kept with affection

4

after each time some more leftovers are collected
on a makeshift oven of broken bricks
rice-flowers blossom and spill over

5

there was a reason behind leaving
just as there's always a reason for leaving
enroute I diligently look for a way back

6

let the lips ajar
so the tongues will get to know each other
blood will be shed and
some history of serendipitous moments

7

when the wind blows it makes an ocean
when it stops, a mountain
with a city on its back and a jungle in its heart
paused right there
now let it be decided
which way the water will flow

Translated from Bengali by Rukmini Banerjee

CHAPTER FOURTEEN

What Happens in My Body When I Choose You

SUSAN RAFFO

Until recently, I've been pretty lucky. My movement work and paid work have mostly been aligned. This means that I've been able to weave between the boundaries of friendship and labor, of work and home, of personal political integrity and the political integrity of my job, without too much contradiction. It's been like swimming in a vast and glorious ocean of making change, moving between friendship and project planning, from gossip to goals, all without too many stumbling blocks.

A few years ago, I started a job that, for the first time, meant that I had to make decisions that were strategic to the change we wanted to make but weren't always, at face value, aligned with my political and personal beliefs. It has been a hard job, asking me to stretch and to grow in ways that I haven't always appreciated. And within it, I've noticed the need for a different kind of boundaries. For the first time, I felt the need to keep my closest friends separate from the work that I am doing. For the first time, I didn't want it all to weave together.

At its core, I think this is about the difference between transformative movement work and working within systems to make the change. Moreover, the meaning of "friendship" is very different in both.

Friendship isn't a single state—it's a continuum, a process, a biological reality. My neighbor's cousin who "friended" me on Facebook because she likes craniosacral therapy (and I am a craniosacral therapist) is a friend in the light sense: there is some kind of intimacy exchanged, a feeling of connection that is meaningful to her and which brings my body closer to her body. So she reached out with a virtual tap and we are connected. That's one end of friendship, a moment of claiming, of intimacy, amid absolute separateness. At the other end are the friends I don't hide from, the very, very few people I depend on to have my back for the long term—to think with me, to remember my family story and refer to it, for whom my life and my existence matters, no matter how shitty I am, no matter how many mistakes I make, no matter how pissed off at me they get. This doesn't mean a lack of critical acceptance—it means commitment. It means staying in for the hard work and not leaving unless it is dangerous to your body to remain. This kind of friendship means that literally, at the most cellular level, I become part of you and you of me.

Eight hundred thousand years of evolution have taught our bodies that in order to survive, we need to be part of a pack. When we are vulnerable, curled up and licking our wounds, we need someone to watch over us so that we can rest. We cannot find enough food or time and we cannot reproduce or take care of our children without connecting to someone else, preferably more than one with a few standbys. Depending on where you were raised and your cultural tradition, this pack is called your family, community, tribe, or your kin. In good and easy times, it's not hard to connect with people who aren't part of our pack. But in hard-edged survival times, the world gets small and our bodies turn to those most likely to get us through.

Our pack is there to help us survive. Period. And surviving isn't a cognitive brain thing, it's a glorious mess of instinct and learned behavior, of culture and genes. When the shit hits the fan, my Facebook friends are only pixels on a page. I know who is in my pack and who is not—even if we never actually talk about it.

Just because our packs are who we depend on to survive doesn't mean they are people who are part of our transformation. As we are born and grow up, they are the carriers of every kind of shit and glory from one generation to the next, teaching racism—both external and internalized—along with reading and writing. Sharing the secrets of assimilation and lying along with a recipe for bread. Modeling through action and words how to hold on to a sense of self even when every system around you is telling you that you don't matter. Unintentionally and with enormous impact, our pack passes along the herbal remedies that our grandmother used because healthcare was not available or because it was better than public healthcare, as well as every handy tips and trick and secret weapons that they have successfully used to breathe another day. We are here because of what they handed down to us, shared among us.

We all have the packs that raised us first, our families or systems of origin. We carry them wherever we go. Friendship is different. It's about the pack we choose, not the pack we are given. These are the people we choose to help us survive. This "choosing" is not always cognitive, meaning we don't always think it through with clear examples of how they make us a better or safer person. But we definitely choose them, the relationships deepen with every point of struggle and change that we go through together.

Again, at the best of times, we can share our heart with all kinds of people, getting bits and pieces of what we need from a lot of different sources. We feel big, spread out with a complex personality that reflects back at us from a wide array of people. In survival times, it just becomes a smaller group. We lean into our pack because they are there for us, supporting us even if they don't completely meet all of who we are. It's the difference between who is "us" and who is "them" in a moment of hardship. Generally, in survival moments, the difference is clear.

The implications for movement work are huge. Trying to make change as a radical within the liberal non-profit industrial complex where white supremacy, sexism, and class hatred are the casual norm, means being very specific about who is us and who is them. For me with this new job, it has meant leaning hard into my pack so that I can stay some amount of grounded while trying to squeeze change, like water, out of the cement of constant resistance. Working in the liberal non-profit industrial complex is not movement work. It is like making sure that people are still being fed while they are organizing the longer-term work of liberation. And to be clear, food within this analogy is just the energy that's going to get the body through another day, not necessarily food that makes you strong or makes you well.

I hear a lot of language about movement building and community, but often it seems to mean creating the spaces where like-minded people can learn, work and play together, and enjoy each other's company. It doesn't necessarily mean building a pack, building the deep connections that will remain even when the shit hits the fan. And because we don't do this, we lose our vision for the movement to petty causes, infighting, or compromises that take us to places we never meant to go. This was never meant to be easy.

Remembering that our first pack, our family or systems of origin, passes along everything they have learned to survive, means remembering that we inherit a legacy of historical trauma and resilience along with language and recipes. This is fundamentally who we are, the things that have been passed on to us from our ancestors. If we are lucky, we have language and context for it, some kind of reflection or ritual that means we know who we are and where we come from. Since the intent of the US colonization is destabilization, most of us living in the US either don't know these fundamental things or we secretly worry that we don't know enough to claim ourselves. This is intentional. It's part of how colonization works—and it works on the bodies of both the colonized and the progenies of the colonizers.

So this is what we inherit, it is where we begin. The very systems we are seeking to change are right here, in our bodies. Trauma is both a cause and an effect of centuries of domination and violence. All of what we have inherited—what we call culture and what we call home— is created through this generational passing over of trauma and strength. We constantly move in and out of highly stressful moments of survival because the systems around us and within us are constantly reinforcing and resisting the dehumanization that is the American dream.

So what is movement work? Movement work is healing the trauma and lifting the resilience that we have individually and collectively carried. It is messy and painful and time consuming and not at all supported by the goals-and-outcomes thinking of the non-profit world. It demands a deeper level of intimacy than any of us feel safe engaging with outside those we have already named as being like "us."

And it means being open to the fact that the trauma caused by the systems outside and inside us are always operating.

And so we have to both widen and deepen the "us." There is no other way. Eight hundred thousand years of evolution means that my body literally cannot hear, see, or understand you if I am under great stress and you are not someone I have already let in. During those times of survival, I can only interpret your actions in ways that will help me survive this moment. It doesn't matter what story my mind is telling, my body is on high alert and if you are not absolutely safe for me, then you are someone I have to manage so that I can get through this moment. The body reacts differently from that of the mind's understanding of what is taking place, its reaction is based on what has been experienced and learned in the past and not on assessing the complexity of a present moment. For the body, the survival response is just as strong whether it's a tornado coming across the field toward my home or a moment in a meeting when someone says something racist and the meeting is called off. Depending on how I have learned to survive these moments, the same reactions come back into play. Get out of there, fight back, stop and look around for someone else to do something, disappear. The body just wants to survive; it doesn't want to negotiate the best response for long-term change.

Movement work has to change the patterns in the systems around us and the systems within us. We can't do any of that work alone. Building movements around friendships means building movements not with Facebook friends but of packs.

What does this mean? It means we start our work recognizing that generations of systems of domination have caused significant individual and collective trauma. Without shame or judgment, we look to create spaces that are attentive to this truth. Within the cycle of violence, the perpetrator's actions also come out of trauma. The greater systems that we struggle within have been working on our bodies, all of our bodies, even before first contact. What is powerful about this is that, in recognizing the traumatic impact of generations of oppression, we build the space for healing. The incredible damage of centuries of oppression is not only physical but also emotional and psychological.

This damage impacts our ability to envision the other world that is possible. It limits what we can do. It gets in the way of love.

So where does a pack come in? Very simply, individuals cannot heal alone any more than we can guarantee our basic needs ourselves. As much as I might write about change and my desire to change, there is a big part of me that wants nothing to be different. The survival strategies I learned growing up in my particular pack are constantly looking for ways to reframe themselves, re-negotiate themselves into not changing. Change *hurts*—from feeling my body waking up to the things it has shunned to sensing the impact of my actions and my people's actions on other bodies, really feeling that, *being* that, it hurts and if at all possible, my body doesn't want to hurt.

Work that centers on the deepening and growing of relationships in an honest and constructive way so that someone has our backs and at the same time call our shit without leaving us—this is where we start to shift the systems that we carry inside. And this shifting inside helps us to change the systems outside. One feeds the other.

This is how we build movements that transform, rather than movements that place one band-aid after another over an infrastructure that should have come down a long time ago.

CHAPTER FIFTEEN

Friendship Is Not Magic
Online Echo Chambers in the 2014 Scottish Independence
Referendum

JEREMY MATTHEW

On the late morning of 19 September 2014, social media in Scotland
was unusually quiet. Pro-Independence blogs like *Wings Over Scotland*
and *Bella Caledonia* had not been updated since the polls closed the
previous night. The constant churn of 'Yes'-related posts on Twitter
had, for the first time ever, swung to 'No' according to *The Herald*'s
'Twitterendum' graphic,[1] and the Saltire-waving crowds that had gathered in George Square on previous days were mostly dispersed, now
outnumbered by satellite uplink vans and journalists preparing reports
on camera for international news bulletins with the buildings of central
Glasgow in the backdrop.[2] The emotional euphoria that captured so
many supporters of Scottish independence both on- and offline was
palpably deflated. How could this have happened? With so much
energy and enthusiasm among the 'Yes' supporters before the vote on
whether Scotland should become an independent country, it seemed
as if a bubble had been burst. And indeed, it had—this was a bubble
that trapped supporters of independence. Pro-independence conversations and opinions were engaged and enthusiastic within that bubble,
but the energetic interactions of independence supporters and activists
seldom travelled outside its walls. 'Yes' activists won the conversation
on social media and spread their message across their friends and followers but despite doing much better in the final vote than the polls
from a year or two earlier had predicted, the Yes campaign still lost
the referendum. Social media, at the time of the referendum for an

independent Scotland, was isolated in an echo chamber of friend and follower networks, and the Westminster-friendly headlines appearing in every newspaper instead reflected, even more closely, how the majority of the electorate voted on polling day. Could this mean that social media and the communications between friends and followers are ineffective in leading to political change?

The concept of the echo chamber is not new or particular to networks of friends on social media. The idea that groups of individuals may exclude different viewpoints or perspectives that are oppositional or relate to different topics from their preconceived interests and beliefs has been observed more broadly among human interactions in general. Indeed, the phenomenon was first identified in the 1960s,[3] and in later decades the concept of individuals blocking out viewpoints which they disagreed with could be observed in early 1990s TV-audience research where it was found that the viewers ignored or forgot the political ads they disagreed with,[4] or in the era of Internet and blogging, in the early 2000s, with only a very small number of users visiting pages with information that challenged or expanded upon their pre-established interests.[5] The idea that the Internet assists the creation of and enhances the strength of echo chambers is also not new, with Cass Sunstein arguing at the beginning of this century that the capabilities of the Internet further 'allows people to sort themselves into innumerable homogeneous groups, which often results in amplifying their pre-existing views'.[6] Echo chambers and the propensity for groups to develop exclusionary discourses is fairly well documented, but arguably the manner in which social media platforms operate further enhances the likelihood and effect of echo chambers than prior technologies. Contrary to the promise of the Internet facilitating the wider dissemination of information, social media locks information down into isolated bubbles of users, increasing the likelihood that those users will interact with information that already conforms to their pre-established interests and beliefs. This is not always the fault of Facebook's algorithmic tailoring of displayed content but is further reinforced by such functionality. As Geert Lovink argues, 'rather than foster new public engagements, online discussion tends to take place within "echo chambers" where groups of like-minded individuals, consciously or not, avoid debate with their cultural or political adversaries'.[7] In the case of pro-independence activists in the Scottish independence referendum, the echo-chamber effect was particularly noticeable in the experiences of several activists and was the result of conscious choices which were then reinforced through social media algorithms. But pro-independence communication was relatively exclusive to social media networks largely due to a lack of pro-independence information available offline.

Perhaps unsurprisingly, the largely London-based British news media establishment reflected the perspectives of the local political institutions more closely than the perspectives of readers in Scotland, a common concern regarding contemporary journalism in many countries.[8] Even though the Scottish editions of London-based papers would be in Scottish newsstands, the editorial stance of regional editions would often be similar if not identical, and the London editions were also the most visible online. For example, in the regular 'The Papers' section on the BBC's website display the front pages of the UK national press each morning, the London editions are always favoured over any regional differentiation in the front-page content. Occasionally, in the final run-up to the vote during the last two weeks of the referendum campaign the BBC would also show a small number of Scottish editions on their 'The Papers' section but this was rare and irregular, and almost always not the case throughout the longer campaign. Notable exceptions to the regular London editions would be the 16 September edition of *The Daily Record*, 'The Vow' front page, but the London-based partner of *The Record*, *The Daily Mirror*, also had its front page featured on the BBC as normal. By the time the polls opened on 18 September, only one major newspaper in the UK had published an editorial in favour of Scottish independence (the Glasgow-based *Sunday Herald*), with all other national news outlets either claiming objective neutrality (such as the TV stations and *The Independent*), or published editorials favouring a No vote (such as *The Daily Mail*, *The Guardian* and *The Telegraph*). However, Yes activists were most clearly disappointed by what they perceived as an anti-independence bias in the BBC's reportage, leading to a large protest in front of the BBC office in Glasgow on 14 September, and the #BBCBias trending on Twitter through the final days of the campaign. Many activists around Scotland in the final days of the campaign noted a particular sense of disappointment and heartbreak for the BBC's coverage but leftist campaigners from the Radical Independence Campaign also reserved some ill will for the anti-independence stance of the left-leaning *Guardian*, a publication they believed ought to have been on their side but instead sided with the Westminster consensus.[9] With the news media establishment in the UK and Scotland so thoroughly anti-independence in their editorial stance, many pro-independence activists and campaigners turned to social media as a way to communicate their views. However, for these pro-independence Yes activists, social media platforms—run by for-profit technology companies, dependant on advertising—may have become too much of a crutch as the goals and objectives of social media companies did not necessarily align with their aims.

On page one of Facebook's initial public offering (IPO) filing, the company describes its mission statement by claiming that 'People use Facebook to stay connected with their friends and family, to discover what is going on in the world around them, and to share and express what matters to them to the people they care about.'[10] This statement, given a highly prominent position in material created for financial regulators and investors, reflects the view that social media is a fundamentally democratizing force on public discourse, what can be characterized as a 'utopian' argument regarding online communications and their effects on politics.[11] This line of thinking, first popularized during the early days of the web in the 1990s, has continued in the popular discourse during political news events involving citizen journalism through social media.[12] However, reality is more complicated, and the way that social media platforms like Facebook are designed and operated makes the statement from Facebook somewhat self-contradictory. After all, while Facebook states in its IPO filing that connecting friends is its 'mission', an IPO document itself is really about the potential for profitability and returns on investment. Facebook aims to create profits for its shareholders, and it seeks to earn these profits through increasing user engagement with the platform in order to monetize user data. Through the management of the platform's capabilities and functions, Facebook prioritizes the ability for users to 'stay connected with their friends and family' and as a result limits the potential for users to 'discover what is going on in the world around them'. What users get instead are their own views of the world reflected back at them. Or as Tufekci argues, 'By holding on to the valuable troves of big data, and by controlling of algorithms which determine visibility, sharing and flow of political information, the Internet's key sites and social platforms have emerged as inscrutable, but important, power brokers of networked politics.'[13] This is not to say that Facebook directly manipulates political discussions with the intent to sway public opinion regarding specific votes, but it does mean that its algorithms can have an indirect effect on the opinions of the users. The Scottish independence referendum provides an example of how friendships on social media limit the capability for activists to reach outside of their own movement's bubble and instead create an online environment where campaigners and activists are more likely to spend the majority of their time preaching to the converted. The goals of Facebook as a company do not necessarily align with the goals of activists seeking to spread their message of political change.

Facebook as a company is interested in increasing the activity and engagement of users with the platform generally for the purposes of monetizing that engagement through advertising. With that end in mind Facebook is interested in ensuring that users see more content that they are interested in, and less content they are not interested in. What this means in practice is that the algorithms which tailor a user's news feed will respond to their activity, displaying more content that is identified as similar to other posts the user has engaged with (such as clicking 'like', commenting on, or clicking on links posted), and lessen the visibility of the content that the user has not engaged with in some way. Exactly how the Facebook algorithms work is a closely guarded trade secret—analogous to Colonel Sanders' secret herbs and spices—but outside observers have been able to infer a number of activities which can trigger these algorithms. For example, a post from a friend with a reply containing words like 'Congratula-tions' is highly likely to be displayed on a user's news feed, because it is more likely to be regarding an important life event (such as a new job, a marriage, or a child).[14] Such finely grained shifting of displayed content based on word usage also works for political opinions: users who are liberal are less likely to see links on their Facebook feed to Fox News or the *Telegraph*, and users who are conservative are less likely to see links from MSNBC or the *Guardian*. Eli Pariser describes this echo-chamber-enchasing effect as a 'filter bubble', where 'every "click signal" you create is a commodity, and every move of your mouse can be auctioned off within microseconds to the highest commercial bidder.'[15] In the context of the Scottish referendum, users who support Scottish Independence are more likely to see posts containing phrases like 'vote Yes' or 'Yes Scotland' and much less likely to see posts containing phrases like 'vote No', 'Better Together', or 'No Thanks'. Such differentiations may have been further reinforced for pro-independence users, in particular, due to the fact that anti-independence campaign first decided to name itself 'Better Together', and then later in the campaign more frequently using the slogan 'No Thanks', while the official name for the pro-independence campaign remained as 'Yes Scotland'. Information of Google searches in Scotland through Google Trends suggests that this consistency made the Yes campaign much more recognizable in online discourse. At their peak in mid-September 2014, online searches in Scotland for the terms 'Better Together' and 'No Thanks' combined were 10 per cent less frequent than 'Yes Scotland' according to Google Trends.[16] While what users post on social media and what they search on Google is likely to be different in terms of exact word usage, it is possible that pro-independence campaign phrases on Facebook were also more identifiable (and thus likely to be given higher priority by the Facebook algorithm) than the more fractured anti-independence campaign phrases which may have received a lower priority as a result—particularly for supporters of the Yes campaign. In other words, it's possible that the way an algorithm deals with key words and political talking points may have an asymmetric effect, and impact one side of a political argument more than the other, potentially further decreasing the chances that Yes- and No-leaning users will see posts from other users they disagree with.

Facebook's photo identification algorithms may have also potentially played a part in the definition of like-minded groups by

Facebook, due to the popularity of users adding supporter badges to their profiles. These badges would usually take the form of the word 'Yes' in a coloured (usually blue and white) circle added to a corner of a profile image or avatar. Facebook's photo detection and face tagging algorithms have been growing increasingly sophisticated in their abilities to recognize faces in recent years, and it seems very possible that recognizing relatively simple badges that reflect a user's support for a social or political movement is well within their abilities.[17] While gathering data on private Facebook profiles is difficult, this behaviour was also observable on Twitter, where series of seven different 10-minute snapshots using the #indyref hashtag taken between 15 and 17 September 2014 show that 30 per cent of users had either a Yes or No badge on their avatar but of that group 80 per cent were Yes badges. This ratio remained broadly consistent across every 10-minute snapshot of #indyref Twitter activity, spread evenly across the three days before the vote. This ratio also largely coincides with the 'Twitterendum' chart that claimed to measure pro- versus anti-independence sentiment on Twitter, usually showing around 80 per cent support for 'Yes' on any given day. While the methodology behind the *Herald*'s chart was not clear, this corresponding data of supporter levels across a number of samples suggests that active Twitter users were indeed pro-independence by a very wide margin. Clearly Yes activity, without a home in the established mass media, found a home on social media. But in finding this home, Yes activists and supporters made themselves much more identifiable, and much more easy to ignore by those users they most wanted to convince.

There is also evidence from discussions with pro-independence activists that their Facebook news feeds were much more likely to be filled with pro-independence posts and had fewer anti-independence posts. Of a group of 13 Yes supporters and activists interviewed in the final two weeks of the campaign, almost all reported that their social media feeds displayed far more pro-Yes than No posts. Some activists also expressed trepidation when it came to interacting with No supporters on social media, usually encountering such posts in public areas of social media that were inhabited by 'trolls', users who were either being deliberately provocative or hostile, or users who weren't interested in having a sincere exchange of views. A small minority of these Yes activists did deliberately go out of their way to find areas where No supporters discussed their views, such as on particular sub-reddits (sub-forums within the Reddit platform), but almost all activists interviewed had some reservations when it came to engaging with anti-independence supporters on social media. However, this was not true outside of social media space, because these activists also had a great deal of enthusiasm about campaigning door-to-door, distributing pamphlets, staffing campaign booths, attending demonstrations and spreading information about Scottish independence to 'undecided' or anti-independence voters in the offline world. Indeed, the Radical Independence Campaign had a fairly strong social media presence on Twitter, Facebook and other platforms, but also made arguably an even heavier effort to campaign via offline events and spaces, such as regular meetings and discussion nights in multiple Scottish cities, rallies, canvassing and door-knocking. Evidence of Yes activists attempting to communicate their views was just as evident in physical spaces as it was in digital spaces. Despite this, social media was, partially due to the algorithms of platforms like Facebook and partially due to deliberate decisions by users, a much more insular and isolated space for communication between Yes activists. This is perhaps typified by a point made by one Yes activist in Glasgow's Yes Bar on the night of the referendum, where she noted that she did have friends and family members who she knew were not in favour of independence; nevertheless her Facebook feed was almost always displaying pro-independence posts. Clearly her offline friendships were telling her something quite different from her online ones. If pro-independence activists and campaigners in Scotland wish to communicate their ideals of civic nationalism based on the establishment of fairer and more democratic political institutions, then the idea of the public needing to get the message in a broader way than targeted social media posts means that the Yes team needs to get the message out not through social media and blogs but via other far-reaching means of mass communication. The enthusiasm among activists for campaigning both offline as well as online suggest that this is entirely possible, but activists should not fool themselves into thinking that social media represents a key area to get the message out. Social media is for discussion among supporters, not for convincing people or encouraging them to think outside of their own bubbles. In other words, if you want to connect with others that share your own opinions, spending time with your friends on social media is a good idea. But if you want to change how everyone else views the world, it almost certainly is not.

Friendship on social media is not a magic bullet for political change. Networks of friends and followers on social media do fill a vacuum left by establishment media and allow the spread of information that follows alternative news agendas. But essentially, it is difficult for social media to win elections or change broader public opinion when other forms of media are largely publishing pro-establishment narratives. Activists in Scotland did indeed spend a great deal of time canvassing door-to-door and making public demonstrations visible on the streets of Scotland's cities, and the increased readership of the pro-independence *Sunday Herald* reflects the demand for alternative viewpoints in other less-digital forms of media. Developments after the referendum such as the growing membership of the Scottish National Party and the Scottish Green Party, and the establishment of the daily pro-independence paper *The National* reflect a greater engagement with offline politics and activism, and these factors could in the long run prove that Scottish independence may eventually be supported by the majority. But social media in isolation faces significant barriers to wining the argument for independence activists due to the bubble-forming nature of online communications through for-profit social media platforms. Facebook and Twitter are not designed to spread messages to a wider public, they are designed to increase user engagement and, therefore, enhance profitability. Thus far the best way these companies have found to increase user engagement is to give them what they want to see the most—information that already conforms to a user's pre-existing viewpoints.

Notes

1   See 'Twitterendum: How Your Tweets and Our Stories are Driving the Debate', *The Herald Scotland* (6 March 2014). Available at: https://goo.gl/AL995N (last accessed on 23 July 2017).

2 Observations, anecdotes, interviews and data from social media and the web mentioned in this chapter are results from field research in Scotland gathered during September 2014 in Aberdeen, Edinburgh and Glasgow.

3 R. Michael Alvarez and Jonathan Nagler, 'Party System Compactness: Measurement and Consequences', *Political Analysis* 12(1) (Winter 2004): 46–62

4 For a detailed analysis, see John William Cavanaugh, *Media Effects on Voters: A Panel Study of the 1992 Presidential Election* (Boston: University Press of America, 1995).

5 Markus Prior, 'News vs. Entertainment: How Increasing Media Choice Widens Gaps in Political Knowledge and Turnout', *American Journal of Political Science* 49(3) (2005): 577–92

6 Cass Sunstein, *Echo Chambers* (Princeton: Princeton University Press, 2001), p. 2.

7 Geert Lovink, *Networks Without a Cause: A Critique of Social Media* (Cambridge UK: Polity Press, 2011), p. 2.

8 Bernd-Peter Lange and David Ward, *The Media and Elections: A Handbook and Comparative Study* (New Jersey: Lawrence Erlbaum Associates, 2004).

9 See an editorial published in the *Guardian* (12 September 2014), 'The Guardian View on Scottish Referendum'. Available at: https://goo.gl/-JWhGWB (last accessed on 23 July 2017).

10 Facebook Inc, 'Form S-1 Registration Statement', United States Securities and Exchange Commission, Washington DC (1 February 2012). Available at: https://goo.gl/NCffeA (last accessed on 23 July 2017).

11 Josephine Berry, 'What Is to Be Screened—Net Utopians and Their Discontents', *Afterall: A Journal of Art, Context and Inquiry* (1998): 66–73.

12 For example, see Peter Huck, 'We Had 50 Images Within an Hour', *Guardian* (11 July 2005) Available at: https://goo.gl/QT5nvX (last accessed on 24 July 2017).

13 Zeynep Tufekci, 'Engineering the Public: Big Data, Surveillance and Computational Politics', *First Monday* 19(7) (2014). Available at: https://goo.gl/m1xZMQ (last accessed on 23 July 2017).

14 Caleb Garling, 'Tricking Facebook's Algorithm', *Atlantic* (8 August 2014). Available at: https://goo.gl/oigoYi (last accessed on 24 July 2017).

15   Eli Pariser, *The Filter Bubble: What the Internet Is Hiding from You* (London: Viking, 2011), p. 7.

16   See Google Trends Comparison Report, available at: https://goo.gl/-L9YfLw (last accessed on 24 July 2017).

17   John Bohannon, 'Facebook will soon be able to ID you in any photo', *Science* (5 February 2015). Available at: https://goo.gl/-b8BwmF (last accessed on 24 July 2017).

CHAPTER SIXTEEN

Con Vivere
Friendship as the Means to Live Fully

NILA KAMOL KRISHNAN GUPTA AND SHAMIRA A. MEGHANI

When we began to talk about writing this piece together, our thoughts turned first to the spaces in which our friendship has developed. We both love to cook for our friends, and some of the earliest spaces of our friendship were of sharing food that we prepared together, around a big table, in company with other queer of colour scholars, activists and allies, in the privacy of someone's home. Our first sustained conversations were at a Race Revolt reading group: from where we developed our networks of queer people of colour, moving from texts to activism. But in the time we have known each other, our lives have taken us both some distance away from the town we met in, and our online interactions have become the more regular space of friendship. Rather than mesh our differences into a single voice, we have chosen to represent ourselves through an exchange which also reflects our online interactions. Our discussion here is inspired by the importance of both the dining table and online spaces, and the way that these sustain us in our lives and work. These are the spaces where we practice some of the 'million different ways to fight'.[1]

SHAMIRA. The scene of the dining table is much more than a functional surface for sharing home-made food. Rather than move immediately towards the writing table which might seem more appropriate for producing an essay, we oriented most easily and unquestioningly towards the space of the dining table. It is where we developed mutual support and self-care alongside—and intertwined—with our critical thinking, fusing visible and less visible forms of activist strategies. Around the dining tables of our homes, the movement between friendship, nurture, criticality and strategizing has been seamless. What brings us together also orients us towards particular spaces. As Sara Ahmed suggests 'the very direction of our desire ... might also be a matter ... of how we inhabit spaces, and who or what we inhabit spaces with'.[2] She points out, too, that 'other social orientations, which affect what we can face at any given moment in time' might orient us towards particular kinds of tables.[3] Re-orienting these words somewhat, towards the need for starting points that are shared and unspoken, we come to the (imagined) conviviality of the dining table.

For us, that conviviality—from *convivium*: 'a feast'—is often, but not only, a feast of our inherited (and sometimes rediscovered) South Asian foods. Our conviviality includes feasting over new ways of making that inheritance fit our animal rights and environmental food politics. But this Latin root for feasting, *convivium*, itself emerges tellingly from *con vivere*: 'with' and 'live'. At the dining table, we also make ourselves the space to *live*, and spaces for *living with*. Together, in something that combines friendship, extra-familial kinship, activism, intellectual and creative work, we work to dispel our self-doubts and make space for our validity. Though explicitly not a space free of challenge, the dining table is one which allows us to begin without the explanations that other spaces often demand of us, explanations that orientate us too far from ourselves.

It is where we have been able to make time for talk in which the parameters are, for once, ours. In doing this, we claim an activist inheritance from the feminist publications of Kitchen Table Press. Ahmed describes these as a 'reorientation device', and indeed, the process of orienting ourselves towards our validity has required the reading of critical texts by women of colour as a device.[4]

The dining table setting is a very specific and valuable space for our friendship. The trust enabled has been the starting point for us to take greater risks in understanding power as it flows through circuits of gender, sexuality, ethno-raciality and class. Convivial thinking around the dining table has enabled us to develop strategies against the effects of trauma—in life, activism, and writing. Through this conviviality we make space for our experiences and resist the normative coursing—the harm—of pervasive whiteness and hetero- and gender normativity.

NILA KAMOL. We both love to cook and engage with the nurturing and creative aspects of cooking together, but we're also wary about the way in which people of colour are often reduced to a fetishized accessory to prove the liberal inclusiveness of white supremacist imperial cultures, and how this often happens around our 'exotic' cuisines. Sharing food in a domestic setting refuses to take part in that kind of consumption and helps us return to our own focus, bodies, thoughts. This also acts as a withdrawal of labour—activist, intellectual, physical, emotional, creative—from contexts that have expected and even demanded labour but been unwilling to reciprocate.

Sharing food at home has often involved cooking varied South Asian dishes, as we've both consciously oriented at times towards certain foods we've grown up with in our different diasporic lived experiences. This isn't (only) a nostalgic 'rediscovering' but, rather, a speculative practice, pursuing possibilities. Our food, friendship and political practice resist the oversimplification of our diasporic experience.

Cooking and sharing is also a sensory embodied experience: the smells, sounds and flavours, the labour of chopping, mixing masalas (generally feminized and/or attributed to lower caste or class), the holistic comfort of eating together. Feminized labour is often expected or demanded rather than chosen. Of course, our friendship does not exist outside patriarchy but we consciously choose and collectivize the labour. Technical specifications help here too—the food we cook often requires simmering time, thus allowing conversations that have been happening alongside cooking to also come into the focus!

SHAMIRA. Talking in these spaces has allowed both of us to begin to make sense of different but very intense and embodied experiences of growing up in the diaspora, where the politics of skin, race, ethnicity and gender constructed our senses of ourselves.

I was 10 when I first noticed the beginnings of vitiligo on my face. It's a skin condition in which melanin disappears in odd-shaped patches, causing the appearance of increasing, creeping, whiteness. The impact of this is particularly striking if you have dark skin, and allopathic medicine have no cure for it. Some experiences resulting from this still stand out because they contributed to my sense of self, identity and criticality. At primary school, a black British female classmate asked me about it and then commented that I was 'becoming more normal'. Positioning both of us firmly outside 'normality', her words centred whiteness as the default for Britain. It collided with earlier experiences of racism which I had been taught by my mother to counter with the resisting phrase: 'Black is beautiful' (I was called 'blackie' before I was called 'Paki'). Having vitiligo allowed me to experience the differences between ethnicity and phenotype viscerally, even as it soon prompted a sense of being 'unhoused' in my body. And this fragmenting of a previously unified experience (of phenotype and ethnicity) only continued as the implications sank into my long-since tomboyish self. My parents, seeking cures, talked with the one or two people they knew with vitiligo. One spoke of me and herself within earshot, pityingly, 'It's such a shame that she's so young. At least I was married already when it happened to me.' I knew instantly that I was 'unmarriageable', and outside some parts of our community's (unenforced) norms.

I had a strong sense of self as soul, from the esotericism of my Muslim upbringing, and it helped anchor me to a core sense of self that was not going to be judged by or loved for appearance. In some ways, it liberated me from normative gendering, although I wore make-up to cover the vitiligo. Into my teens, and outside of girls' school, I often passed as a boy—a continuity beyond childhood that no one really objected to. And *in* girls' school, with no boys to challenge, I, along with others, occupied masculine roles, in temperament if not clothing (even today, I can wear very feminine clothing only with a sense of being in drag). Gender expression, whether masculine or feminine, has for me always been, in part, a performance—something that I put on in relation to a sense of self—and this contrasted with the reiterated gender performativity that surrounded me.[5] Learning, much later, after the vitiligo had largely disappeared of its own accord, to theorize gender, I found a language for what I had already experienced. But my sense of self continues to be distanced, at times, from embodiment. When I am called to it by racism, embodiment is all too real—called to it by normative gendered expectations, I don't find that I fit.

There are very few convivial spaces in which I find easy kinship, and don't have to compromise quite uncomfortably to 'fit in'. Friendship that allows me to be dis/embodied in whatever form I find myself is precious. This *is* the skin I'm in. Friendship and its complex conviviality enables my scholarly processes. It has shaped my work by allowing me to ask questions that reflect a resistance to identify visibility as the only marker of the politically 'real'. Connecting with Nila, and some others, I can contribute to their processes as they do mine. That way, we stay productive, that is, our voices continue to be heard where they might not have been otherwise.

NILA KAMOL. Growing up in the 1970s and 80s in England, coercive gendering was so normalized as to be invisible (and largely, still is). As an adult, I found my way to materials and communities that rejected cis-sexist constructions of gender. I am a genderfucker—my relationship to gender norms is playful, mocking, alienated and subversive. I also use 'trans', 'transgender' and 'non-binary' when appropriate.

But back then I was 'obviously' a girl. To succeed at 'girlness' was to be subordinate to boys and to achieve prettyness—blonde hair, blue eyes and, of course, white skin. My black hair and brown skin defined me as the ugly 'other'. Until my late twenties I also had severe eczema, covering my face and body—unsightly, painful and constantly itching. I was literally never comfortable in my skin.

I was a 'Paki'. This is a hate speech term in British English applied to anyone who looks South Asian. My skin colour was constantly characterized in- and outside school by racist peers and adults as being the colour of shit. The abuse marked my skin, the literal point of my interface with the world, as an abject waste product, something dirty. Much later, I would realize that the placing me in the category of 'girl' acted out a comparable but much less recognized violence—that of compulsory gendering.

The liberal, middle-class progress narrative that influences the UK migrant as well as sexuality/gender communities (albeit in very different ways), suggests that in young adulthood one is able to move (via university) to more 'progressive' or 'high-status' locations. During my twenties and thirties, I was able to use class and education privilege to make choices about where I lived. But as I 'succeeded' I moved into a world ordered by white English (upper) middle-class 'progressive' norms. This world knows not to use hate speech and, in fact, uses this to distinguish itself from working-class and non-white cultures which it demonizes as backward. It reifies its own power by refusing to name it, instead blaming the oppressed constituency, a dynamic contiguous with my early experiences of racism.

Searching for resources to counter this violence I found *Race Revolt*, a collaborative print zine discussing race, ethnicity and identity in queer, feminist and DIY punk communities.[6] For the first time I saw myself, desi and queer, reflected in angry, critical, powerful narratives. I was inspired to make my own interventions against the racist norms of the LGBTQ spaces I inhabited.

These actions immediately met with overt bullying and something much more insidious: a form of systemic gaslighting. Gaslighting identifies a very specific kind of emotional abuse and manipulation. The abusee's reality is denied or manipulated in order to undermine their sense of self so that they become reliant on the abuser. Axes of cultural hegemony (in this case, white supremacy) rely on such gaslighting to maintain their dominance.

The cumulative trauma has the effect of alienating me from my body and agency. My friendship with Shamira has long provided space to repair the damage and come back to myself, my body, mind and desires—to recover, create and act in the world.

SHAMIRA. Our experiences of growing up in Britain were both unusual and utterly ordinary. We find that we negotiate the hostilities of our diasporic experience by thinking, theorizing and processing, which I think can leave us some distance from our bodies. Friendship is a space for both critical work and repair. There's no simple opposition of the intellectual and the sensory in how we talk, and the digitization of our kinship—the result of distance—has resulted in new ways of relating but with continuities. Online, it's not unusual for our friends to pile in. We can find ourselves around a virtual table quite quickly! It's a disembodied experience that is nourishing because of the joy of connecting.

NILA KAMOL. Coming to trans and race consciousness has been a syncretic process, one fuels the other and I find myself much more able to push away models which are of no relevance to me. I still have to navigate oppressive systems and the effects of trauma, both of which continue to materially affect me in precarity of housing, health and income.

'Living with' another brown gender-variant person is rewriting my relationship to my skin and body. I can refuse the 'ugly' label and the abjection forced upon it. I am learning to love my genderfucky brown disabled body, a hugely powerful act, refuting the abusive 'truths' of my childhood.

SHAMIRA. I feel as though I've spent a lifetime learning to appreciate the value of who we are beyond being non-individuated objects of political attention and invisibility. That home is a country which has not begun to come to terms with Empire and its legacies defers the ordinary comforts of home for diasporans. Connecting together over lost mother tongues, food and culture, becomes a form of sustenance that helps counter the distance and disembodiment produced by objectification, exoticization, internalized racism and c/overt racist discourses that have been with us formatively and beyond. The connections we make through friendship turn us away from being 'repulsed by the evil of [our] skin' and towards beauty.[7] Writing about life and friendship in collaboration has been challenging and revealing—both individually, and for the friendship itself.

NILA KAMOL. It has been difficult but also powerful to collaborate during a period in my life when I'm dealing with homelessness and several other serious life issues. I've surprised myself and Shamira with my ability to create and collaborate in these circumstances, but the process has also sustained me. To be a brown queer/trans person with disabilities on a low income is an ongoing creative act of survival.

Writing this piece together has enabled us to articulate a lot about our friendship which has hitherto been more organic. This piece is a snapshot of our friendship and the part it plays in sustaining our critical and activist work at this moment in time. It has in itself been a small act of sustaining each other through a difficult period of time. As with friendship, we've used digital tools for collaborating over distance. It therefore stands as a microcosm of how our friendship and activisms have developed.

Our real-life and virtual dining tables bring us back into our brown queer/trans bodies, which are nourished by each other. We resist collapsing our 'difference' into simple 'representative' narratives, and are part of (but make no claim to represent) the complexity and variance of diaspora experience. To be embodied in a space of queerness, politics, passion and activism that centres around brownness is beautiful and radical in a white supremacist hetero-patriarchal world. We're at home, with each other and in ourselves, and that is a resistant act.

Notes

1   Leah Lakshmi Piepzna-Samarasinha, 'A Time to Hole Up and a Time to Kick Ass: Reimagining Activism as a Million Different Ways to Fight' in Melody Berger (ed.), *We Don't Need Another Wave: Dispatches From The Next Generation Of Feminists* (Emeryville, CA: Seal Press, 2006), p. 178.

2   Sara Ahmed, 'Orientations: Toward a Queer Phenomenology', *GLQ* 12(4): 543–74; here p. 543.

3   Ibid., p. 547.

4   Ibid., p. 572.

5   Judith Butler, *Bodies That Matter: On the Discursive Limits of "Sex"* (New York: Routledge, 1993), p. 95.

6   *Race Revolt Zine* was created by Humaira Saeed and Heena Patel. For a brief note on the publication, see their page on the *Grassroots Feminism* website. Available at: https://goo.gl/5tWqVk (last accessed on 21 July 2017.)

7   Al-Noor Peera, 'History Part One'. Available at: http://-www.peera.com/-word.html (last accessed on 14 April 2015).

CHAPTER SEVENTEEN

Friendship Is an Invisible Blood That Keeps Us Real

MA MERCEDES ALBA BENITEZ

All my friends are freedom fighters, survivors, some of them professionals in social issues, we are all activists, artists, teachers, housekeepers, employers, some times we keep distance, long silences, but when we meet again, we open our hopes and dreams, we make each other true, we are mirror, we can not lie to each other, we love the movement of the soul in freedom, we have seen the magic, growing from our shoes and each other's smiles. Friendship is in many ways for me the proof that I am alive, an open book, my friends when I am alone, thousands of miles away from them is the food that keeps me wandering around my own soul and world, this place that would be nothing without the knowledge of my collective being. My friends speak many languages: Spanish, Japanese, French, Russian, Finnish, Quetzal, Italian, English, Chinese, Portuguese, Hindu, Catalan, Swedish, friendship is a real privilege that I got, I have not only shared food and drinks with them, but dreams, realities, struggles, boycotts, complots, love, desire, freedom, poetry, my soul. I don't know if I am a good friend but I have had the best ones, lots of them have died, as a young feminist activist in my country, Mexico, in the late 1980s, lots of my most-loved male friends, we wanted to be respected, to be proud of our love our sexuality, they all died of AIDS, I do remember them, I do continue the struggle, because of them I am proud and keep going, keep painting, writing, loving, denouncing, I will keep living searching for a better world and the human being that is inside me. I have no choice but to keep surviving even over my pessimism and dreams, because my friends all over the world, those who can not reach with my finger, those who let me alone in this dimension, those who are never tired of constructing a better world, taught me that dreams "Do come true!"

I take this paper to mentions some of my dear friends whose who let me here, with their wishes and desires in my red suitcase, who killed themselves because pain is sometimes a wounded animal, a beast that eats the soul, those beautiful souls who died of AIDS, those who have been killed because of their commitment to justices.

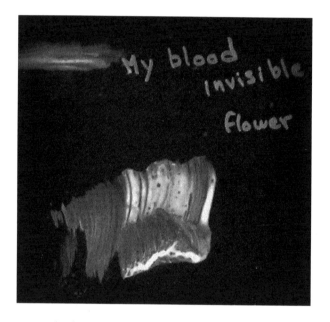

FIGURE 17.1 'My Blood Invisible Flower' by Ma Mercedes Alba Benitez, 2015.

I never say goodbye, we will meet again, thru a "virtual" world, with technology or without it! That is the power of friendship, my lovely friends: Heber, Javier, Juanita, Maricarmen, Susana, Felipe, Juan, Gerardo, Luis, Maria, Pepe, Geronima, Clio, Carlos, Sebastian, Pablo, Patricia, Gustavo, Sonia, Neil, Israel, Samuel, Rafael, Paul . . .

CHAPTER EIGHTEEN

Thinking the Relational Character of *Commoning* to Understand Political Activism

CESARE DI FELICIANTONIO

1. The Relational and Emotional Dimension of Activism

Feeling upset after the meeting with the support group. As always the meeting started with people introducing themselves, briefly describing their life histories, their problems with the banks or the mortgages, (. . .). Then a woman led the conversation, I never met her before but apparently she has been attending the support group for years already. Her words were heartbreaking, describing the importance of PAH, especially the support group, in her recent past, when she was going to have her house repossessed by the bank—together with a huge debt still there—and, at the same time, being diagnosed with a serious health problem requiring long, expensive and exhausting treatments. She described herself as desperate, without any more energy, really believing her time was over (. . .), then she arrived to the PAH and, for her a kind of new life started. 'The PAH has been a real balsam to me. You saved me, you brought me back to life, back to the will of believing, hoping, feeling and fighting,' her words today. Then she addressed to the newcomers, inviting them not to feel alone any more, 'I know you don't trust anyone any more,' she said, 'but here it's all about us—we take back our lives, our problems, no one will solve the problems for you but everybody will help and take care of you in facing and solving them' (Fieldwork notes, 4 November 2014: author's translation).

This long quotation from fieldwork notes in Sabadell, Catalonia, Spain, in the second half of 2014, reveals the double emotional dimension linked to being part of PAH (*Plataforma de los Afectados por la Hipoteca*, Mortgage Victims Platform), one of the most important social movements active in Spain since 2009. On one side, people arriving at the PAH feel desperate, alone, as they risk to lose the most important material good they have been working towards and hoping for, the house, which involves a crucial emotional dimension—the idea of 'home' playing a main role in the formation of (self-)identity among different contexts and phases of the life path (Easthope 2004; Ronald and Elsinga 2012; Waitt and Gorman-Murray 2011; Wise 2000). On the other, completely discouraged by the institutional setting, these same people assemble together to find a self-organized material solution to their problems, thus developing a collective sense of empowerment, possibility and action (Álvarez de Andrés *et al* 2015; Colau and Alemany 2012). So desperation and hope, and more generally emotions and feelings are the key factors in analyzing and understanding the raising of this social movement that has been able to make *collective* and *public* the sense of *personal* failure and abandonment usually associated with financial meltdowns.

Focusing on these emotional and affective dimensions of sociopolitical activism and participation, the chapter discusses how the extraordinary success of the PAH can be explained through the practice of *commoning*, meant here as a relational practice of putting resources in common. In this respect, the shared resources are represented by the life experiences, hopes, emotions and time of the people involved, thus going beyond the purely material dimension usually associated to the commons (Ostrom 1990). The chapter then follows the recent attempts to analyse the commons in their everyday situatedness (Bresnihan and Byrne 2014; Huron 2015), emphasizing the role of emotions, affects and relational ties as the ultimate commons to rely on for people dispossessed from their life aspirations and basic material needs. This way, it responds to recent calls for considering the role of affects and emotions in shaping spaces of activism (Barassi 2013; Brown and Pickerill 2009).

The remainder of the chapter includes three sections. In Section 2, I briefly describe the dramatic dimension of the housing crisis in

Spain and Catalonia, focusing on the grassroots' response to it as represented by the PAH. Basing on fieldwork data collected in Sabadell, Section 3 discusses the importance of the relational dimension in shaping the reproduction and success of the PAH, thus the practice of *commoning* is re-conceptualized as a relational action of putting life in common. Finally, in the conclusion, I stress the need to consider the relational character of the commons.

2. The PAH: 'Mortgaged' Lives Fighting for the Right to Housing

Following former dictator Franco's will to build a 'country of property owners', in the last decades Spanish political elites have made homeownership one of the main goals of both national and local politics (Colau and Alemany 2012; Garcia-Lamarca and Kaika 2014; López and Rodríguez 2011), the result being an increase of homeownership rate from 78.5 per cent in 1991 to 87 per cent in 2007 (Palomera 2014). Thanks to the large availability of credit in global financial markets, this process was made possible mostly through mortgages and predatory lending (Garcia-Lamarca and Kaika 2014). This is the reason why Ada Colau and Adriá Alemany have introduced the concept of 'mortgaged lives' to refer to the housing bubble and the homeownership boom in contemporary Spain.

From 'mortgaged' these lives rapidly became 'foreclosed' and 'dispossessed', as the housing crisis severely affected the country since 2008. Catalonia represents the most affected community (the administrative divisions of the Spanish country) of the current housing crisis: from 2008 to the third quarter of 2012, Catalonia registered 112,514 dispossessions—79,043 of them were mortgage executions, corresponding to 31 per cent of dispossessions of the entire country (Colau and Alemany 2013); only in 2012, the evictions rate was 8.96 per 1,000 inhabitants (ibid.). In the period between 2007 and the third quarter of 2012, Barcelona has been the most affected province of the country, registering 46,835 mortgage executions; Madrid has been the second with 44,616. In this dramatic ranking, Catalonia is represented also by Tarragona, occupying the 7th spot at the national level with 15,052 mortgage executions (ibid.).

Given an inadequate response of public institutions entrapped by the mantra of austerity, the main response to this dramatic situation has arrived from grassroots' mobilization, spearheaded by the PAH. PAH emerged in Barcelona on 22 February 2009, initially as a response to the dramatic increase of foreclosures and evictions, and its primary aim was to block evictions and assist people during the foreclosure process. So the PAH was initiated as a movement of homeowners who were unable to repay their mortgages because of deteriorating economic and financial conditions with the rapid increase of unemployment. Moreover, predatory lending had targeted specific low-income groups and neighbourhoods that were missing the basic requirements to repay their mortgages (Palomera 2014).

The experience of the PAH was not completely 'new', as it relied for its foundation on the experience of *V de Vivienda*, a social movement born in 2006, active mostly online, struggling for the right to decent housing. The main feature connecting the two movements is the importance accorded to public campaigns; in the case of V de Vivienda, their slogan was 'You will not have a house in your fucking life' and the symbol of a yellow balloon representing the real estate bubble. However, the years of V de Vivienda were still the years of boom in homeownership and easy credit, so although being prefigurative of the imminent crisis, V de Vivienda did not receive massive grassroots' support. On the contrary, a rapidly deteriorating phase has permitted the fast proliferation of the PAH, currently made of 226 nodes all around the Spanish country.[1] Being the most affected community in terms of dispossessions, Catalonia is also the most active within the PAH with 76 nodes of the network.

The political strategy and repertoire of the PAH is made of a variegated range of actions, campaigns and groups, the primary one being the emphasis on mutual aid, self-support and self-assessment. Indeed, the PAH rejects the neoliberal model of NGOs substituting the State and providing services and assistance mainly thanks to the work of 'specialists'. On the contrary, the PAH is based on the idea that 'you are the best assessor for yourself' and that uniting personal experiences, knowledge and time is the best way to fight an oppressive system that leaves people on the streets. So people in trouble arrive at the PAH assemblies and receive help only if they are available to share their time, knowledge and efforts with others and build the network as well. 'Once you arrive at PAH you know that you won't be fighting alone any more'—is the main motto repeated by PAH militants in Catalonia. The result is a process of self-empowerment of people who believe that it is possible to challenge the power of banks and financial institutions, and there is a collective way to fight the sense of loneliness and failure associated with foreclosure and dispossession. This explains the brave series of political actions and campaigns realized by PAH activists, from banks' occupation to exhausting negotiations with banks to obtain social rent for households losing their house.

In this process of self-empowerment and increasing popular consensus and activism, the PAH has been able to reshape its primary aim, thus addressing its claims not only around homeownership and the mortgage question but also around the issues of housing and precarity, thus involving the people who could never afford (or did not want) to enter the mortgage market. So the main battle of PAH now concerns the right to decent housing in all its forms, resulting in a strongly inclusive process for diverse subjectivities: from low-income migrant households who were subjected to predatory lending or could never become homeowners to the former middle-class who lost their homes because of the job loss. Basing on the case of the PAH Sabadell, one of the most well-known and active nodes of the network in Catalonia, the next section is going to discuss how such successful process has been made possible through the practice of relational *commoning*.

3. The PAH Sabadell. A Tale about the Commons

The local node of the PAH in Sabadell was created in February 2011, thanks to the engagement of a group of militants from the leftist/autonomous scene of the city[2] who had heard that people from Sabadell suffering with mortgages, foreclosures and evictions had contacted the PAH node in Barcelona. After a first public meeting attended by around 40 people, the weekly general assembly has grown more and more—it is now attended by around 200 people and dozens of newcomers every week seeking a way to avoid losing their home (owned or rented). The organization of the node follows the principles of the overall network: it is completely horizontal, people are asked to present their situation in the assembly and there is a process of self-assessment by all the people present based on their previous experience. Indeed the basic idea is that the ultimate decision on how to intervene is up to the person involved in the repossession/mortgage execution, but this results from a collective discussion in which the others try to share information and explanations. Once started, the procedure on how to help is re-discussed collectively by the assembly time after time according to the legal deadlines of the repossession/mortgage execution process. Collective actions and campaigns are also organized to support individual causes, from blocking evictions to providing a new shelter through squatting in vacant flats owned by banks.

Since the weekly meeting has grown so much in terms of attendance, making it difficult for people in need to have the chance to discuss their problems, the assembly has decided to dedicate a special weekly meeting for newcomers in order to give them information and avoid the frustration/awkwardness in sharing personal stories with hundreds of people. Moreover, this has been envisaged as a measure to better help non-native Spanish speakers in order to avoid language-based misunderstandings. However, with the amount of people taking part in assemblies increasing, the PAH Sabadell militants have started to reflect on how one of the crucial dimensions of their political action was getting lost: the relational/emotional side. Indeed one of the most acknowledged dimensions linked to loss of home is the risk of losing self-trust, serious psychological depression and even suicide attempts (Currie and Tekin 2011; Libman *et al* 2012). These dramatic facts follow the sense of personal failure usually associated with the loss of home; as a matter of fact, one of the main features of the 'neoliberal reason' (Peck 2010) is reducing every kind of socioeconomic personal event during life to a matter of personal responsibility, thus producing anxiety and continuous uncertainty (Dardot and Laval 2014b). In order to avoid people continuing feeling alone, abandoned and 'failed' despite taking part to PAH meetings, the militants decided to create a new group: meeting on a weekly basis to discuss any kind of personal issue far beyond the problems with mortgage. In the months I had the chance to stay with the support group, we discussed a wide range of issues from the children's education to the anxiety caused by the precarious conditions of the job market, from problems in kinships to everyday racism. From my experience, I can state that the ultimate goal of the group is taking care of each other, everybody investing their time, energies and experiences to discuss and solve someone else's problems. Indeed, all the support for weekly meetings concerns *you*— when you arrive everybody wants to know more about you, your story, how your life is doing; you share thoughts, experiences, anxieties. If someone's concerns require more time to be addressed and discussed, the support group remains to assist you. The basic rule is that there is no prefixed time limit for the meetings: 'the meeting is over when there is no one else left in the group who wants to share their issues' is a frequently repeated motto. The concrete result of such a process is that every week people who arrive at the support group start to regain their energies, determination and will: from sad and faded, their attitudes quickly turn to passion and joyfulness.

To give an example of such a process, I quote from an interview with one of the assiduous attendants of support group meetings. At a first glance V.G.F.[3] could appear as someone who lived their life to enter the world of the 'new petty bourgeoisie', in a country where accessing homeownership is the distinctive characteristic of this class (Aalbers 2015; Ronald 2008). After years of employment and financial stability in the household, the systemic meltdown started in 2007 and resulted in economic hardships, first due to the loss of job, and later, loss of the property for failing to pay the mortgage. With no material support and feeling desperate about losing the house, they arrive at the PAH as the ultimate step on the terrible path leading to the loss of everything they own:

> I was desperate when I arrived at the PAH, I did not believe that there would be any solution, that anybody could help us, (. . .), but, above all, I was feeling guilty and shamed to narrate my story to others, I blamed myself because I had not been able to do it, everything was getting lost, my world, my affects, the conviction and trust in your possibilities. (. . .) So when I arrived I was not really able to speak, I was too shy, too angry, I could not accept and believe that I had *failed*. (. . .) I felt intimidated, you know, you have spent your life just thinking of yourself and your household interests, you wanted to achieve something, have a stable position, (. . .), arriving here was a real shock, so much pain, so much

desperation. (. . .) But we were many, and every week new
people arriving, (. . .), at the beginning I was feeling somehow *different* from the others, but then you know the others,
you speak with the others, you learn from them and you realize we come from the same world, a world of people deceived
by the promises of banks and finance, (. . .) people who do
not want to leave their lives in the hands of those who make
profit, (. . .), here I learnt how the change is possible, how
we can take back our lives—first, our homes—but we have to
fight together, day by day. But this has been the most reward-
ing experience of my life, producing change, (. . .) the way I
see and think about the others' lives and experiences has completely changed. I'm part of something now, a large family
taking care of me (Personal interview on 10 November 2014;
author's translation, emphasis added).

I define this process at work, as highlighted by V.G.F.'s words,
as *relational commoning*, thus conceptualizing 'common' not as a noun
but as a verb, a collective action of sharing with the others our life
experiences, stories, feelings and emotions. In a neoclassical perspective, the commons have usually been depicted as the basic pools
of material/natural resources a community can count on (Ostrom
1990). More recently, the commons has become the main concern of
a growing literature, mostly linked to post-Marxism and autonomous
thought, emphasizing how the commons has been put at work under
informational, knowledge-based capitalism (Dardot and Laval 2014a;
Hardt 2010; Hardt and Negri 2009) with new forms of enclosure-
raising (Hodkinson 2012). Although recognizing the importance of
such perspectives, I want to highlight here the symbolic value of *commoning*, meant as 'the fluid, continuous and relational ways in which
the living commons, past and present, are produced. Commons understood as a verb indicates the limitations of understanding the commons as a noun, as a static, physical resource, such as a bounded plot
of urban space' (Bresnihan and Byrne 2014: 11). *Commoning* emerges
then as a practice in a context shaped by a dramatic crisis, such as
the Catalan–Spanish one, with thousands of people experiencing the
traumatic experience of losing a shelter. Spoilt of material resources,
these people arrive at the PAH meetings feeling guilty and alone—thus
the only resources left to share with the others are life experiences,

emotions and feelings and time. In this sense, the *common* represents a set of relational, emotional and affective resources that can be shared to engage in a process of collective self-empowerment and mutual care.

In the case of PAH Sabadell, this relational dimension is made explicit in the main mottos of the group: 'You won't be alone any more' and 'Once you are part of the PAH, you will never find yourself on the street without a shelter'. Although it may sound rhetorical, the last motto has become possible thanks to the brave and tenacious engagement of the militants, not simply blocking evictions but also squatting in vacant flats. The Obra Social PAH—the squatting campaign of the network whose name paraphrases the old name of banks branches aimed at promoting affordable housing—in 2013, had supported, among other things, the occupation of a vacant building owned by a bank and offered shelter to more than 140 people who were evicted from their properties. In 2014, the constant pressure of PAH Sabadell led to a historical success: the bank-owned building was ceded to the *generalitat* (the Catalan administrative system) for several years and the *generalitat* recognized a social rent—according to their incomes— to the families living there. This landmark success has favoured the support to the Obra Social PAH within the Catalan PAH, thus leading to the monthly workshops on knowledge and skills about squatting organized by the PAH Sabadell.

This series of successful campaigns would have not been possible without cultivating the relational/emotional side of the engagement, this process of 'cultivating subjects' (Gibson-Graham 2006) embodied by the support group in the case of the PAH Sabadell. As stated by one of the activists during the presentation at the weekly general assembly: 'Support group is where you come to learn you are not alone, to learn that PAH is a group of people who have had similar problems and similar anxieties but all together we have learnt a way to face them' (Fieldwork notes, 15 October 2014; author's translation).

The result of such an involvement is that most of the participants of the support's activities, such as V.G.F., refer to PAH as 'the PAH family'—'A family of people who are there to listen to you, to take care of you, to give you suggestions, to cry and laugh with you' (Personal interview with a PAH activist, 28 October 2014; author's translation). Friendship, personal and emotional reward, and a deep sense of belonging to a community become then as the key factors driving *commoning*—as a practice that leads so many people to be involved in assessing and taking care of the others' troubles and situations.

4. Conclusion: Thinking the Relational Character of the Commons

The dramatic mortgage and housing crisis hitting Catalonia and Spain for the last several years has brought thousands of people to organize groups within the PAH to fight together, claiming the right to decent housing and life, challenging 'the violence of financial capitalism' (Marazzi 2011). I have argued here that the success of the movement depends on its capacity to create a space of *relational commoning*, meant as a practice to put life in common, going beyond a purely material perspective on the commons. Recognizing that the commons is socially produced (Federici 2010; Linebaugh 2008), is the first step towards an approach that emphasizes the emotional and affective dimensions attached to the practice of *commoning* for people gathering together in order to instil hope, trust and the will to pursue living. Indeed the isolation and individualization featuring the subjectification process influenced by neoliberalism (Dardot and Laval 2014b) have made them desperate, guilty of having failed to achieve what a so-called responsible person should. Fighting together each day, taking care of the others' needs and problems, making *collective* and *common* what was previously perceived as a personal tragedy to build new affective institutions of friendship, trust, mutual aid and confidence. Thus, the members usually refer to the PAH as 'the family'. This shift in the perspective about the commons can open new ways and possibilities to analyse the everyday resistance to hegemonic institutions in urban contexts in which strangers come together, as recently pointed out by Amanda Huron (2015). The PAH activists have engaged with a process of sharing all that left to them—experience, time, knowledge, their affects and empathy—to oppose the violence of a system that wants us to remain isolated and always 'responsible' for what happens to us, hiding the inequalities in the social system that does not encourage the sense of mutual aid, support and trust. *Relational commoning* emerges then as a practice of care, opening the way to a 'world-making' politics (Muñoz 2009) assigning priority to affect, friendship, trust and sharing.

Notes

1   Data available on PAH website: https://goo.gl/CSRwg1 (last accessed on 1 August 2017). The PAH nodes are regrouped for communities following the administrative division of the Spanish State.

2   Like the rest of Catalonia, Sabadell has a long-standing leftist/ autonomous tradition highlighted by squatted social centres engaged in a wide series of activities for the local community.

3   Names of respondents have been withheld to protect their privacy.

Works Cited

AALBERS, Manuel. 2015. 'The Great Moderation, the Great Excess and the Global Housing Crisis'. *International Journal of Housing Policy* 15(1): 43–60.

ÁLVAREZ DE ANDRÉS, Eva, María José Campos Zapata and Patrik Zapata. 2015. 'Stop the Evictions! The Diffusion of Networked Social Movements and the Emergence of a Hybrid Space: The Case of the Spanish Mortgage Victims Group', *Habitat International* 46: 252–59.

BARASSI, Veronica. 2013. 'Ethnographic Cartographies: Social Movements, Alternative Media and the Spaces of Networks'. *Social Movement Studies: Journal of Social, Cultural and Political Protest* 12(1): 48–62.

BOURDIEU, Pierre. 1984. *Distinction: A Social Critique of the Judgement of Taste.* Cambridge: Harvard University Press.

BRESNIHAN, Patrick, and Michael Byrne. 2014. 'Escape into the City: Everyday Practices of Commoning and the Production of Urban Space in Dublin', *Antipode* 47(1). Available at: https://goo.gl/MfEpVq (last accessed on 1 August 2017).

BROWN, Gavin, and Jenny Pickerill (eds). 2009. 'Activism and Emotional Sustainability'. *Emotion, Space and Society* 2(1): 1–69.

COLAU, Ada, and Adriá Alemany. 2012. *Mortgaged Lives. From the Housing Bubble to the Right to Housing.* Los Angeles, Leipzig and London: Journal of Aesthetics and Protest Press.

———. 2013. *2007–2012: Retrospectiva sobre desahucios y ejecuciones hipotecarias en España, estadísticas oficiales y indicadores.* Available at: https://goo.gl/giLsFS (last accessed on 1 August 2017).

CURRIE, Janet, and Erdal Takin. 2011. 'Is the Foreclosure Crisis Making Us Sick?', *National Bureau of Economic Research Working Papers*. Available at: https://goo.gl/dvU8CA(last accessed on 1 August 2017).

DARDOT, Pierre, and Christian Laval. 2014a. *Commun. Essai sur la révolution au XXIe siècle*. Paris: Editions La Découverte

————. 2014b. *The New Way of the World: On Neoliberal Society*. London: Verso.

EASTHOPE, Hazel. 2004. 'A Place Called Home'. *Housing, Theory and Society* 21(3): 128–38.

FEDERICI, Silvia. 2010. 'Feminism and the Politics of the Commons' in Team Colors Collective (ed.), *Uses of a Whirlwind: Movement, Movement, and Contemporary Radical Currents in the United States*. Oakland: AK Press, pp. 283–94.

GARCIA LAMARCA, Melissa, and Maria Kaika. 2014. '"Mortgaged Lives": The Biopolitics of Debt and Homeownership in Spain'. *Transactions of the Institute of British Geographers* 41(3): 313–27. Available at: https://goo.gl/kw5Fo7 (last accessed on 1 August 2017).

GIBSON-GRAHAM, J.K. 2006. *A Postcapitalist Politics*. Minneapolis: University of Minnesota Press.

HARDT, Michael. 2010. 'The Common in Communism'. *Rethinking Marxism* 22(3): 346–56.

————, and Antonio Negri. 2009. *Commonwealth*. Cambridge: Harvard University Press.

HODKINSON, Stuart. 2012. 'The New Urban Enclosures'. *City: Analysis of Urban Trends, Culture, Theory, Policy, Action* 16(5): 500–18.

HURON, Amanda. 2015. 'Working with Strangers in Saturated Space: Reclaiming and Maintaining the Urban Commons'. *Antipode* 47(4): 963–79.

LIBMAN, Kimberly, Desiree Fields and Susan Saegert. 2012. 'Housing and Health: A Social Ecological Perspective on the US foreclosure Crisis'. *Housing, Theory and Society* 29(1): 1–24.

LINEBAUGH, Peter. 2008. *The Magna Carta Manifesto: Liberties and Commons for All*. Berkeley: University of California Press.

LÓPEZ, Isidro, and Emmanuel Rodríguez. 2011. 'The Spanish Model'. *New Left Review* 69: 5–28.

MARAZZI, Christian. 2011. *The Violence of Financial Capitalism*. Bellinzona: Semiotext(e).

MUÑOZ, José Esteban. 2009. *Cruising Utopia: The Then and There of Queer Futurity*. New York: NYU Press.

OSTROM, Elinor. 1990. *Governing the Commons: The Evolution of Institutions for Collective Action*. Cambridge: Cambridge University Press.

PALOMERA, Jaime. 2014. 'How Did Finance Capital Infiltrate the World of the Urban Poor? Homeownership and Social Fragmentation in a Spanish Neighborhood'. *International Journal of Urban and Regional Research* 38(1): 218–35.

PECK, Jamie. 2010. *Constructions of Neoliberal Reason*. Oxford: Oxford University Press.

RONALD, Richard. 2008. *The Ideology of Home Ownership: Homeowner Societies and the Role of Housing*. Basingstoke: Palgrave Macmillan.

———, and Marja Elsinga. 2012. *Beyond Home Ownership. Housing, Welfare and Society*. London: Routledge.

WAITT, Gordon and Gorman-Murray, Andrew. 2011. '"It's About Time You Came Out": Sexualities, Mobilities and Home'. *Antipode* 43(4): 1380–403.

WISE, J. Macgregor. 2000. 'Home: Territory and Identity'. *Cultural Studies* 14(2): 295–310.

CHAPTER NINETEEN

Friendship As a Mode of Sustainable Change in the Ready-Made Garment Sector in Bangladesh

LIPI BEGUM AND MAHER ANJUM

Through in-depth interviews, this essay documents the unique stories of Alyia, Mussamat and Jesmin, three garment factory workers and members of the National Garment Workers' Federation (NGWF) in Dhaka, Bangladesh. These individuals share their anecdotal journeys of friendship and engagement with social change to make the ready-made garment sector in Bangladesh sustainable in the aftermath of the Tazreen Ltd. and Rana Plaza factory disasters in 2012 and 2013, respectively. Through stories of rebellion, resilience and learning, this piece draws attention to the paradox of how gender-neutral friendships in the ready-made garment sector empower workers as they speak up against low-paid production and uncertain working conditions shaped by global market forces in an effort to make it a safe, fair and sustainable place of work.

The Ready-Made Garment Sector in Bangladesh

In the past 30 years the Bangladesh ready-made garment (RMG) sector has grown tremendously. In 1978, some 130 employees of one of the first four garment factories were sent to South Korea for management training; by 1985, 700 factories were in operation. Ten years later the manufacturers' association listed some 2,400 registered factories (Amin et al. 1998); and in 2011, the RMG sector in Bangladesh was forecast to double by 2015 and triple by 2020 (McKinsey 2011). It has been placed as the largest export earner of Bangladesh and includes 4,825 garment factories, employing over 3 million people. The great majority (85 per cent) of workers are women (Sikder et al. 2014), many of whom travel alone from smaller villages around the capital city of Dhaka in search for better standards of living. The movement of manufacturing base from developed nations in the West to countries like Bangladesh in the East is based on low production costs and plenty of unskilled labour, usually women. The fast growing sector is met by the challenges of establishing minimum wage, securing preferential trade agreements, safer working environments and the right to organize through trade unions. For Bangladeshi garment factory workers, this means being left in a paradoxical position of control and freedom.

On 24 April 2013, over 1,100 people were killed and thousands more injured in the collapse of the Rana Plaza garment factory building in Bangladesh, which housed major global brands. This was less than six months after the Tazreen Ltd. fire in November 2012, where more than 150 people died in a fire that swept through the garment factory. The disaster was the result of poor maintenance of fire and safety standards and, therefore, entirely preventable. Among the multitude of responses to these tragic incidences, President Obama suspended the long-term US Generalized Scheme of Preferential (GSP) trade benefits for Bangladesh. This was a marginal loss[1] but triggered a wider socioeconomic loss due to a profound negative country image.

Over 1,000 factories were inspected in 2014 and less than 2 per cent were deemed to be unsafe (Bangladesh Accord Foundation 2014). While low wages have yet to be regularized, these inspections on health and safety measures show that from a structural perspective the overall state of the sector is robust and successful. However, apart from a small number of short films and articles by international human rights groups,[2] this story of robust success of the RMG sector in Bangladesh has stretched little beyond the narrative of the unskilled, uneducated and poor sweatshop worker.

Amartya Sen argues that the sectors growth achievement is not entirely transparent, yet he points out sustained positive change in gender relations as a noteworthy contributing factor (Sen and Drèze 2014). Sen does not elaborate on these gender relations and calls for further investigation. We believe noteworthy factors can be found in Bangladesh's strong historical ethos of gender-neutral friendships as a mode of learning (education), rebellion and fighting for social justice—a history often overlooked in the face of negative publicity.

Historically, Bengal—what is now Bangladesh and West Bengal, India—has had its fair share of quiet revolutionaries. Through education, Begum Rokeya Sakhawat Hussain established the first Muslim girls' school after having become literate with the help and friendship of her brother and continued her education after marriage under the guidance of her husband (Hossain 2013). In the tale *Teen Kanya* (Three Daughters) by Nobel Laureate Rabindranath Tagore (as in many of his other works), modernization and opportunity for social growth is charted through themes of gender-neutral friendships and resilience (Tagore 1977). Moreover, Bangladeshis are taught from an early age to celebrate the poet Kazi Nazrul Islam, known as the 'Bidrohi Kobi' (Rebel Poet) for his lifelong passion to fight oppression (including gender) and strive for political and social justice (Langley 2007).

This article does not seek to provide a detailed history of political resistance in Bangladesh and cannot raise the voices of all its garment factory workers, nor does it tries to undermine the fundamental challenges and positive global initiatives undertaken to improve the sector. Instead, it is through embodied dialogues that this article demonstrates the role of friendship as an instrumental mode of rebellion, resilience, learning, and ultimately a sustained mode of social change for Bangladesh's RMG sector.

Amader Jatra, Our Journey

Amader Jatra means 'our journey' in Bangla. 'Jatra' is commonly used word by our interviewees to reinforce the personal and cultural context of the recorded stories. We are met by Alyia and Mussamat and other workers sitting in small groups outside NGWF's head office in Dhaka, Bangladesh. We learn that Friday was their only day off and so they could come to the office for training sessions. The demand for such sessions exceeded the number of rooms available, hence we are met by a large crowd sitting outside.

The NGWF was set up in 1984. With more than 27,000 members, it is the largest trade union federation in the Bangladeshi garment sector and they have 18 women on their 30-member Central Executive Committee. The NGWF works hard to strengthen the trade-union movement across Bangladesh, it promotes workers' rights through targeted campaigns and by lobbying the government, factory owners and multinational corporations for stronger legislation and enforcement. The NGWF also offers legal advice and carries out training sessions for workers around labour rights with a focus on women and leadership (War on Want 2014).

FIGURE 19.1 (FRONT ROW, RIGHT TO LEFT) Aliya, Jesmin, Mussamat, Amin and a group NGWF workers attending training sessions in December 2014.

We speak to Amirul Haque Amin, president of NGWF, who lends an insight into gender development in the garment sector. Amin believes women workers are not *shimaboddho* (limited) in their pursuit for positive social growth. With a sense of pride he states:

> Our females are empowered, therefore, development and independence is a good thing. They can earn for themselves, they can create their own voice. Garment workers were family burden but not any more, they can be decision makers in their family. They make the choice when they want to marry and take an extra 5 years. In the earlier generation decisions were taken by parents, now it's taken by them (Personal interview with Amin).

We learn that garment factory workers are anything but passive as the media predominantly portrays them, yet we also learn that their situation is far from perfect. Amin explains the challenges of overcoming unfair pay, gender discrimination and rights to promotion. He tells us '85 per cent top-level managerial positions are taken up by men and bottom-level operators and helpers are women'. These facts do not surprise us, we can relate to them, there are some universal issues at hand, for even in developed countries unequal pay and gender discrimination remain strife.

Amin continues to speak freely: 'All factories in the world are this way, what is different in Bangladesh is our cooperative collaboration and working together'. We learn that things are different from what is portrayed in the global media, contradicting America's reason for withdrawing the GSP. Amin argues that 'we assist the worker and ask what the women need. I am quite optimistic. The disasters have made their voices bigger, they see themselves in the disaster, and think: this could happen to us, we need to change things'. Inspired by Amin's discussion, we go on to interview the workers.

Bidrohi, the Rebel

The conversation starts off with Alyia Begum. Alyia's journey in the garment sector began in 24th November 1985 after she left school with a HSC (Higher Secondary School Certificate) qualification. Alyia did not plan her career in the garment sector, she took it up through the suggestion of her male cousin. Alyia started as an operator, progressed to a training operator and then a training supervisor. Alyia speaks of her journey of rebellion as that of a *bidrohi* (rebel), a personal rebellion driven by a sense of collective-individualism, self-determination, and strong friendship networks. Alyia tells us her career development would not have been possible without the early encouragement in her second job from her South Korean boss who treated her 'like a daughter', she recalls, '*shekhan theke amar jatra shuro*' (from there my journey began).

Alyia tells us that she 'had no clue of foreign buyers, I liked her even though she was a foreigner . . . even though she was an outsider, she called me "Ma'am", I felt *lajja* (embarrassment) but it felt good.'

Alyia's positive feeling from being called 'Ma'am' by a figure of authority is an early sign of Alyia embracing change through friendship. Alyia's story of her friendship with her boss demonstrates the role of friendship as a mode of resilience against anxieties of globalization and political instability during a time of growing prejudice against Bangladeshi immigrants in South Korea and Bangladeshi nationalist mistrust of foreign trade. This friendship also highlights the importance of mentorship, as she was guided and supported to dream and aspire to do more than what she was doing. During a time when very few female workers held supervisory and management positions, Alyia's friendship with her foreign buyer gave her the motivation and courage to become an inspiring female authority figure herself. Alyia goes on to recall having '50 trainees under her management within one year'.

As we continue to follow Alyia on her career journey, it becomes evident that she has grown up with the industry; her early friendships which depended on technical support and mentorship have helped her develop an inspirational leadership style strongly rooted in the foundations of friendship. The power of this leadership style is apparent when Alyia recalls the collective bargaining power of her friends (colleagues) in the face of political instability and global inequality. She tell us how in 1990, during her tenure at AC Garments,[3] she got into 'many fights', yet support from her friendship network gave her the confidence to dispute unequal pay. She recalls her friend and *bidrohi*, Nabi Miah, helped her stand up to police and threats from her autocratic boss and file a case with Bangladesh Garment Manufacturers and Export Association (BGMEA) against unfair labour practices. Alyia tells us that this was 'not common for a woman at the time', however, she was 'determined to stand up for her friends'. Alyia successfully managed to secure 70 jobs for her friends and colleagues, but it wasn't enough for her. She left the job and joined another garment factory later that year.

For Alyia, mentoring and friendship allowed her to build her own career. From the very beginning, she demonstrated the qualities of a leader nurturing success through support and friendship networks. Alyia effortlessly combines self-determination and collective-determination. She wraps up the conversation, giving us a list of friends who played an important role in her success, going on to say 'I can't remember them all' and proudly states her 'fearlessness', her sense of self-actualization and her belief in executing the *odhikhar* (right) to fight for her friends.

Rokkha, to Safeguard

For others, friendship became a protective tool against feelings of insecurity and instability. This was particularly evident in our conversation with garment workers Mussamat Phurkan Akhter and Jesmin Begum. Mussamat recalls starting work in the RMG sector in September 1995, she tells us she 'used to match numbers, then I was an operator . . . it's quite hard with a lot of people to oversee'. She is proud of her achievements; however, she also enunciates the hardships and coping mechanisms that she has had to develop over the years. Mussamat speaks of joining the garment sector to 'help out her family', and that her sister had joined the factory with her but left after three months. Unlike Alyia, Mussamat, recalls 'not eating for two days' and 'crying a lot', but having to 'continue working to support her mother, her ill brother and his family'. Mussamat talks about her friendship with her co-worker Runa, and how Runa motivated her to stay in the factory: 'Runa consoled me, she made me understand about continuing to work even if I was away from my family'. For Mussamat this friendship was essential to her mental resilience while away from her family.

Mussamat tells us, 'Ever since those days . . . of Runa making me stay, I have remained in the garment sector'. Mussamat has built her friendship network ever since: 'Today I have come in to visit Alyia'. Mussamat shares less of an overt collective spirit. Unlike Alyia, she is matter-of-fact and there is a sense of hardship in her voice and a greater sense of physical and mental struggle in her experiences. She describes her 'visual impairment' which has made her actively strive for a sense of security. She speaks less of her friendships, but tells us that she is 'tougher because of her friendships with people like Runa who have treated her like a sister'. Mussamat explains how she still continues to visit Runa even though their lives have taken different paths, 'Runa has kids and a husband now, I go round for food, the whole family knows me, and her children call me Aunty'. She explains how she 'never married nor had kids because of her eye problem'.—'I thought if I have children, if it gets worse, who will look over me? If I have beautiful kids, how will I provide for them? I cannot let them beg. I decided I will work for myself and be on my own.' There is a similarity between Alyia and Mussamat here—despite their strong sense of self determination they are also concerned for others. For example, when Mussamat questions whether it is possible for her to adequately provide for a family despite her visual impairment, she essentially reveals her core values and her desire to do good for others.

Compared to Alyia who described the support of her husband as tantamount to her mental well-being and success, Mussamat is pragmatic. She reveals she is happy with her life and her friendships and goes on to defy patriarchal stereotypes by explaining that 'garment workers don't want to marry, people assume we are all the same, leaving their family. I want to support my brother and his kids and get them educated . . . In two years' time, I will have my health plan and I will move to the village.' She continues to speak of her family as friends and Runa's kids as her family; however, she speaks of friendship in practical terms: something you do, something you seek to safeguard yourself and others. In Mussamat's case, it helps her cope with life changes and provides the support towards pursuing unconventional life choices.

Shikkha, Learning

Garment worker Jesmin also recalls starting work in the garment factory to support her family. Jesmin started in BDC Garments, in 2000, to support her mother who had separated from her father that year. Jesmin speaks of her quick promotion from a 'helper to an operator within 15 days'. Impressed by Jesmin's promotion, we ask her how that was possible; to which Jesmin replies that she is 'a quick learner' and that she 'bought a sewing machine and learnt everything at home in the evenings.' Jesmin is modest and makes it sound extremely easy. We shortly learn that friendship with Dolly, her operator-manager at the time, played a significant role in developing her ability to strive for several promotions within a short period. Jesmin recalls Dolly as someone who paid attention to her abilities and saw potential in her: 'Dolly used to ask me about my qualifications. I told her that I was at secondary level, but she was impressed by me more than my educational qualification. She used to teach me and encourage me to do well.' Jesmin's friendship with Dolly is similar to Alyia and her South Korean boss—both friendships were initially based on a mentor and role-model dynamic. We are able to analyse that such mentor and mentee dynamics have played out into long-term friendships and are essential to successful careers within the RMG sector and for collaborative practice. Jesmin explains the importance of Dolly's friendship to her career, 'Now I am in a higher position than Dolly's but we still stay in touch, we don't work against each other, we still put our heads together to achieve critical successes.'

Like Mussamat and Alyia, Jesmin has grown up with the industry, initial years of networking with positive role models and supportive friendships have shaped her attitude towards dealing with hardships and instability later on in her career. Jesmin states, 'Like Dolly, I want to help others.' She recalls how this realization dawned on her the day that the Rana Plaza fire incident occured. Jesmin was working that day on a 7 a.m. shift when she heard that 30 people had died at Rana Plaza:

> When I heard 30 people were dead, we had to go. Rana Plaza is burning, I need to find my colleagues, I have to go . . . I sneaked my mobile in and got the news about Rana Plaza . . . Couldn't find a rickshaw. Where I found a car, I got into the car. Where I had to run, I ran 9 km, 10 km . . . we all went. We made a scene, drama, used pregnant women to get there, we had to lie about emergencies about my operation. We were clever about it, to get there. We couldn't get in. I called two strong male friends, one stay behind and one stay ahead so we can get in. I showed my visiting card [member of Garments Federation card] and got through. Everyone started helping each other, and I could understand the importance of help and support only then (Personal interview with Jesmin Begum, author's translation).

Jesmin's friendships during the Rana Plaza disaster helped her to deal with a crisis without feeling defeated. She describes the support from her male colleagues, whom she refers to as 'Brother Murad' and 'Brother Atiq', who coached her to believe that while she is educated and young, she 'should value working and earning to protect herself from a rapidly changing and unstable sector'. Unlike Mussamat who does not want to marry or stay in Dhaka, Jesmin is still young; she continues to learn and is still hopeful and optimistic about staying in the big city of Dhaka and exploring the opportunities it has to offer.

Aparishim, Limitless

The journeys of Alyia, Mussamat and Jesmin are a snapshot of how thousands of factory workers in the Bangladesh RMG sector are paradoxically bound by the capital forces, yet are limitless in negotiating a sense of survival, pleasure and resilience within these global forces. Central to this social agency is the creation of a web of empowerment through gender-neutral friendship networks. These networks not only enable garment workers to exercise their political visions and remain resilient within unstable and uncertain working conditions but also demonstrate best practice of how friendship networks are essential to effective leadership styles and collaborative learning practices within collective cultural contexts.

For Alyia and Jesmin having a mentor within the friendship circle has been a significant factor in helping them progress towards leadership roles. In both cases, the women had non-gender-biased mentors who spotted their individual abilities and talents.

One of the things that all three women pointed out when interviewed was the 'level of education' they had or didn't have. Alyia and Jesmin had completed high-school level. They competed with men and excelled rapidly within the factories progressing even to managerial positions. In the case of Mussamat, her lack of progression was partly due to her disability of being partially sighted, but also the fact that she did not have the opportunity to complete school and, therefore, felt less confident to compete for higher positions. However, Mussamat is not a woman to be pitied; throughout her years of work at the factory, she has made plans for her future and is looking to retire in the next few years. If it was not for her work in the garment factory, this would not have been something she could have achieved.

If we are to sustain the long-term success of the RMG sector in Bangladesh, it is essential that effective and context-specific working styles such as friendship and mentoring are better understood by all members of the global supply chain and are publicized as best practice examples of collaborative learning to shift power from the corporation to the creator. Like Amin, we are sad that factory disasters have had to open the eyes of the world to Bangladesh as a destination for innovation, but true to our historical roots, our future is in our cultural past as optimistic, *bidrohi* (rebellious) and *aparishim* (limitless) global learners.

Notes

1   This is due to the small volume of exports and the lack of import restrictions on Bangladeshi goods in the US. The GSP allows exporters from developing country to pay less or no duties on their exports to the US.

2   Refers to the other human rights groups which focus on garment factory workers, for example, War on Want (London), Rainbow Collective (Dhaka), Labour Behind the Label (Bristol), etc.

3   Names of the factories and factory workers in this chapter have been changed to protect the privacy of the research participants, except in the cases of Alyia, Jesmin, Mussamat and Amin, who have consented to identify themselves.

Works Cited

AMIN, S., I. Diamond, R. T. Naved and M. Newby. 1998. 'Transition to Adulthood of Female Garment Factory Workers in Bangladesh: Adolescent Reproductive Behaviour in the Developing World'. *Studies in Family Planning* 29(2): 185–200.

BANGLADESH ACCORD FOUNDATION. 2014. 'Accord Makes Good Progress Towards Safe Factories in Bangladesh Factories'. *Bangladesh Accord Foundation*. Available at: https://goo.gl/g8fGXz (last accessed on 2 August 2017).

BBC NEWS ASIA. 2012. 'Dhaka Bangladesh Clothes Factory Fire Kills More Than 100'. *BBC News Asia* (25 November). Available at: https://goo.gl/-D72Z7v (last accessed on 2 August 2017).

HOSSAIN. 2013. 'Rokeya Sakhawat Hussain (1880–1932)'. *Bangladesh Golden Book*. Available at: http://goldenbookbd.com/rokeya-sakhawat-hussain-1880-1932/ (last accessed on 3 March 2015).

LANGLEY, W. E. 2007. *Kazi Nazrul Islam: the Voice of Poetry and the Struggle for Human Wholeness*. Dhaka: Nazrul Institute.

BERG, Achim, Saskia Hedrich, Sebastian Kempf and Thomas Tochtermann. 2011. *Bangladesh's Ready Made Garments Landscape the Challenges of Growth*. McKinsey and Company. Available at; https://goo.gl/hgP4Pf (last accessed on 4 August 2017.)

TAGORE, Rabindranath. 1977. *Collected Poems and Plays of Rabindranath Tagore*. New York: Macmillan.

SEN, Amartya, and Jean Drèze. 2014. *An Uncertain Glory India and its Contradictions*. New Delhi: Penguin.

SIKDAR, Mehedi Hasan, S. Kabir Sarkar and Sumaiya Sadeka. 2014. 'Socio-economic Conditions of the Female Garment Workers in the Capital City of Bangladesh'. *International Journal of Humanities and Social Science* 4(3): 173–9.

WAR ON WANT. 2014. 'Demand Justice for Victims of Bangladesh Building Collapse', *War on Want News*. Available at: https://goo.gl-/1sd7Pf (last accessed on 5 August 2017).

CHAPTER TWENTY

Personal and Political
Friendship as a Feminist Methodological Tool in the Recovery of Anandibai Jaywant's Life and Writing

VARSHA CHITNIS

In the summer of 2011, I travelled to India in search of women's narratives on the experiences of gender within the structure of caste in western Indian city of Baroda.[1] I was particularly interested in looking at the writings of Anandibai Jaywant, a well-known writer from Baroda. However, the difficulty I faced in locating her books, which were either missing or completely absent from the existing libraries and archives in the city, led me through a fascinating journey. This chapter is a result of my quest for Jaywant's life and work, and enumerates not only the process through which I have been able to partially rediscover her life and writings but also engages with questions of feminist methodology and activism. In this chapter, I explore the possibility of considering women's friendship as an archive in the process of locating and recovering women's histories. I argue that adopting feminist methodology for the retrieval of women's lives and writing beyond the conventional archives has been a form of feminist activism, I argue that friendship between women should be considered a potential resource in the retrieval and restoration of women's histories. In examining the five-decade-long association of Jaywant with Akkasaheb Mujumdar,[2] I trace an archive that has preserved not only their friendship but also their life histories.

I begin with brief biographies of Jaywant and Akkasaheb and examine the context of their association and friendship. The biographical details outlined here are drawn from Jaywant's handwritten, unpublished autobiography 'Jeevandarshan' [Glimpses of (My) Life], and her typed, unpublished biography of Akkasaheb. For Akkasaheb's biographical description, I also rely on my interview with her grand-daughter-in-law Saroj Mujumdar. In exploring the relationship between Akkasaheb and Jaywant, I posit women's friendships as a source of feminist history. I also highlight the intergenerational relationship between Akkasaheb and Saroj Mujumdar to open up space for a new feminist rethinking of friendship.

Anandibai Jaywant

Jaywant was born as Anandibai Korde in Baroda in 1894 in a Marathi-speaking, upper-caste, Chandraseniya Kayastha Prabhu (CKP) family. Educated till the fifth grade in Marathi, she was married to Prabhakar Jaywant of Dahanu in Maharashtra in 1909. Anandibai was the second wife of the widower, who was about 11 or 12 years her senior. He was studying to be a lawyer but only after a year of their marriage, he passed away from typhoid. Anandibai was 15 at that time. Her father-in-law could not bear to see her sorrow, so he sent her back to Baroda with her brother. In Baroda, Jaywant confined herself within the four walls of the house. To take her mind off her sorrow, she began to read. Since childhood, she had been very fond of reading, and with the help and support of her brother, who brought her a different book each day from the library, she continued to read. Jaywant was also passionate about art, and loved to draw and paint. Their *shipayi*, or helper, who worked as a peon in Baroda College, got her discarded pieces of drawing paper, pins, and pieces of pencils and erasers. Jaywant began her art on these scraps of paper. She went on to win prizes and medals at various art exhibitions, including one held in London. She thus spent her days reading and drawing.

When she had exhausted the available literature in Marathi, at her brother's suggestion, she learnt to read Gujarati and soon exhausted the library collections in this language. Subsequently, she also learnt English, Hindi and Bengali with the help of dictionaries and translation aids, and read many books in these languages. Soon her quest for reading had transformed into a desire to write. She began writing but it took her many years to find the courage to share her written work.

Her first publication was a short story that appeared in the Marathi women's monthly *Gruhalakshi* in 1929. Her first novel *Kulakatha* [A History (of my Life)] was published in 1932. Her first novel on 'women's condition' was *Urmila*, which I have not been able to locate. By the time her second novel on women's issues, *Unmilan* [The Blossoming], was published in 1956, she had written and published two collections of short stories, a historical novel and three novels on social issues in Marathi, and a novel and several short stories for children in Marathi and Gujarati. In addition to writing and painting, she was fond of singing, embroidery and knitting, and is said to have been an exceptional cook. The 1975 edition of Ravi Bhushan's *Famous India: Who's Who* featured Jaywant as a writer and an artist. She passed away in 1984 at the age of 90.

Akkasaheb (Lakshmibai) Mujumdar

Akkasaheb was born in 1894, as Lakshmibai, in Miraj, Maharashtra. She was the daughter of Sir Gangadhar Rao Patwardhan, the ruler of Miraj. Her mother, Shri Umabaisaheb was the daughter of the prominent 'Engineer Jog'. Although she was born in a rich family, Lakshmibai was very humble and polite, says Jaywant. She was married to Dattatray Mujumdar (Abasaheb), the only son of Sardar Chintaman Narayan Mujumdar of Baroda, at the tender age of 8 or 9. After her marriage, she came to be affectionately called 'Akkasaheb' in her marital home. Akkasaheb was Abasaheb's second wife; his first wife had passed away soon after their marriage. Akkasaheb's parents chose the Mujumdar family because Abasaheb was pursuing an LLB degree, and it was very rare to see an educated (degree-holding) son among rich families. Furthermore, Abasaheb's mother Janakibai was the sister of the noted physician, Dr Nanasaheb Deshmukh.[3]

The young Akkasaheb noticed the difference in the environments between her natal and affinal homes. Her maiden home was the dwelling of a king and they had insurmountable wealth. However, her mother, the Ranisaheb (or Queen) was a disciplined woman and she ensured that the entire household behaved in the same manner. She imposed both discipline and humility in her three children. Ranisaheb also ensured that the children did not idle away their time and kept them busy in one activity or another. Contrarily, even though her marital family was not as wealthy, it enjoyed royal privileges. This meant that Akkasaheb did not need to engage in any kind of work around the house, but it also put severe restrictions upon her freedom in certain ways. In Miraj, she had enjoyed much freedom, which she found lacking—even at that young age—in her marital home. Furthermore, her education had also been discontinued after marriage.

Akkasaheb's husband, Abasaheb Mujumdar, was a health aficionado. When he was to take his final examination for LLB, he was so ill-prepared that he wanted to forgo the examination that year and appear in the following year. However, at his father's insistence, he took the exam and to everyone's surprise not only did he pass but also scored the highest marks in his class. Abasaheb's father was so thrilled at his son's exceptional performance that he wanted to gift him something special. Abasaheb asked for a communal swimming pool to be built in the *vyayamshala*, gymnasium, run by Narayan Guru. It came to be known as the Mujumdar *haud*, pool, and was enjoyed by the neighbourhood community for many years. In 1915, he began a journal *Vyayam*, dedicated to physical culture and exercise.[4] Later, he also edited the voluminous *Encyclopedia of Indian Physical Culture* (1950) wherein Akkasaheb (as Lakshmibai Mujumdar) wrote the section on games for women and girls. In addition, Akkasaheb also took the pictures that have been showcased in this volume. Her brother, the then ruler of Miraj had gifted a 'powerful camera' for this task. Jaywant notes that Akkasaheb captured thousands of pictures which she then developed and printed herself before selecting the ones to be included in the *Encyclopedia*. At that time, Lord Tennyson's XI had come to Baroda to play a cricket match and Akkasaheb had gone to the cricket ground to take the pictures of the team. She had also managed to capture a photograph of Prince Dhairyasheel Rao Gaekwad of Baroda. She travelled across India to photograph various sports events and exercise positions. In addition, she also travelled extensively with her husband to procure articles for his journal and for the *Encyclopedia*. Before the English edition was published in 1950, Akkasaheb and her husband were instrumental in the publication of the 10 volumes in Marathi.

Akkasaheb was a strong, determined and brave woman. Jaywant narrates an incident where Akkasaheb wanted to witness the coronation of Fatehsinghrao Gaekwad II. However, the invitation to the coronation ceremony was not extended to women—not even to Lady Krishnamachari, wife of the then Diwan Sir Krishnamachari of Baroda, the chief minister of the province. On account of the Sardar status of her family, Akkasaheb sought an audience with Queen Mother Shantadevi (mother of the crown prince Fatehsinghrao II) and asked her permission to view the ceremony. Shantadevi neither granted nor denied her request, which Akkasaheb construed as a silent acquiescence. On the day of the coronation, accompanied by her daughter-in-law and Jaywant, she watched the ceremony from one of the passageways to the Darbar (or king's court), after which the three women quietly went to the balcony to view the rest of the event for which they were invited. Jaywant has used many other incidents in her biography to characterize Akkasaheb as a fearless and determined woman. She also narrates incidents that showcase Akkasaheb's generosity and philanthropy.

Jaywant and Akkasaheb's Friendship

Jaywant had first seen Akkasaheb in the Morbi Theatre in Baroda in 1912. However, they met more than a decade later, in 1924, after an art exhibition was organized in Baroda. Jaywant's entry to this exhibition was a hand-embroidered lion on silk. Akkasaheb was one of the judges at this exhibition. Her co-judges were keen to confer the first prize to another entry whose artist was known to them. But Akkasaheb demurred. She thought that Jaywant's entry was the more deserving of the first place and she made her opinion known to the panel of judges. In the end, Jaywant's silk lion won the first prize. After this competition, Akkasaheb invited Jaywant to the Mujumdar *wada*, or mansion. She believed that since the lion was impeccable, Jaywant must have been trained as an artist. She wanted Jaywant to teach to her niece, Yamutai Bivalkar, who was living with them at the time. Jaywant confessed that she had no formal training in art, and that she was a self-taught artist. However, Akkasaheb insisted and Jaywant began visiting the Mujumdar *wada* to tutor her niece. Unfortunately, two years later, young Yamutai passed away. Jaywant thought that she would not be needed at the *wada* any more. But Akkasaheb wanted her to continue to visit them and teach her instead. This was the beginning of a friendship that lasted for more than five decades.

In her biographical tribute to Akkasaheb, Jaywant recounts the many trips on which Akkasaheb dragged her into conversations and travel plans. By all accounts, including her own, Jaywant was a quiet and reserved person; Akkasaheb on the other hand, was outgoing and outspoken. She would not hesitate to speak out, for example, even in the presence of Sayajirao Gaekwad III, the then Maharaja of Baroda when he was visiting them at the Mujumdar *wada*. Abasaheb and Akkasaheb used to even organize trips: sometimes to places of Hindu pilgrimage, or holidays at picturesque places. They also invited their friends and the tenants of the *wada* on these trips, at no cost. Jaywant recapitulates many of their travels together. Often Akkasaheb insisted that Jaywant came along. Jaywant recounts one particular instance when she did not want to go, but given her quiet and docile nature, could not refuse Akkasaheb. In the end, however, she had a great time and recounts with fondness the joys of the entire tour.

Saroj Mujumdar, the granddaughter-in-law of Akkasheb, also recalls their relationship with fondness. For over 40 years, Mujumdar says, Jaywant (who was called *Mastereenbai*, Lady Teacher, in the household) came to the Mujumdar home exactly at 2 p.m. Initially the purpose of Jaywant's visits was to teach Akkasaheb drawing and craft skills. But later the scope of their meetings and association expanded. Often they read and discussed books. Akkasaheb even made notes in the margins of her books, which is one of the reasons why Mujumdar has preserved her books with love. They read everything from mythology to philosophy to contemporary novels and discussed them all. Sometimes they also spent time doing needlework or artwork. It appears from the prefaces to Jaywant's books that Akkasaheb also encouraged her to write more, and often sponsored the publication of her writing. Their relationship was thus, at various times, of teacher–student, artist–patron, biographer–subject and, of course, friends.

Friendship as a Feminist Methodological Tool

Feminist historian Geraldine Forbes identifies the need to locate and preserve women's documents as a first step in uncovering women's history in India.[5] Drawing on her work in the subcontinent since 1979, Forbes highlights how the recovery and reading of women's documents has been key in providing an alternate history of Indian women when the dominant narratives of India in the West were influenced by Katherine Mayo's *Mother India* (1927) or Mary Daly's *Gyn/Ecology* (1978). The recovery of women's writing has been an important part of feminist social, political and academic activism. In many instances, the recovery of women's writing and their histories have required the use of novel methodological approaches to look beyond the confines of conventional archives. Feminist scholars have used women's memoirs, family photographs and oral histories, to not only include women in the narratives of history but also to provide a counter-history to the dominant narratives. Similarly, in my work I continue to utilize the connection between feminist methodology and feminist activism—or, rather, feminist methodology *as* activism—to highlight the role of friendship between women as an important source of feminist history. I argue that uncovering these relationships between women, which have resulted in the preservation of women's documents and histories, is (or should be) an important aspect of feminist academic activism. Such feminist activism also helps identify relationships and connections between women across generations, as I explain here. To this extent, my work falls in line with feminist political and historical scholarship that identifies the scope of friendship beyond the realm of personal or individual to identify its political potential.

Anandibai Jaywant was my grandmother's aunt, my great grandfather's sister. Thus, my connection to and search for her work is both personal and academic, for it is through my memories of my grandmother that I trace my investment in Jaywant's work. When I went to Baroda for my doctoral fieldwork in 2011, I was convinced that it would be quite easy to acquire Jaywant's written work. Not only had she lived in Baroda her entire life but many of her books were published there as well. In addition, Baroda has a large Marathi-speaking population and a significant CKP community. Thus, between private collections and the libraries of Baroda, I was confident of finding her books and recovering her life history.

But when I failed to locate her books in my home and in the libraries at Baroda,[6] I contacted all relatives, friends, other members of the Marathi-speaking community, and the President of the Marathi Vangamay Parishad (a Marathi literary association), but none of them had any of her books. Neither did Jaywant's nephew Shrikant Korde and his wife Shubhada, with whom she had lived until her death. Shubhada Korde informed me that she had given away an entire stack of books and paintings to her nieces who were also interested Jaywant's work. After multiple unanswered and unreturned phone calls, I was finally able to get in touch with one of them who informed me that she had lost track of the books after she lent them to another relative, now deceased.

I contacted Shubhada Korde again; she was cooperative and very keen on helping me trace Jaywant's books. It was then that Korde told me about Jaywant's lifelong association and friendship with Akkasaheb. Korde thought that the latter's family might have some of Jaywant's books. However, her husband was less optimistic. He doubted that anyone in the Mujumdar family would care enough to retain such old books. He argued that Jaywant's books would be treasured by a generation that knew her and appreciated her work. Since no members of that generation were alive in the Mujumdar family any more, the chances of finding her books there were very slim. But as a last resort, Korde took me to see Akkasaheb's granddaughter-in-law, Saroj Mujumdar. A very active, dynamic and strong woman in her own right, Mujumdar had not only retained all of Akkasaheb's books in her library but also meticulously catalogued them. She knew exactly how many of Jaywant's books she had and which ones, and was glad to share them with me.[7] Although Mujumdar only had 7 of the several books that Jaywant had written—it was a start. She also showed me a set of 36 pictures depicting various episodes from the life of the mythological hero Krishna which Jaywant had painted as a gift to Akkasaheb. The home of Saroj Mujumdar thus became a repository of artefacts, an archive for charting the life of Jaywant, and her friendship with Akkasaheb.

But the material contents of this archive, the books and the paintings, are founded on friendship between women: on Akkasaheb's friendship with Jaywant, and on the intergenerational friendship between Akkasaheb and her granddaughter-in-law. When I interviewed Saroj Mujumdar in December 2011, a few days after our first and rather unplanned meeting, I realized that there was a close relationship of mutual admiration and affection between Akkasaheb and her. Mujumdar came into the marital home as a young woman of 18, and it was Akkasaheb who not only urged her to continue her education in Baroda but also supported her through it. When she graduated with a bachelor's degree, Akkasaheb gifted a specially made piece of jewellery. According to Mujumdar, Akkasaheb was very progressive such that she and Mujumdar got along better than Mujumdar and her mother-in-law. It is on account of this respect and admiration for Akkasaheb that Mujumdar has preserved her possessions, including Jaywant's books. In turn, Akkasaheb's close relationship with Jaywant is the reason that Jaywant's life and work is cherished and preserved by Mujumdar. In the absence of her own immediate family, Mujumdar became the surrogate family through which Jaywant's heritage is being preserved. It is also on account of my interview with her, and my interest in the life of Akkasaheb that Mujumdar recovered Jaywant's biography of Akkasaheb. Meanwhile, as a result of my interest in Jaywant's life and her work, and my now reacquainted relationship with Shubhada Korde, she managed to retrieve a handwritten copy of Jaywant's autobiography, 'Jeevandarshan'. These two texts are not only useful in recovering the lives of these two women but also provide an alternate insight into the history women's lives in Baroda.

On the one hand, this chapter calls for identifying and utilizing friendship as an important archival source in feminist methodology. On the other hand, it is also an endeavour to expand the scope of the meaning of friendship to include intergenerational relationships of love, respect and mutual admiration which might elude the conventional understandings of friendship. Saroj Mujumdar's association with Akkasaheb was within the traditional setting of a familial relationship. However, their affinal relation to each other does not exhaust the scope of their relationship. I argue that it is important to identify and acknowledge such relationships which are founded on love, mutual respect, admiration and constant support, within the purview of friendship. Even though Saroj Mujumdar might not characterize her relationship with Akkasaheb as one of friendship on account of the deference she was expected to have towards the latter, such intergenerational relationships of women can provide new directions for thinking about friendship. This could be especially useful in those contexts where 'friendship' might not be the socially accepted or appropriate term to define such relationships. In saying this, my intention is not to impose friendship in a context wherein it is absent but, rather, open up new spaces of feminist activism by identifying new possibilities for feminist rethinking of friendship.

Notes

1   Although Baroda has been officially renamed Vadodara, I have used Baroda in keeping with the period to which this article pertains. Also, since my research involves Marathi-speaking women and Marathi literature, Baroda is more commonly used in the region.

2   I use 'Jaywant' for Anandibai Jaywant in the tradition of academic writing, but 'Akkasaheb' to refer to Lakshmibai Mujumdar, as she was popularly known in Baroda.

3   Anandibai writes that the famous artist Raja Ravi Varma was a close friend of Dr Deshmukh, and that he had painted a picture of Janakibai with a young Abasaheb which was still displayed in the Diwankhana at the time Anandibai wrote the biography.

4   Namrata R. Ganneri, 'The Debate on "Revival" and the Physical Culture Movement in Western India (1900–1950)' in Katrin Bromber, Brigit Kraweitz and Joseph Maguire (eds), *Sport Across Asia: Politics, Cultures, and Identities* (New York: Routledge, 2013), pp. 121–43.

5   Geraldine Forbes, "Locating and Preserving Documents: The First Step in Writing Women's History," *Journal of Women's History* 14(4) (2003): 169–78; here, 169.

6   I found just one title in the Hansa Mehta Library at the M.S. University of Baroda and one at the Oriental Institute.

7   She informed me that she had recently lent them to a professor of Marathi in Baroda who was working on a literary history of the city.

Works Cited

FORBES, Geraldine. 2003. 'Locating and Preserving Documents: The First Step in Writing Women's History.' *Journal of Women's History* 14(4): 169–78.

GANNERI, Namrata R. 2013. 'The Debate on 'Revival' and the Physical Culture Movement in Western India (1900–1950)' in Katrin Bromber, Brigit Kraweitz and Joseph Maguire (eds), *Sport Across Asia: Politics, Cultures, and Identities*. New York: Routledge, pp. 121–43.

JAYWANT, Anandibai. (n.d.). 'Jeevandarshan' [Glimpses of (My) Life]. Unpublished Memoirs. [Marathi]

————. 1970. 'Ek Aagli Vyaktirekha' [A Special Biography]. Unpublished Manuscript. [Marathi]

MUJUMDAR, Dattatraya Chintaman (ed.). 1950. *Encyclopedia of Indian Physical Culture*. Baroda: Good Companions.

MUJUMDAR, Saroj and Varsha Chitnis. 2011. Personal Interview. Baroda, December 9. Digital Recording.

CHAPTER TWENTY-ONE

Conflicts and Intimacies
Rethinking Friendship and Transnational Solidarity

SAM BULLINGTON

In 1997, my research and romantic partner, Amanda Swarr, and I spent the summer in Cape Town, South Africa, doing pre-dissertation research on queer communities. We were not sure what to expect in the first nation in the world to have officially recognized sexual orientation in its Constitution. "What will I find?"—I wrote in my journal prior to our departure. "Will I even be able to find queer communities? How will I gain access to them and to diverse perspectives within them?" Our first research strategy focused on queer-identified spaces and we systematically visited twenty-five venues—from bars to bookstores, sex shops to coffee shops, baths to restaurants—interviewing business owners, employees, and patrons. We situated ourselves in a largely gay male neighborhood downtown, staying at a guest house on the same block as the three major gay dance clubs. As a result, we spent the majority of our time with gay men—especially with Cape Town's three drag troupes— and had not yet developed a strong rapport with any queer women.

Across the street from the guest house, a restaurant attracted our attention for it had a large rainbow flag prominently displayed in front. During our interview with one of the owners in the kitchen of the restaurant, Amanda and I mentioned how there were only a few lesbians we had encountered during our month of preliminary research there. He responded, "You should meet my friend, Megan," whom he knew from a gay business associate, and within minutes, he was holding out the phone to me. Megan asked a few questions about our research and, by the end of the conversation, had agreed to set up a get together for us. She indicated that she would "invite friends with opposing ideas" so that we get a range of responses.

Megan and Denise picked us up from the guest house as promised. They hustled us into the car and fired questions at us for the 20 km distance from downtown Cape Town to their house in Bothasig, a mostly Afrikaans white middle-class suburb. By the time we had arrived at our destination, they had offered to let us stay in their home for our dissertation fieldwork.

Megan and Denise were relatively new to Cape Town, they had moved from Johannesburg and were very energetic, driven, and organized, which they characterized as quintessentially "Joburg" traits. When we met them, they were establishing their own desktop publishing business, working out of their home on what felt like a graduate students' schedule. A typical day would find them bustling about their small rented house—Denise at the computer, Megan wheeling and dealing on the phone, or barking commands to Denise. They worked in a panic—on deadline—almost every day. It was strangely comforting and familiar to Amanda and me.

Because they were new to the city, they appreciated Amanda and me as friends. They were anxious for us, and wanted us to spend time with them. The room we stayed in became known as "our room" and much of our time together felt like double dating. We spent many hours discussing relationships, with Megan frequently comparing herself to me, and comparing Denise to Amanda, at least partly because of the same age difference (seven years) in both couples. We rented videos together, made dinner together, and walked their dog on the beach together.

We found immediate connection with Megan and Denise due to commonalities of race, class, and lifestyle which facilitated our incorporation into their household. As the intimacy and trust in our relationship grew, conversation sites shifted from "guest" areas like the living room and dining room to more informal spaces like the kitchen and bedroom. Most of our discussions consisted of trading stories. Even when we were interviewing them with a tape recorder, when Megan would finish explaining an aspect of her life, she would turn to Amanda or me and say, "And what about you?" They were interested in our stories, our opinions about gay life in the US, and our perspectives on gay life in Cape Town.

Despite our apparent commonalities, we frequently disagreed about what it meant to be gay and the role that gay identity plays in one's life. Like other South African gay women of their race and class, Megan and Denise found the term "lesbian" to be vulgar and abhorrent, seeing their own gay identity as a description of their sexual preference only, and they did not position themselves as part of any wider social change movement.

By contrast, our initial encounters with Monica and Trish were a disaster. We met them the day after we met Megan and Denise, at the end of a long day. After an entire day of interviews, we arrived at the offices of Out in Africa, the South African lesbian and gay film festival, for our final interview of the day. The director of the film festival provided a rich discussion, even suggesting films for the International Lesbian Studies course I would be teaching when I return to the US. However, from our questions, she decided we needed to hear the "black perspective." She took us across the hall to see two women she had yelled at earlier asking them to turn down the music. We barged into their apartment where one woman was unenthusiastically slumped on the couch watching *Days of Our Lives* and the other was in the kitchen preparing dinner. The director introduced us and left us there.

We were tired and uninspired and felt bad about interrupting their evening. They were engrossed in their soap opera and lethargically answered our tepid questions, made worse by the fact that Trish spoke little English and they both had heavy Afrikaans accents characteristic of Cape Town's "colored" community. Though I perked up upon learning that Monica was one of the activists I had read about in an excellent anthology on South African lesbian and gay lives, it was not enough to offset our overall desire to leave. We were supposed to meet Megan and Denise shortly thereafter, back at our guest house which was some distance away.

It slowly became clear that the subject of Monica and Trish's exchanges in Afrikaans was the extra food they had put on for dinner so that we could stay. Although it was obviously a burden, they were trying hard to be hospitable; when we eventually announced that we had to leave, it was clearly an insult. None of the communication was clearly stated between us, and this pattern repeated over the next few weeks. Numerous times when we visited Monica and Trish, Monica would disappear into the bedroom, make a phone call in Afrikaans, and commit us to social plans without telling us what she was doing; invariably we would have to decline because we already had plans with someone else. One day we arrived and Monica was very angry. Apparently, we had agreed to plans with them without realizing it and had never shown up. On another occasion, upon leaving them I remarked "See you later," not appreciating that they would interpret my casual American farewell as a literal statement and prepare food for our return.

Our miscommunications led to endless ruptures in our relationship. Trish and Monica expected to see us every day, which was impossible if we hoped to continue our research in the short time we had in Cape Town. Further, Megan and Denise expected to spend a lot of time with us as well and, because of their work schedule, that was mainly spent at their home. Because they resided quite a distance away from Cape Town, we were isolated at their house and dependent upon them for transport back to town—that they could not always readily provide. On one occasion, Monica and Trish invited us to a women's dance attended by mostly colored and black lesbians, but we were unable to attend because we were in Bothasig with Megan and Denise and could not get back on time. Being so torn by dual obligations often made any communication with Trish and Monica uncomfortable. I found our encounters to be unpredictable and exhausting and began to dread them.

However, a coalitional meeting of Western Cape lesbian and gay organizations to discuss the building of a shelter for homeless gay youth proved to be a turning point in our strained relationship. The meeting was held in Guguletu, a black township outside Cape Town, and Monica had strongly discouraged us from going as tensions between black and colored activists had been brewing, Monica was afraid that conflicts would surface at the meeting and that she did not want us to witness. I was uncharacteristically persistent in my desire to attend the meeting largely because I wanted to meet Monica's brother, another major gay activist I had read about, who was coming down from Johannesburg especially for this meeting.

Attending that meeting and debriefing later in their kitchen completely transformed our relationship with Monica and Trish. We discovered strong common values and shared political visions and commitments. Although we did not have comfortable cultural similarities, we felt immense respect for their activist work. They had risked their lives during the anti-apartheid struggle, been rejected by their religiously conservative families in order to develop a life together, and had committed themselves to gay and lesbian community in Cape Town, especially those who were poor and racially marginalized. They had co-founded the first multi-racial gay and lesbian organization in Cape Town, as well as organized the first lesbian and gay pride march, and, despite their limited resources, continually opened their home to gays and lesbians who had nowhere else to go.

Whereas Megan and Denise had little experience with gay men, no reflections on the impact of AIDS on their lives, and little political involvement, Monica and Trish solidly linked their gay activism to struggles against other oppressions—those based on race, class, and HIV status, for example. Somehow during that meeting in Guguletu, we had proved ourselves and won their respect while they garnered our emotional attachment. I remember getting out of the van when we returned from the meeting and instead of having the urge to flee, I just felt like lingering. That evening, we ordered a pizza together and talked and laughed late into the night. Tensions dissolved and a new level of intimacy emerged.

From then on, we had a daily relationship with Monica and Trish. We began to have inside jokes with one another and watched the daily installments of *Days of Our Lives* together. We supported Monica when she was nervous about her driving lessons, and Trish took us on the train to her township and meet her family. I began to have things that I only wanted to tell them, or even discuss issues that I knew only they could appreciate. For example, when, just days before our departure, Amanda and I learned that one of the drag performers that we had become close to found out that he had AIDS, we were devastated, and the only people we could trust to really understand this were Trish and

Monica who had not long before lost a close friend to AIDS—a drag queen whom they took in and cared for until her death.

While with one white middle-class lesbian couple we quickly established mutually comfortable interactions, yet later discovered some fundamental differences in values. With another, a working-class "colored" lesbian couple, our initial interactions were disastrous and fraught with cultural misunderstandings, yet through shared political commitments, we developed rich and intimate connections that have led to long-lasting bonds of friendship and extended family. When we returned in 1999 to do our dissertation research, we lived with Monica and Trish for several months while we were looking for our own apartment and ultimately chose a place just down the street from them. We regularly had meals together, helped host their holiday gatherings and other special occasions, worked for the community dances with Monica—arriving with them to set up and unpack equipment in the wee hours afterward, went to work with each of them on a regular basis, and we even attended their wedding. From the US we helped the AIDS organization they co-founded to win their court case against the pharmaceutical industry, learning in the process that our own university held the patent to a very expensive anti-retroviral medication that prompted us in turn to co-found our own organization to pressurize the university to not enforce its patent in the Global South. The current courses I teach in Global Health are rooted in the activist work I shared with Trish and Monica. When Monica went back to school to finally complete her education that had been interrupted by her anti-apartheid activism, we helped edit her papers over the Internet.

With brief return trips to South Africa every few years, we have been able to maintain and continue to grow the intimate bonds we had initially forged, despite the dramatic new configurations in our personal lives. Amanda and I broke up in 2005, as did Trish and Monica not long after. In 2007, Amanda brought her new partner along to meet Monica and Trish while it was my first return to South Africa after going on testosterone. In 2012, I returned alone not as an academic but for a shamanic festival, visiting Monica in her new residence with her new partner. By 2014, our most recent trip, Trish and Monica were living together again, though as family not as lovers, and the four of us—now getting older—reminisced continually about our 17-year-long friendship. Even Trish and Monica's families consider us a part of them. Monica and Trish helped organize the South African launch of Amanda's book about our research while I worked on editing the book that the four of us have been working on about Trish's life since 2000. As our personal and professional lives have ebbed and flowed, and our activist passions have evolved into new areas of societal need, one element of our lives has remained constant: the deep love and respect that the we have for one another.

CHAPTER TWENTY-TWO

My Summer in Cape Town
Or, I'm Sorry for Losing You

ALOK VAID-MENON

This poem explores an opportunity of *lost* friendship. I spent the summer of 2011 volunteering and conducting research with Gender DynamiX, the first transgender advocacy organization in Africa, located in Cape Town, South Africa. As a trained academic in the United States I came in with pretentions of *professionalism* and *ethics* that I soon realized are antithetical to activism and social justice friendship. This poem is a critique of the ways in which the academic industrial complex creates the researcher–subject dichotomy as a mechanism of control, circumvents the possibility of friendship that transcends the recorded interview, requires both the material and affective labor of the subaltern, and manipulates and steals the stories of oppressed people. This poem is a call for activist academics to envision new ways of relating to our 'subjects' as *community*, and perhaps even more radically—as friends.

They will ask you
Whether your project can inflict 'harm'
And you will respond: 'minor discomfort' to expedite the review process

Her name is Cym,
And the arc of her smile mirrors her painted eyebrows,
On Mondays she asks you what you did over the weekend.
You do not tell her. You are guilty of the conversion rate:
How you can afford a club, a skin, a language that she never will.
She wants to know what it feels like to live in America

If you have a handsome boyfriend there who will buy you dinner
sometimes

In your field research class, they will teach you about the importance of
obtaining consent.

Cym cannot sign your form
So she communicates with the earnestness of hazel eyes
Smiles, tells you how she used to let heroin and men
Inside of her and sometimes couldn't tell the difference,
Laughs
Tells you how the cops would beat her in men's prisons

In the international research workshop they will tell you not to get
involved in your subjects' personal life.

Your palms are sweaty, do not let them smear the ink.
Keep writing as she laughs and encourages you to ask more questions

An aneurysm is a blood-filled bulge in the wall of a blood vessel.
When the size of an aneurysm increases, there is a significant risk
of rupture,
often resulting in death.

A researcher is an ambitious distraction at the back of the room.
When the amount of information increases, there is a significant risk
of an epiphany,
often resulting in a published paper.

She will die suddenly nine months after your interview.
You can still remember the scent, her smile

———————

1

Dear Cym:
In America I am learning how to think that I am better than you.
In fact, I am majoring in you.
Don't worry, they don't use your name, keep it confidential

2

I am turning your body into a new theory
Academics work like Johns sometimes, don't worry,
They will pay me to use you,
I promise I will cut you some of the profit in my acknowledgements.

3

My thesis will be in English,
In the accent you heard on re-runs of *Friends*, Cym I'm sorry we
weren't friends,
but I wanted to keep it *professional*
I promise I will print it on the whitest paper I can find,
So they can see the black in your words

4

I will bury you in a library,
I hope you will find home there
In this haunted house of quotations
Hanging on the shelves like skeletons

Listen to the recorded transcript on repeat,
Feel her laughter crawl into you,
Watch it spark the timber wood of your bones,
And burn your paper in the flames

And cry because we refuse to let people inside of us in fear of
imploding

And cry because you have the story of a woman nested in the back
of your throat and you do not deserve it.

Dear Cym:
What I really meant to ask is:
What theory did you use to stay warm at night?
Is, *Can you teach me?*

CHAPTER TWENTY-THREE

On the Path of Friendship

MARY ADKINS-CARTEE AND KARNI PAL BHATI

Introduction by Mary Adkins-Cartee

Talking about friendship excites me. To speak of friendship in a context of neoliberal domination and globalization, continued white supremacy, patriarchy, capitalism, and imperialism is to claim the right of our relationships to exist outside of what bell hooks so often refers to as "white supremacy capitalist imperialist patriarchy's" sanctioning. As such, developing and speaking out about friendship is a subversive action.

Friendship is a topic that I have been deeply invested in, and have been influenced by the work of bell hooks, Cornel West, Todd May, Audre Lorde, and C.S. Lewis in this respect. I've also been fortunate, as a Caucasian/white female living in the industrialized world (the US, with stints in the UK and Canada), to develop deep and enriching friendships across lines of race and gender, sexuality, ability, age, and culture. In this piece, I hope to explore, with my friend, mentor, and teacher Dr. Karni Pal Bhati, one of the closest "friends of my mind" (hooks and West 1991), the various powers and potentialities of friendship.

Dr. Bhati and I first got to know each other at Furman University in the fall of 2005; he taught two seminar courses I took up as a fourth-year undergraduate student: one in Modernism and Postcolonial literature and theory, and one in South Asian literature and film. Dr. Bhati was the first professor who encouraged me to apply to academic conferences and to share my academic work with a wider audience, and he continues this tradition now with this publication. He also encouraged me to apply to the 2007 Association for Commonwealth

Literature and Language Studies conference which was hosted by the University of British Columbia in Vancouver, BC. On account of that conference, two years later I became a graduate student at the University of British Columbia in an MA program entitled Society, Culture, and Politics in Education.

A Dialogue between Friends

This section draws in part on the dialogical tradition of writing established initially by James Baldwin and Margaret Mead in their 1973 A Rap on Race, *continued by bell hooks and Cornel West in* Breaking Bread: Insurgent Black Intellectual Life *in 1991, and continued into the twenty-first century by Mumia Abu-Jamal and Marc Lamont Hill in their 2012* The Classroom and The Cell: Conversations on Black Life in America. *This part of our writing proceeds, therefore, as a dialogue between us, guided by questions to which we respond.*

What do you think some of the most salient moments of our friendship have been so far? How have these moments influenced you—personally, politically, and/or academically?

MARY. I don't remember the moments specifically, but the feeling of the moments, during my senior year at Furman—moments when I came to your office to discuss essay proposals for your classes. It was perhaps the first class I'd taken where the topics were entirely open-ended, and while other students found this frustrating, I was thrilled. I could write about anything that interested me concerning the class readings? Wow! How completely refreshing!

And I remember that you seemed genuinely interested in my thoughts. To have the affirmation of a professor whose thinking I held in deep regard moved me, and gave me the confidence.

I also remember the first conference you ever invited me to—it was a conference on Postcolonial Literature, in Savannah, Georgia—a few classmates and I presented with you. One of the first nights, you and a couple of other professors invited us up to one of the hotel rooms to have a glass of wine before dinner. I was just 21 that year, and I felt so grown up and sophisticated—having wine with my professors. I recall that time with great fondness.

And then, of course, Vancouver. What a life-changing event—the Association for Commonwealth Literature and Language Studies (ACLALS) conference in 2007—it goes beyond words. I was just entering my second year of teaching high school after finishing my undergraduate degree, I was 23, not yet enrolled in a postgraduate program, and I had to fight the administration of the high school to participate in the conference because it took place during the first week of the school year. At first, they gave me a flat-out "No." I wouldn't accept that; so I put together a portfolio of scholarly articles concerning teachers' engagement with professional development in their content areas and presented my argument to my principal because I'd "done my homework," he agreed to let me go.

I remember the strangeness of the experience, and how different everything seemed. I navigated my way between the airport and the university simply by asking strangers for directions. I ended up making a pit stop for change for the bus in Richmond, British Columbia, and then asking students for directions to Gage Towers once I was on the (huge!) campus. At that time, the US cell phones (or at least mine) did not operate in Canada, and I remember finding you and Raina through a series of emails from a computer kiosk in the dormitory lobby.

And I remember the colors. Blue, deep forest green, gray everywhere. Brown. Never having visited the Pacific Northwest before, everything was surprising. I was surprised by the signs on paper-towel dispensers in the university bathrooms that reminded people to be mindful of how many trees they had used to dry their hands. I was surprised by signs on the buses that illustrated, with stick figures, people experiencing 'bad karma' for not recycling. I was surprised by the diversity of the people and the general liberalism of the culture (as compared to South Carolina and US culture, at least). There was an ethos there that was intoxicating, and I had to know more about it.

Of course, our experience in Vancouver led directly to my application to the Society, Culture, and Politics in Education program at the University of British Columbia (UBC), and I went on to live in Vancouver for two years while I worked on my MA.

I had begun, through you, to think of doing postcolonial literature in a graduate program, but as I continued to teach, I realized that I wanted to apply the social-justice focus of postcolonial studies to education, and the program at the UBC was the perfect place to explore these issues.

Gaining that experience, and that degree, has furthered my work for social justice in and outside of my current classroom, and I endeavor to teach "about and for" social justice (Benson 2010) in both professional and non-professional contexts.

KARNI. Responding to this question makes me think of the evolving ways in which I have learned to relate to people across boundaries of age, cultural belonging, role (student–teacher). My own experience as a student in India, and even in the US was such that I could not easily bring myself to see my teachers as friends. There were boundaries that could not to be crossed. Teaching undergraduates in the US, especially in my upper-level courses which are focused on texts from South Asia or other non-Western parts of the world, made me realize that teaching is a form of conversation between students and the teacher. Even while I was guiding and, to an extent, controlling the conversation, both students and I were aware—in our more self-aware moments—that because I related to the culture represented in the text in a relatively more intimate way than them, I was a friendly, or, rather, a friend-like guide. This made me see my pedagogy in terms of a form of friendship rather than a hierarchical relationship with students, which can sometimes have unintended consequences, I will admit.

I remember the first serious conversation you and I had after class. The course was Modernism, Modernity, and Empire. You were very receptive to the critique of empire in ways that went beyond simply blaming the imperialists. You were perhaps making connections between different ideas you had picked up in other courses, or your own life experiences, in a way that you were already attuned to the idea that the operation of power cannot be isolated from the representational regimes which shape dominant forms of knowledge. I think I could sense that you were seeing it as an ethical issue of the present rather than that of the colonial past. I was also gratified that instead of being put off by my open-ended and somewhat experimental pedagogy, your interest in the issues raised by the course material made you welcome it as an opportunity to explore ideas, and to deepen your interest in a critique of society. I have to say that I was fortunate to have you in class because your welcoming my open-ended assignments not only legitimized my pedagogy but also made it more acceptable to students, including some of your friends who were to take my courses the following year.

Our conversations continued after you enrolled for the South Asian Cultural Studies course the following semester and graduated that spring. You were selected to teach at a high school in the area. I was impressed with your sense of idealism and passion for social change. I wanted my son and daughter to meet you, which they did, and thought well of you too. And then you asked me to observe and report on your teaching. I was very impressed with your patience, your dedication, and skill in channeling the energies of a mixed group of students, half of whom were from disadvantaged backgrounds. I saw a new side of you that I could not have imagined, and through you, I found a new respect for teachers like you, who take on the burden of trying to shape the minds of youth on the margins of society.

Later, I was touched by the fact that you thought well enough of me to consult me in some of the major decisions you had to make—the decision to enter into marriage, the decision to resign from your teaching position at the high school (where you were doing very well), and to apply to graduate school in Vancouver. So, yes, I have been influenced by you, in many different ways.

Is love part of friendship? If so, what type(s) of love? The Greeks distinguished between philos *and* eros—*do you think there is truly a distinction between types of love?*

MARY. I absolutely think that love is inseparable from friendship. I also think that the classical Greek distinctions between *philos* and *eros* are perhaps not so clear-cut as the Greeks made it out to be. While *eros* has been traditionally defined to include sexual and physical attraction and romantic love, theorists Audre Lorde and bell hooks have both discussed the ways in which "the erotic" can be conceived of outside of sexual bonding and the ways in which it can be present in teaching, in writing, and in friendship.

For example, Audre Lorde defines the erotic as "a measure between the beginnings of our sense of self and the chaos of our strongest feelings. It is an internal sense of satisfaction to which, once we have experienced it, we know we can aspire" (2007: 54). And this sense of satisfaction may or may not be connected to the physical or sexual; she also states that "the erotic functions . . . in several ways, and the first is in providing the power which comes from sharing deeply any pursuit with another person" (ibid.: 56). A shared pursuit, such as writing or intellectual activity, can be absolutely full of erotic energy that may intensify friendship bonds. The love of an idea, of a piece of art, a shared passion for writing, or the shared love of discursive practice and critical analysis can all become bases for deeply satisfying friendship (*philos*), but this type of friendship is surely not absent of *eros*—of passion.

Furthermore, bell hooks states in *Breaking Bread* that "we must think of not just romantic love, but of love in general as being about people mutually meeting each other's needs and giving and receiving critical feedback" (hooks and West 1991: 56). The idea of intellectual and critical feedback as the basis of friendship, or as Todd May puts it, drawing on Talbot Brewer, the "development of *universally self-affirming evaluative outlooks*" (2012: 88), can be a form of passionate connection—even love—just as powerful as any romantic love may entail. This type of love can have a profound impact on one's life.

KARNI. What you say here is very well put and well supported by contemporary scholarly work as well. I think there is often an overlap between *eros* and *philos*. Eros can begin with *philos*, or grow out of *philos*. Besides, there is always an unselfconscious working of *eros* in *philos* too. As Lorde, whom you cite above, put it eloquently, the "deep sharing of any pursuit with another person" is erotic in a way that is distinct from the conventional associations with *eros*. One may also draw here on Eve Sedgwick's idea of a

continuum that she developed in the context of homosociality—
she suggests that our affective states have to be understood as
located on a continuum rather than in discrete compartments. So,
although there is certainly a distinction between different kinds
of love, it is not a stretch to think of the different kinds of love as
subcategories of something more widely known and experienced
as love.

*bell hooks speaks about "romantic friendships" while Todd May describes
"deep friendships." Do you find there to be a distinction and/or an overlap between the two?*

MARY. I find there to be a great deal of overlap between the two types
of friendships described by these authors.[1] Understanding *eros* as
a type of deep passion Audre Lorde describes, both these types of
friendships are founded on a greater degree of *eros* than perhaps
other friendships enjoy. bell hooks explains that

> [W]hen [her] romantic friendships . . . become visible to
> friends and acquaintances, they often want to suggest we
> are just repressing sexual longing. This is simply not the
> case. We are making a comfortable choice to use eros as
> a basis for strengthening a committed friendship (hooks
> 2002: 209).

She also states that as women under patriarchy are taught to
value romantic bonds more highly than other bonds, romantic
friendships teach us that it is not only possible but also ultimately
fulfilling and desirable to "value all deep bonds equally" (ibid.).

Similarly, Todd May drawing on Elizabeth Telfer, states that
"friendship does not simply involve a sharing and a passion, but
also some recognition that these are in place" (2012: 74). His
emphasis on "recognition" and hooks' emphasis on "choice" are
similar, for recognition is surely required for choice to take place.
Furthermore, both authors reach toward an ineffable quality these
types of passionate bonds entail: May explains that "the depth of
a deep friendship is something that is lived between people more
than measured as a quantity" (ibid.: p. 68).

Moreover, both authors emphasize depth of meaning that
these types of friendship engender. Todd May states, "The liking

of a friend, the engagement in shared activities, the conversation: these lend a vibrancy to living of the kind Wolf describes as necessary for meaningfulness" (2012: 101). And likewise, bell hooks: "In deep, abiding, romantic friendships, commitment to personal growth is a given. The work of healing is shared, the pain and the joy" (2002: 213). Indeed, according to hooks, romantic friendships

> [O]pen up the space where we can develop primary bonds in platonic relationships that are constant, committed, and able to last a lifetime . . . And at the end of the day it is this love that sustains us and gives life meaning (ibid.: 216–17).

In other words, while hooks may put more emphasis on commitment and *eros* in romantic friendships, and while May emphasizes the lived quality, passion, and shared engagement deep friends enjoy, they both ultimately explain how these types of friendships enhance the meaning and purpose of our lives by deepening affective, ethical, and intellectual aspects of our lives.

KARNI. I think of these two terms as parts of different argumentative/discursive contexts. Todd May develops his idea of "deep friendships" as part of a conversation with fellow philosophers while hooks develops her idea of "romantic friendship" as a feminist in dialogue with other feminists and groups of people who may be described as "friends of feminisms." There is also a difference between the two styles of writing. While May's method of developing his idea comes across as professorial and is helpful in exploring philosophic alternatives to the dominant rationality of neoliberalism, hooks seems to be concerned with the lived reality and challenge of conceiving alternatives to patriarchy and heterosexuality that can be liberating for both women and men. There is much to learn from both.

How do you think differences in age, race, class, gender, and/or sexuality, and/or life experience have shaped our friendship? How do you think we have transgressed boundaries and respected boundaries?

MARY. Two quotations that stick out to me that help answer this question: Todd May says, "Just as friendships do not arise within a vacuum, they are not maintained in one. The norms of friendship often reflect the norms of the joint activity in which the friendship arose in the first place" (2012: 71).

Audre Lorde states, "The sharing of joy, whether physical, emotional, psychic, or intellectual, forms a bridge between the sharers which can be the basis for understanding much of what is not shared between them and lessens the threat of their difference" (2007: 56).

In other words, I think it is our shared passion for literature, and for a postcolonial, deconstructionist, and social justice perspective on literature, politics, and life, that has helped the two of us bridge differences of race, nationality, gender, age, and career position. We share a similar take on life even across these differences, and we have learned and continue to learn from our differences because we can trust each other based on what we do share. We have also not sought to generalize our own social locations on each other—respecting the boundaries of difference in order to learn from them, in order not to co-opt or gloss over them. I think we have sought, implicitly, not to judge each other but instead to trust the genuineness of each other's interests and intentions, and to engage critically and intellectually from that place of trust.

KARNI. I have partially answered this question above, but I will add that I have been a slow learner, managing to keep my mind open to learning from you through your intellectual and professional concerns that you are able to connect with our daily lives and interactions with the people we live and work with. You brought such passion and sense of engagement to the things we talked about on our walks around the Furman Lake that I could no longer recall that you were once a student in my class. I see you as a colleague, a fellow traveler in search of a meaningful life—not a life of isolated academic concerns, which is a risk for many at the university level, but one of engagement with the issues of the day at the local, national, and global levels. As our sense of mutual trust grew we were, I think, able to see how our friendship was enriching rather than fraught with a transgressive potential.

What role do you think friendship plays? Is solidarity necessarily more politically oriented than friendship? Is there a politics to friendship?

MARY. It is, personally, through friendships that I have come to imagine possibilities for my life and for living differently and better—academically, politically, and personally—than I ever would have imagined alone.

In speaking of solidarity between black men and women, Cornel West states that "[the black community has] had traditions that were able to channel [a feeling of inadequacy] in such a way that we could remain in that boat with the tension, with the hostility, because there was also love, care, loyalty, and solidarity" (hooks and West 1991: 56). While West is speaking specifically of solidarity across lines of gender within the African American community, his ideas about staying present with "tension" and even potential "hostility" through practices of "love, care, loyalty, and solidarity" are also applicable to practices of solidarity across other lines of difference. Furthermore, Todd May states that while friendship and political solidarity are not necessarily the same, deep friendships help us practice the skills that allow us to enter into political solidarity.

In other words, through friendship and love and loyalty, we practice the affective, intellectual, and even erotic capacities and micropolitics necessary for being in solidarity with others who are different from ourselves. And indeed, Audre Lorde describes how "[She has] a particular feeling, knowledge, and understanding for those sisters with whom [she has] danced hard, played, or even fought. This deep participation has often been the forerunner for joint concerted actions not possible before" (2007: 59). While solidarity might be more explicitly political than friendship, as the feminist saying goes, "the personal is political," and understanding friendships as "assemblages" (in the Deleuze-Guattari sense), one may not desire to draw such a binary (perhaps patriarchal?) distinction between "friendship" and "solidarity," as each may flow productively into and help create the other. With whom we choose to share our lives as friends, as well as the dynamics of "deep participation" in friendships, are always political, too, and may contain the (erotic) seeds of deeply rooted actions—including, potentially, the creation of concepts (for example, Deleuze and Guattari, *What is Philosophy*) and writings (such as this one)—"not possible before" (2007: 59). Friendships create and are created by what Gilles Deleuze and Felix Guattari call "micropolitcs," but the micro is always embedded within, affecting and affected by macropolitics as well (1991: 213).

KARNI. Solidarity is clearly a form of friendship, a fellowship that is at once a desire to enlarge the sense of self through an accommodation of the collective self and also a consolidation and affirmation of the reconstituted self. I have not been an active member of a group of individuals bound by bonds of solidarity in a struggle of some duration, but I imagine the capacity for friendship as prerequisite to solidarity. We think of solidarity as a feeling born out of a shared sense of injustice or injury suffered by individuals who recognize the source of their injury and build bonds out of a sense of commiseration. It can also be born out of a sense of devotion to a cause of reform, or the desire to transform an existing set of norms or policies.

What role does attraction play in friendship?

MARY. Todd May describes this phenomenon as a "spark," hooks describes it as the presence of non-sexual *eros*. Audre Lorde says there is no distinction between "writing a good poem and moving into sunlight against the body of a woman [she loves]." In a Deleuzian sense, attraction might be seen as a productive desire that brings into possibility of new becomings; however, it is also crucial to honor the ways we are differently embodied. When we embody our friendships, remembering and re-membering and respecting one another's bodies across lines of difference, how do we describe the ethics and politics of embodied friendship?

Because friendship, particularly the intellectually passionate friendships, so often draw upon the erotic energy of the passion for the shared activity, I think there is at least the potential for attraction of various forms to take hold or to develop. This attraction may be an intense mental attraction, an intense emotional attraction, even an intense "spiritual" attraction, if one understands the word "spiritual" as encompassing the whole person and not necessarily as transcendent (hooks 2000). And we know from deconstructionist theory that the idea of a fixed boundary between the "I think" and the "I am" is really a false one, and that, in Deleuzian theory, "I am" becomes "I become/I am becoming." In other words, the borders of the "self" are always in flux, porous, evolving, open, and often transgressive, and often passion, as affect, flows productively between and among friends. It would not, in my view, be uncommon for different types of attractions to spill over into and inform one another. In other words, while I do not think physical attraction is a requirement for deep friendship to exist, I do think attraction of some sort is required, and it would not be inconceivable that various types of attraction could intensify one another. In past relationships, I have certainly experienced situations where what started as friendship progressed into romantic and physical attraction, though this has not been the case with every friendship that I have considered deep or important to me.

KARNI. I think what is interesting about the role of attraction in friendships is that often it is, or can be, quite unconscious. It might even be absent at the beginning, and may develop over time. This is not how we generally think of attraction because we usually see it as overpowering our reason-guided, somewhat staid, lives. But different individuals have different capacities for resisting this reason-guided way of approaching relationships; while some are incapable of even conceiving of alternative ways of being, others are capable of taking the risk to be led by their hearts, as the cliché goes. Likewise, one can be attracted to qualities other than looks; one can be drawn to someone's intellect, or idealistic activism.

Perhaps 'attraction' is only another name for *eros* as we have discussed earlier.

Dialogue with Scholars

In this section we repond to ideas on friendship in the work of different scholars that appeal to us.

MARY. In *Friendship in an Age of Economics: Resisting the Forces of Neoliberalism* (2012), Todd May discusses how "deep friendships" may provide ground for resisting neoliberal domination (2012: 123–43). Friendship carries revolutionary potential. It is not necessarily revolutionary by nature, but it can be both the testing ground and the fuel for revolutionary thinking or behavior—or perhaps a site from which what Foucault would call "revolt" can emerge.

Foucault claims that "it is through revolt that subjectivity (not that of great mean but that of whomever) introduces itself into history and gives it the breath of life" (1979: 133). For Foucault, revolt "is 'anti-strategic': to be respectful when something singular arises, to be intransigent when power offends against the universal. A simple choice, but a difficult work" (ibid.: 134). Friendship offers a tool box and a safe, dry space for storing and developing tools that can be put to service in revolt, or in the insertion of 'subjectivity into history.' Todd May's argument that deep friendship provides a space from which to resist contemporary neoliberalism (and, we as readers might extrapolate, to resist also capitalism, consumerism, patriarchy, racism, imperialism, and other systems of domination) is one example of what such political 'revolt' based in friendship might look like.

Drawing on Aristotle's concept of "true friendship" and Graham Little's concept of "communicating friendship," and his own concept of "deep friendships," May states that "communicating friends . . . both understand and change one another, and these two aspects of friendship interact" (2012: 87). As such, May argues that even though deep friendship is not necessarily in and of itself resistance (to neoliberalism, specifically, as he argues), it provides fertile ground for resistance to neoliberalism and other oppressions because understanding and change between friends lead to trust and motivation. May states that friendship "allows for the bonds between people necessary to solidarity to develop. I can only be in solidarity with those I trust. Friendship trains me in that trust, and in doing so trains me to interact with others in a common project even where I may disagree with them" (ibid.: 137). May also argues that deep friendships of the type he discusses provide us with the motivation to resist neoliberalism because neoliberalism encourages us to see one another in either entrepreneurial or consumeristic terms, and as such, those who have experienced the joys and the character growth engendered by deep friendships have motivation to protect the space of deep friendship from encroachment by neoliberalism and its domination by the figures of the consumer and the entrepreneur (ibid.). Moreover, states May, "a deeper friendship has the resources to challenge norms in a way that shallower ones do not" (ibid.: 85).

Perhaps it is possible, though, that the revolutionary potential within friendship is even deeper than May's (already insightful) argument. Briefly, in his chapter on "deep friendships," May mentions that friendship is not necessarily exclusive of love. And indeed, African American scholar, feminist and cultural critic bell hooks defines love in her book *All About Love: New Visions* (2000) as a combination of characteristics; "To truly love," she states, "we must learn to mix various ingredients—care, affection, recognition, respect, commitment, and trust, as well as honest and open communication" (2000: 5). She also draws on M. Scott Peck's *The Road Less Traveled* (1978) which in turn drew on Erich Fromm's *The Art of Loving* (1956), defining love also as "the will to extend one's self for the purpose of nurturing one's own or another's spiritual growth" (ibid.: 4).

Surely, friendship involves all elements of love that hooks discusses. Where, then, are the boundaries between friendship and love, or *philos* and *eros*, as has been argued by many (Meilaender 1994)? Aside from the fact that Meilaender's chapter on "Friendship between Men and Women" takes monosexuality (gay, lesbian, or straight) as the norm, and gender as a binary Meilaender also describes how, for Aristotle,

[W]hile there can be friendship between lover and beloved, it will not be the highest form of friendship. It will be friendship grounded not in character but in pleasure—and it is, therefore, likely to fade . . . It is important to note that *eros* and *philia* are indeed different forms of love, even if they may sometimes go together (1994: 184).

However, in claiming that "the highest form of friendship" cannot exist where *eros* exists, Aristotle (and by association, Meilaender) reinforces a patriarchal and hierarchical "ranking" of affective attachments and relationships. Feminism, on the other hand, has espoused more egalitarianism among types of relationships; as bell hooks explains: "Most women and men born in the fifties or earlier were socialized to believe that marriages and/or committed romantic bonds of any kind should take precedence over all other relationships" (2000: 136); however, "To love well is the task in all meaningful relationships, not just romantic bonds" (ibid.: 138). Conceptualizing *eros* as simultaneously the privileged bond under patriarchy while denigrating the possibility of "the highest form of" friendship within this bond, achieves what patriarchy so often does with respect to women/womyn, and relationships, that is, to divide the imbricated and complex into binaries, and devalue half the binary, often, ironically, by placing it upon an ostensible pedestal. In the cases of both women and friendship under patriarchy, both are simultaneously ostensibly held up as "exemplars" of morality (think the Madonna–whore binary), yet devalued in the hierarchy. Furthermore, patriarchy operates based on "a paradigm of sexual difference that [has] at its root the assumption that men are inherently different from women, with different emotional needs and longings" (ibid.: 149). Likewise, patriarchy transubstantiates such ideas of "natural difference" into relationships and loves, into the distinction between *philos* and *eros*. Understanding *eros*, in the words of Lorde, as "that power which rises from our deepest and non-rational knowledge" (2007: 53), we may also understand all loves, including but not limited to *philos* and *eros*, as not necessarily "non-rational" but as "super-rational," the powers of all types of love draw on much more than reason only as a way of knowing. Here is May's "spark," which can lead to both meaning and happiness.

One might initially want to draw a distinction between the love between friends and the love between romantic partners or lovers based not just on the *philos*ophical distinction of *eros* and *philos*, but also on the presence of specifically sexual erotic passion. However, even here, hooks points out that "Nowadays the assumption is that something is wrong if an individual feels intense erotic connection with someone and does not allow that *eros* to lead him or her to sexual intercourse. Romantic friendships differ from other forms of friendship precisely because the parties involved acknowledge both, that there is an erotic dimension to their passionate bond and that it acts as an energetic force, enhancing and deepening ties" (2002: 207–8). hooks describes her romantic friendships' commitments, stating that "we may exchange vows of commitment that we deem as important to honor as those we exchange with romantic partners with whom we are sexual" (ibid.: 209). Additionally, we know that many marriages are, or can become, celibate and companionate over time, much more akin to the "romantic friendships" hooks describes. And furthermore, as parts of the US and world society are now in the midst of what some are beginning to call the "second sexual revolution,"[2] now that polyamory and so-called friends-with-benefits relationships are acknowledged and sometimes embraced by many people, even people in committed, previously monogamous relationships, there is not necessarily always a preventative imperative which would bar deeply committed friends from expressing both their *philos* and *eros* physically but non-exclusively. Many might still consider this a radical idea, but it is not so dissimilar from the non-commodified "hippie" sexuality of the 60s and 70s that May discusses, and this once again reaches toward a non-hierarchical approach to friendship and love, attraction, *philos,* and *eros*.[3] Indeed, May also emphasizes the role of equality in friendship; he states that "friendship . . . is a relationship among equals, one defined by mutual trust" (2012: 131).

The only truly distinguishing characteristic of romantic friendships from other friendships, then, is a greater degree of *eros* than perhaps other friendships may enjoy, but this is a question most likely of degree, not of binary separation. Perhaps these romantic friendships are not so different from May's "deep friendships," in that both have a tendency to "bend" each friend's life down a slightly different trajectory than would have otherwise come about, and both involve a profound degree of intimacy and commitment. It is one of the pleasures of friendship to experience this "erotic bending" of one's life direction, and in the best of friendships, one becomes enabled to explore paths one may have wished to take anyway, but perhaps lacked the clarity to pursue. These paths can be both personal and political:

> Deep friendships are best thought of as contributing not just (and not primarily) to the happiness of our lives but to the meaning they display, both to us and likely to others as well . . . Friendships do not only intersect with one's life; they help create it. The shape a life takes is in part a product of its deep friendships (ibid.: 99).

As such, deep friendships, in May's sense, not only lead to a sense of happiness and personal meaning and fulfillment but also impact the actions we take in the world. Friends who share our values, who help us form "evaluative outlooks," inspire, encourage, and support us in taking meaningful action based on our values. hooks and West point out the value of theory (theory created in dialogue with "friends of our minds," as they state) in terms of action:

> Theory ought not to be a fetish. It does not have magical powers of its own. On the other hand, theory is inescapable because it is an indispensable weapon in struggle, and it is an indispensable weapon in struggle because it provides certain kinds of understanding, certain kinds of illumination, certain kinds of insights that are requisite if we are to act effectively (1991: 34–5).

Friends help us theorize our lives, and as bell hooks states, "when our lived experience of theorizing is fundamentally linked to processes of self-recovery, of collective liberation, no gap exists between theory and practice" (hooks 1994: 61).

KARNI. Many have noted that friendship is one of the more complex human relationships, and many have gone back to Aristotle's treatment of the subject. What about non-Western perspectives? I recall having to memorize some couplets from the epic Ramayana by the sixteenth-century poet Tulsidas in junior high school. They were anthologized with the title, *mitra lakshana varnana*, or "attributes of a friend." The opening verse may be paraphrased thus: "It is a great sin to even behold one who is not aggrieved by the grief of his friend. A true friend is one who views his own grave misfortune as inconsequential while seeing the slightest adversity of his friend as momentous."

Among other virtuous qualities listed in the verses that follow are the ability to stop a friend from walking on the path of sin and to bring him to the path of righteousness, helping a friend in times of need, and so on. Unfortunately, these verses would read today like self-help columns in magazines because their concerns amount to being of this nature: how do we know who is a true friend and who is not; what kinds of deeds can be seen as those that are motivated by friendship, etc. Although these verses occur in the epic narrative, Ramayana, in the context of a friendship between Rama and the monkey-king Sugriva, for the modern sensibility they do not go beyond confirming the aphorism, "a friend in need is a friend indeed." They do not lead us to consider the psychological or emotional states of contemporary friendships between individuals.

In the essay, "Friendship in Classical Indian Thought," the political theorist Bhikhu Parekh suggests that unlike:

> [The] anthropocentric and theocentric views of the universe dominant in the West, most Indian thinkers took a cosmocentric view of it. For them the universe was an internally articulated and ordered whole whose constituents were all its equally legitimate 'co-tenants' enjoying the right to exist and to avail themselves of its resources. Human beings, therefore, had a duty of universal friendliness and goodwill (*maitri*) towards the other orders of being (2008: 155–6).

Parekh goes on to discuss the three different forms of friendships in Indian classical thought, each of which have specific
attributes so that the friends produce three kinds of affect: the joy
(*ananda*) of being in each other's company, the assurance of aid
in times of need (*sahaya*), and freedom from fear (*abhaya*) of each
other, including that of betrayal (ibid.: 159–60).

Interestingly, Parekh also finds that given the emphasis on loyalty and a commitment to aid a friend in need, these ancient texts
illustrate some moral dilemmas produced by friendships, which
we might add, are still with us. For example, while friends such as
Krishna and Arjuna, or Karna and Duryodhana in the epic
Mahabharata engage in their youth in "merrymaking, playfulness,
agreeable and amusing conversation, escapades, and disregard of
social convention," this form of behavior goes against the ideal of
"*anasakti*, or total detachment . . . [that] a person aspiring for per-
fection" is expected to live up to. Far from disregarding social or
moral convention such a person, a *samadarshin* (one who "treats
all human beings impartially") must cultivate a form of "detached
love . . . that cares and grieves and has depth and energy but is not
dependent on and possessive about or possessed by its object, love
that is calm and non-emotional, and in full control of itself." As
Parekh points out, this is "how God is supposed to love his creation
. . . and . . . [is what many] Indian saints and spiritual aspirants,
including Mahatma Gandhi, sought to approximate" (ibid.).

Parekh concludes that despite their "fascinating philosophical
discussions," ancient Indian texts seem to neglect "the celebration
of intellectual friendship . . . a friendship based on intellectual
partnership, a shared pursuit of truth and knowledge, mutual
exploration of common problems, delight in the exchange of ideas
and arguments" (ibid.: 164). This is a characteristically modern
view of relationships rooted in the commonality of interests,
whether they be of the nature of a shared commitment to a public
cause, or a shared interest in intellectual or spiritual growth. As
we think of contemporary ways of understanding friendship, it is
interesting to note that ancient views often drew on an analogy
with blood ties implying that the bond between friends is so deep
as to negate their duality—as if two separate selves become one.

This union of souls is precisely the language of the intimacy associated with the institution of marriage which evokes the notion of
one desire in two bodies. As "friendship studies" become more
interdisciplinary and become more broadly "affect studies," a number of other fascinating issues begin to converge. Thus, for example,
one could think of the philosopher Mark Vernon's ideas about
friendship in conjunction with the work of Alan Bray, a scholar of
sexuality in early modern Europe and activist for same-sex rights.
In different ways, they have both pondered the shift in the value
attached to friendship in the West over time. In my reading, they
have argued that both Christianity, as it evolved from medieval
times, and post-Enlightenment modernism which saw the rise of
civil society, had the effect of valorizing conjugal and parental
bonds over all other forms of intimacies such as "voluntary kinship" among individuals of the same sex.

Thus, the conjugal family, and heterosexuality, became the
hegemonic pinnacle of emotional fulfillment, and modern friendships, intellectual or otherwise, came to be understood as part of
the private sphere of our lives and largely of interest only to the
individuals concerned. Far from the pre-modern "material practice of friendship" which could be quite erotic and intimate as we
understand these notions in our supposedly more liberal times,
this relationship has become a matter of individuals being
"just friends," where the affective investment is not only unam-
biguously defined but has also lost the ritual sacramentalization
that was approved by the Church in earlier times, as can be seen
from the example of friends sharing a grave in death. In contesting
heterosexual and patriarchal norms feminist scholar-activists like
Lorde and hooks, among others, have also contributed to a
rethinking of notions of love, "romantic friendships," and the traditional conjugal family; in the words of Lorde, the erotic can be
seen not as destabilizing solidarity with larger social issues but as
"the bridge that connects" the political and the spiritual.

Perhaps it was this very oppositional aspect of friendship that
made it possible for some dissenting intellectuals of the late
nineteenth- and early twentieth-century England to rely on the
affective ties of friendship to create new, other-directed forms of

solidarity in opposition to the dominant imperialist values of the day. This is how the literary critic Leela Gandhi sees the role played by friendship (in her words, "the lost trope in anticolonial thought" [2006: 14]) among dissident and marginal communities of thinkers and artists in Victorian England who "crossed over" in support of anticolonial nationalists like Mahatma Gandhi. She uses the examples of Edward Carpenter, a homosexual and social reformer; Henry Salt, a vegetarian; and the Francophone Jewish French mystic, Mirra Alfassa who befriended the Indian radical anticolonialist Aurobindo Ghosh, as individuals whose dissidence, though marginal, for both the imperialist narrative and the anti-colonial-nationalist narrative, can be seen as "innovative border crossing, visible in small, defiant flights from the fetters of belonging." These "individuals and groups . . . renounced the privileges of imperialism and elected affinity with victims of their own expansionist cultures," they eschewed their "given" community for a cause they valued. In electing "a form of affiliative solidarity that rubs against the grain of obligations to kin, party, or nation," they were living up to E. M. Forster's widely cited motto from the essay "What I Believe" (1938): "If I had to choose between betraying my country and betraying my friend, I hope I should have the guts to betray my country."

While it is possible to counter that these figures were already othered within their own cultures, we must remind ourselves that friendship can bring individuals to acknowledge the otherness all of us carry within ourselves. This otherness can be seen as reaching beyond conventional and instrumental reason—an excess that can be theorized, or metaphorized, but not completely contained. Because it is affective, and like objects of art that we also befriend, so to speak, it perhaps has more to do with the sensorium than the cerebrum. Like Audre Lorde, who sutures the spiritual with the political through *eros*, Leela Gandhi's reading of this alternative ethic of friendship premised on an openness to difference, rejects the dichotomy between spiritualism and politics so that the shared spiritualism of these friends becomes, in the words of a reviewer, "an ethical openness to the undeterminable uncertainties of relations with others that facilitate the intimacy of such connections" (Secomb 2006: 467). This affinity for otherness is both empirical/material and transcendental, and invites, or lures friends to engage in the labor of love to maintain their relationships against competing or conflicting demands, including the demand to recognize, respect, and also when occasion dictates, cross the boundaries of decorum that separate one's own self from that of the friend.

To conclude, all of this is made possible by investing in the pleasure which is not devoid of *eros*, and is derived in conversations with our friend(s) who make it possible to experience our most intense moments of reflection, self-scrutiny, and resolve. This in turn makes it possible for us to think differently, to live more fully, more meaningfully, in ways that are responsive to the time and place we happen to be situated in.

Reflecting on the Role of their Particular Friendship in their Life

MARY. Karni, Raina, and I walk from the student dormitories where we stay for the conference down along quiet sidewalks and find a forest path at the edge of the campus. "Tower Beach," says the sign. This is what we are looking for. We walk down a flight of over 400 stairs—they seemed so strange and eerie then, that first time— past the ferns taller than we are, past the trees that tower above us, past green, damp moss and enormous slugs. It seems to me like we are walking through a land from Paleolithic times—I've never seen anything like it before.

Then, miraculously, we emerge onto a rocky beach strewn with drift logs washed smooth by wind and tide and the misty rains that cover this coast nearly three-quarters of the year. Even in mid-August, the evening is chilly.

We can see Vancouver Island, the big island across the Georgia Strait. The sunset is pink and orange and gold above the blue water, and the sea smells brackish. We can see miles across the Strait—and it seems we are at the waterline of a bowl of liquid surrounded on all sides by mountains. Karni and Raina and I sit. We watch. I tell them, "The only place I still feel like I did when I was a child growing up in church is when I am at the ocean." Karni only nods, but the slightest smile parts his lips and emerges from his eyes. I know he knows what I mean.

We pause for a few moments, sitting there on the white drift-wood log, absorbing the sunset and the water and the mountains and the air, and then we walk down the beach a little further, stopping to investigate the myriad baseball-sized rocks we trod carefully across—cautiously enough not to twist our ankles. The rocks are blue and maroon and gray and brown and green, glistening in the angled sunlight, and dark green seaweed and moss intermingles with them and the clear water that picks them up and tosses them back, clacking them against one another, over and over. I pick up a rock, and I examine its gray-brown hardness, a crease that is almost a forehead furrow across one side, and some dimples pocked into it by tide and time. I show it to Karni, and consider taking it with me, but decide it will be better to leave Nature undisturbed. I lay it down, and we walk a little further, then turn back.

As we begin to head back to the forest trail, Karni shouts suddenly, "Your rock!"

"I didn't get it. It's okay," I say.

"I'll find it," he says, and turns around and jaunts back down the beach faster than I can object.

And before I know it, he returns, a rock in hand, and as I take it, I see it is the rock I'd been examining—my rock.

"Your rock," he states simply. How he found it again—and so quickly—among myriad others, I've still no idea. As he hands it to me, I can't help but notice that he's grinning—shyly and unevenly—but definitely grinning, as I take it. I feel flush inside, and a little embarrassed, and very pleased. Somehow, that rock contained a promise—a promise of future work—of writing, and thinking, and sharing to come. I would hold that rock in my hands in the following two years while I planned my enrollment there at the UBC; I would consider returning the rock to its original place when that degree was finished, but eventually I would decide to keep it simply as a reminder of the promise of one great teacher and a friend to another—a promise of knowledge, of insight, of understanding, an appreciation of all that in human experience and camaraderie cannot be spoken but must be lived and felt mutually. It was a promise of the *eros* of learning and loving and being alive and living in a profoundly human way. That is what you have always helped me to find, Karni, and that ethic always infuses my own teaching and learning and writing and questing, my questioning and my activism, and my sense of this work— academic, intellectual, *and* activist work—always imbricated, and even spiritual work, even in the absence of a strict concept of God or transcendence.

KARNI. We have met after months, or close to a year, though there has been some email or Facebook contact. We walk around the lake catching up on much that has transpired since our last meeting, and finally we sit down facing each other, not tired but giving in to the inviting arrangement of picnic tables and benches, grateful for the change of pace. We pause, peel the fruit, or comment on the small spread between us. And then we resume the conversation about something very powerful or thoughtful that we have read and been moved by.

I feel comforted as I see and hear Mary laugh every now and then because I am not always sure if, as an older person, I am being too intense in the way I muse on my recent sundry experiences of reading or teaching, the state of education, or of the world. But I need not have been, for Mary responds with the right mix of passion, conviction, and inquiring openness that makes me forget the age difference.

Of course, every forgetting is a temporary displacement by other thoughts conscious and unconscious. I am grateful to have Mary's company on this day until our next meeting. We rise and walk on the path again that brought us to this place . . .

Notes

1   I would like to thank Prof. Darrell E. Coleman of Valencia College, Florida, for reading these works, as well as hooks and West's *Breaking Bread* (1991) with Mary Adkins-Cartee and for contributing greatly to

her thinking about these texts, as well as to the topic of friendship in general. With thanks also to Clemson senior philosophy major Will Thompson for reading the Todd May selection with her, and for contributing to her understanding of friendship in many meaningful ways.

2   I would like to acknowledge here however, that this phenomenon largely falls along privileged lines, and that racial, sexual, and other minority groups often risk much more social stigma in pursuing non-monogamous relationship patterns openly. Pernicious racist and homophobic stereotypes concerning the lasciviousness of African Americans, promiscuousness of gays, etc., are still quite rampant. With thanks to Prof. Coleman for correcting me with this insight.

3   It is also important to note that deep friends also respect one another, if love is truly present in friendship. Love, respect, and even a sense of Aristotle's "character" would all demand that in some cases *eros* remains in the emotional, psychic, and/or intellectual realms out of respect for a friend's commitments, especially if any of those are physically or sexually monogamous or exclusive.

Works Cited

ABU-JAMAL, Mumia, and Marc Lamont Hill. 2012. "They Schools: Education and Its Discontents" in M. Abu-Jamal and M. Lamont Hill (eds), *The Classroom and the Cell: Conversations on Black Life in America*. Chicago: Third World Press, pp. 99–117.

BRAY, Alan. 2003. *The Friend*. Chicago: The University of Chicago Press, 2003.

DELEUZE Gilles and Felix Guattari. 1991. *What is Philosophy?* New York: Columbia University Press.

GANDHI, Leela. 2006. *Affective Communities: Anticolonial Thought, Fin-de-siècle Radicalism, and the Politics of Friendship*. Durham: Duke University Press.

HOOKS, bell. 1994. *Teaching to Transgress: Education as the Practice of Freedom*. New York: Routledge.

———. 2000. *All About Love: New Visions*. New York: Harper Perennial.

———. 2002. *Communion: The Female Search for Love*. New York: William Morrow.

———, and C. West. 1991. *Breaking Bread: Insurgent Black Intellectual Life*. Boston, MA: South End Press.

LORDE, Audre. 2007. *Sister Outsider: Essays and Speeches by Audre Lorde.* Berkeley: Crossing Press.

MAY, Todd. 2012. *Friendship in an Age of Economics: Resisting the Forces of Neoliberalism.* Lanham: Lexington Books.

MEILAENDER, Gilbert. 1994. "When Harry and Sally Read the *Nicomachean Ethics*: Friendship between Men and Women" in Leroy S. Rouner (ed.), *The Changing Face of Friendship.* Notre Dame, IN: University of Notre Dame Press, pp. 183–96.

PAREKH, Bhikhu. 2008. "Friendship in Classical Indian Thought." *India International Centre Quarterly* 55(2): 152–67.

PREMNATH, Gautam. 2008. "Review of Leela Gandhi, *Affective Communities: Anticolonial Thought, Fin-de-siècle Radicalism, and the Politics of Friendship.*" *The Journal of British Studies* 47(1): 233–35.

SAID, Edward. 1978. *Orientalism.* New York: Vintage Books.

SECOMB, Linnell. 2006. "Review of Leela Gandhi, *Affective Communities: Anticolonial Thought, Fin-de-siècle Radicalism, and the Politics of Friendship.*" *Postcolonial Studies* 9(4): 465–69.

VERNON, Mark. 2005. *The Philosophy of Friendship.* New York: Palgrave Macmillan.

CHAPTER TWENTY-FOUR

Kissing Friends

IGNACIO RIVERA

When I was a little girl I daydreamed of my future husband. Even though I had no idea what having a husband meant, my family, media and society-at-large fed me the desire to want one and therein lay the fantasy. My cousins and I would create the scenarios. We'd play house, invent pregnancies, give birth, and care for children. My girlfriends and I would giggle about it. We'd even play-out the intimacies— kissing, holding hands, and sexually experiment what this "end-all" relationship would one day look like. A serious boyfriend, or ultimately a husband, seemed to be a good portion of society's life plan for most girls. Be good, go to school, meet a nice boy, date, get engaged, get married, and have children. Then, repeat. Our families prepared us for our next family and we were expected to do the same.

When we come into this world, we come into our first vital relationships. For some, that is immediate blood family, extended blood family, and/or adoptive family. Our second most important interpersonal connection is friendship and our third is partnerships, lovers, and marriages. Each of these hold important roles. Although one thing is clear, whether we have strong family ties or the same best friend since grade school, I learned that my husband would take centerstage. After all, this is what I've–we've been working toward. The intensity of friendship connection we have as youngsters disintegrates to an extent as we get older and navigate toward our "ultimate" sexual partners.

This was once my trajectory but the family plan hit a bit of a snag when it came to me. I traveled many trails until I finally navigated to the one meant for me. My sexual orientation, gender identity, beliefs on monogamy and marriage made it difficult for me to experience or let alone want those predetermined ideas about love and family. On my journey, I found something different. I found partnerships, relationships, and desires that nurtured me beyond the idea of owning property, marital status, and monolithic love. My shift in wanting or needing an end-goal traditional romantic/sexual relationship created space for me to tap into a resource I'd always had—friendships.

The meaning of "friend" has evolved. It seems to hold profound meaning in our development and is thus encouraged by our parents. As we get older, the ideas of best friends, or their worth, diminishes. To my parents, the sound of a 40-year-old calling someone their best friend rings socially immature or even childish. I don't agree. Friends have been an extremely vital part of my life. The secrets we've disclosed, the intimacies we experience, the connections we share are incomparable. Social mores tell us "blood is thicker than water." The very presence of blood keeps us tied to one another. The same could be said for "the law." Legally binding marriages, hell, even commonwealth marriages hold more value in this society than friendship. Blood needs no reason. Law creates and safeguards unions. It can also deny them when one does not fit the mold. We don't have to have anything in common with our blood family. Whether we like them or not, love or hate them, we find ourselves attached—obligatorily, legally, and/or morally. Although some friendships hold a certain degree of obligation and moral tetheredness, it is primarily structured in likeness, love, connectivity, commonality, struggle, and community. Friends for many are the second parents and siblings to the ones we have, the ones we never knew, and the ones we've lost. The difference is that we choose or find them.

The first time I experienced a loving supportive bond outside of my neighborhood, blood family, and comfort zone was with my best friend Aimee. I learned the possibilities of bond beyond blood. The love, respect, honesty, and care we shared, modeled what years later became my chosen family structure. We were two girls at the peak of our adolescent discoveries, cutting the umbilical cord of our childhoods and experimenting. I had never met anyone like her. She was weirdly honest. It was a nice change from all the "bonchinchosas" (Spanish *feminine* term for gossipers) I was used to. She supported me when I came out as a lesbian, then came out as trans years later. She took me in when I left home, when I got pregnant as a teenager and later became my daughter's godmother. I felt that our communication, the way we cared for each other, how we laughed and took risks, elevated my expectations of friendship. We nurtured and protected each other. We held each other in the roughest of times and pushed through it together. Aimee was my friend but she was also family to me. I guess you could say, Aimee was one of the first people I considered chosen family. She has been my chosen family for 27 years.

Our friendships are multifaceted. Marginalized communities have long used the vehicle of friendship as a core tool for survival in the face of social ills. Friends, chosen/found family, gangs, separatist groups, houses, leather families hold a significant place in an individual's life. They are intentional communities of support. Whether that support is protection, validation, survival, or surrogate families, they see us in ways that others won't or can't. Even for those of us who have the privilege of maintaining ties to our blood family, friends and the like offer an extension of us that surpasses blood. Friends have been my survival and I for my friends. As my sexual orientation, gender identity, ideas about monogamy, acceptable sex practices, and "valid" relationships evolved, so did my navigation of friendship. What once was dire for support around poverty and teen pregnancy soon progressed and grew into being a place of visibility, love surrogacy, and movement building. It fueled my activism, nourished my creativity, and was held together by desire.

Questioning led me to my friends. Questioning the rules about whom I can love, how to have sex, and what gender roles to subscribe —only to name a few. I found and sought like-minded people. Through this questioning, I uprooted dialogues, became angered, found a voice and a place. I found activism and unconventional love. The realm of friendships is where I learned about honesty, disclosure, raw vulnerability, and accountability.

At one point in my life, I truly believed that I would be alone forever. According to society's definition of companionship, my chances seemed dismal. I convinced myself I wanted what I was told and I worked hard at it. Then I blamed myself for not trying hard enough. "Regular" relationships didn't fulfill me completely as I was told they should. In my struggle, I found polyamory and things became clearer. I came to know others on a similar path. As I've moved further along I've come full circle, so to speak. I've come back to "friends." The group so important in our infancy as to teach us social skills and integrate us successfully into society, has come to bear its rightfulness in my adulthood. The very people I grow with, politic with, and call my chosen family, are the ones I am in love with. Each are connected to me in some fashion, be it queerness, race, trans-ness, polyamory, kink, art, and/or activism. Each is unique. I give and receive the very things we are told we only find in our soul mates. We crack ourselves open— bare bone, flesh, and blood. These are the people I laugh with, cry with, get advice from, are critiqued and held up by. These are the people I share my body and kink with. These are the people who see every inch of me. These are the people I cuddle and these are the people I fight alongside: I am never alone. My chosen family fills my life in a way that I have never found (consistently) with one person. What I've discovered is that, in this moment, I am my own primary partner. The love of my life is my daughter. I do not wish for marriage. I do not wish for forever or happily-ever-after. I have come to accept that my way of loving–loving my friends, my chosen family, is a political act. It breaks "protocol" and disrupts the status quo. As a trans identified, independent polyamorist, valuing friendship(s) has been key. Even as my gender-fluid identity positioned others to question their sexuality and place me in a vortex of sexual confusion, friendship helped me maintain my sanity, break isolation, find intimate connections and re-frame love, intimacy, power exchange, and what sex could look like.

The concept of friendship has not received the proper attention or accolades it so-rightly deserves. Seen as a travel-through from blood family to lifelong partners, the role of the friend had not been truly acknowledged as the anchoring tool it has so long operated as. I propose that friendship at its core is a mechanism for survival—specifically love survival. It cradles invisible, marginalized, and expendable communities and within that, offers acceptance, growth and movements in oppression disbandment. In this age of queer "normalization"—with same-sex marriage as the primary queer agenda, coupling as the one true acceptable form of companionship, and "kink" eliminated from human sexuality—friendship offers me hope. My childhood dreams of my future husband seem like a distant trip. One I didn't ask to go on. I've since re-routed. I've visited many places. Some I'd like to return to and others, not so much. I've mapped out my own path and friends have been all along that path. There is no "X" that marks the proverbial spot—end of the road. No all-mighty, singular way of companionship and loving. My friendships, my chosen family, have been my sustaining life force that in its very denial as legitimate bonding has outlived acceptable forms of love.

CHAPTER TWENTY-FIVE

Untitled

ALEXIS PAULINE GUMBS

> I can't tell you how much it means to me that all of you exist
> and are doing your work. I can't begin to tell you my brother.
> Maybe sometime I can.
>
> Audre Lorde in a letter to Joseph Beam, January 1987.

Audre Lorde was known for sending small gifts, especially from her
tax returns to her sister and brother comrades to support their literary
and activist work. Each of the people that I honor in these poems took
a very Audre Lorde approach to support my furthered connection with
Audre Lorde. I wrote these poems (and many more) in gratitude to
the people who supported my journey to St. Croix to visit the final
home and resting place of the black feminist lesbian warrior poet
Audre Lorde a few years ago. But friendship is more than the exchange
of money and poems. These are people whose existence helps me to
love the revolutionary parts of myself and whose very presence on the
planet is a cause of joy and celebration for me. These are people who
I think about with affection and care even and especially when they
are far away. These poems come out of the same energy that caused
me to panic when the Egyptian government blocked Skype, my only
real-time access to Mai'a and her daughter Aza amid the Tahrir Square
movement, the energy that causes me to smile deep in my heart when
Darnell posts a picture of his new haircut or a link to his newest article,
to squeal in inaudible decibels when Mecca is in the room, or when
she sends an email that her new book is out, and to light a candle for
Lamar on the eve of his dissertation defense or on the birthday of his
grandmother. I can't say what it means to feel reflected in the living
and work of black geniuses across the planet or what it feels like to be

tangibly supported, not only by their work but also by their support of my work. But I can begin. So here are the poems . . .

such rainbow

For Mai'a and Aza
After Audre Lorde's "Prism"

no such rainbow
light breaks prayer
listening for plague
peals back skype longing
no such hell
no such wake up bell

untrue

there is a prism
crystal walking
revolutionary refract

there is a vision of pink hair
and cheering
girl voices squared in Tahrir
don't sleep

if you don't know
you don't know

how hustle blows wind to
sand cut clarity
how late nights flame artful into home
how moonlit blessings
from silenced gods
make it all possible

we are taking such brightness to bed
dreams to art
we are choosing to clash open in color
glass our wishes into poems
art to dream late in morning
sand moon into glass
sleeptalking prayer

bruised gift of the future
we are holding it in our fists

burnt tribute of realness
we are wearing it on our faces
we are catalyzing sun

we are waking up ready
for such rainbows as this

―――――

To Be Brown

For Darnell Moore
After Audre Lorde's "Thaw"

we season language
into sweet potatoes
deep heavy whole
with so many rooted eyes

we reason lust
into underground
unbroken something else
always saying reach

all around us
worlds are cracking
shells are breaking
birth is calling out our name

down here we grow
syllable by syllable
digging affirmation
watering prayer to
ancestor mud
we know
who the ground will wake
into all our green belief
when the sky will recognize
our measured blues

how the people will dance
into heat shaped light

you and me brother
we remember why

and
what a bright thing it is
to be brown.

––––––––

What it Means

For Mecca Jamilah Sullivan
After Audre Lorde's "Girlfriend"

read your cybernetic name
air traffic neon
landing stripped to faith
way home in the dark

taken   delicious
just plain right

need to know
all year long
another press pencil to bone
push black keys to re-cord chords
otherwise forgotten

badly madly radly
in it

spirit in flight
let's make a phone book
a hotline
for those of us who know
this is what it means to live
forever
silence touchtone born again to witness
beloved voices haunting into word

––––––––

to walk it

For L. Lamar Wilson
After Audre Lorde's "Dear Joe"

we like our legends
dead
our luminaries weak
enough
to fit between
the lines

but you brother
lilting perfect
flower stem tribute

believe in us so
damn
daily

you

throw dirt on the road
to walk it

you stowaway crawlspace
for love

you crooked crossroads
where gender falls
apart

where midnight grasps the hand
of the mourning and wakes up

walk it

say fuck the pretense
this my name in cursive
dancing cross your face
this kiss cool cheek of essex
faced away from joe still waits for
burning up

this the light sprite of just right
who will pronounce your name love
and then love again
until you learn it

refuge from the name drop sun-tea of striving
you touch ghosts
the way they want
to be
touched
swirl the jangled street
into homecoming
here to recognize
the small place
where skin can meet skin
is infinite

and we might live
but that is no reason to give
up
and we might die but that is no reason to
stop

you

lean heavy in the drunkening sweep
of shared air
tar thick days restarting
glean caress out of tree branch missing sky

you

dry mud tracks to tears
stretched legion to come back through
heaven lifted to laces

you

dirt road enough
to walk

CHAPTER TWENTY-SIX

Jack and Jaime

Making Love, Making Revolution

JAIME M. GRANT AND JACK HARRISON-QUINTANA

JAIME.

You know the great joke Jack tells about the beginning of our relationship is that he asked me to lunch about a dozen times and I said yes and cancelled on him 11 times. Which says a lot about Jack—his persistence, his singular sense of purpose once he decides he's going to do something or get to the finish line.

I was horrified when you first told this story at a going-away party for me. Not just because of the behavior but also because I had *no recollection* of this—a further indictment of the monumental self-centeredness and sense of self-importance that the story points to.

I know you don't tell the story to call me out in this way—the story lays the groundwork for a generous, pivotal punchline that started our relationship. But I have thought about it so many times since, and thought about how it also reveals how and why you became so important to me as a collaborator and an intimate friend.

When I met you, I had just had my daughter at 46. A ridiculous, miraculous leap of faith that was a near medical impossibility! I was madly in love with my then partner. My son, Reilly was almost 9, and adjusting to two new precious people in a life I had constructed with me and him as its center. I was also in a new demanding job that I loved.

All of that to say, at 46, you really have the scaffolding of your life in place. There can of course still be outrageous new entries of beings and love and shifting core concerns—as evidenced by my recent insane leaps of faith. But opening oneself to someone new—bringing new people into the family and into my very carefully chosen inner circle—well, it's a very high bar. To say nothing of carving out the time for a lunch.

In my lifetime as an activist, I have taken mentorship very seriously. Intergenerational relationships with pivotal lesbian thinkers and activists a generation or two ahead of me changed my life, influenced the trajectory of my career and sense of meaning and purpose. Without these women, my life would be dust. Nothing. In fact, it's fairly likely I wouldn't have made it. And there are probably half a dozen or more queers a generation or two behind me who would say the same about my role in their formation and resilience.

It's life-saving and generative on both ends—intergenerational relationships. They keep the young ones off the shoals of indifference and help us make use of our time and resources better; they keep the elders from ossifying in our critical perspectives and our future casting.

So, this lunch that you wanted to have. I have had many of them, on both ends of the lunching. And I take them seriously. You were just absolutely hitting me at a time in my life where I had precious little room for them.

So finally, we went, and apparently, I said great things, and about a year later, you wound up as my intern, sharing an office, with two little desks across a room from each other, dreaming queer dreams and hatching very real plots and projects that would literally change the queer world and have huge impacts on our lives.

So when did I know that we'd become family? That our love and admiration and desire for each other's thoughts and feedback and warm shoulder would become indispensable?

I don't have a moment (and I am quite sure you are going to have several memories you pull out of your bag that have been crucial)—

but here is what became clear to me early on that made me begin to rely on you more and more, and feel fed and nurtured and loved within our collaboration.

First of all, you went the extra mile to get me whatever I needed without making me feel like either an idiot or a tyrant. This is no small feat. I'm hugely forgetful, terrible with details and my family life was crunched beyond belief, with many of those needs spilling over into the workplace. You picked up all of these pieces with aplomb. I have said in many workplace retreats: *I want to be appreciated for my significant strengths and I want my deficits accepted and adjusted for. I don't want to be tortured and denigrated for them.* I never, ever had to say this for you. From the very beginning, you were super excited about my strengths—they clearly fed you. And all of the swirling mess around them—you just picked them off as you could, adjusted, cooperated, were helpful in any and every way you could be.

And I could see that this was not because my deficits landed in your "strengths" column. This is probably another reason why we love each other—we are both big-picture thinkers. We live by the broad brush, the giant hopeful, and just worlds we are straining toward. The details bog us down. The only place we want to be precise and layered is in our critique, our analysis. How did we get here? How are we going to find a way out? How is THIS work going to get us there?

But being my intern meant many, many hours of going over horrific, minute details of poorly organized projects and research (that neither of us created). You were the big corrector, the great annotator, the person who got difficult projects over the finish line. Often you were doing work that was blindingly awful. Drudgery. But you never complained. You'd plugged in your earphones, tuning in to some obscure sci-fi, or a *My Little Pony* episode, or Harry Potter fan fiction, and pressed on. In our first year of working together, I felt so grateful for this on so many occasions, I was brought to tears.

And as we began to check off a lot of difficult "To-Dos" from the list, our emotional and intellectual connection really started cooking.

Some of the highlights of those two years across the desk included reality-checking with each other around cruel behavior, internalized oppression, and wellness among other movement colleagues around us. We were working on a number of challenging collaborative projects and we'd get off of a hard phone call or out of a tough meeting and break it down for each other. Often, we'd provide helpful grounding or supportive critique around our own contributions to the conversation or conflict. Very early on, I appreciated that you were not someone who thrived on trashing and that you had a real desire to develop skills—to improve your own strategic interventions on projects, and to sidestep difficulties that could not be solved by logic or direct engagement.

It was around then that our shared belief in therapy and attending to trauma-healing sessions emerged as a key point of connection.

JACK.

My mother is a therapist of some repute in our hometown of Chattanooga, Tennessee, and one of the many pearls of wisdom she's shared with me over the years about mental health is that having a skilled therapist is good, but having close friends is infinitely better.

I feel much the same today about the concept of mentorship. I have undoubtedly been blessed to have been mentored by some of the fiercest queer activists—most of them lesbians and queer women, a demographic fact that I find to be both a funny coincidence as well as a deep reflection of who is the leading edge of justice and liberation for people like me (that is to say, *not* a coincidence at all).

But the thing that separates my relationship with Jaime from some of the other mentorship I've received is that we are also friends and while mentors are good, I've found that friends are infinitely better.

I still remember the day she took me out to breakfast and broke the news that she was leaving me and our work in the DC to move to western Michigan and open a social justice center. I literally thought my life, to say nothing of my career, was ending on that very day. But it turned out that her not being my formal boss anymore allowed new dimensions in our personal and professional relationships.

About a year later, we were talking on the phone with me crouched over the copy machine in our old DC office building and her walking across the college campus she'd set up shop in and the topic of what people think about our interracial intergenerational cross-gender relationship came up. We've always joked about it because people have never known quite what to think of us. Amusingly, people have often made the assumptions that we're sleeping together. Or even more than that. When she first moved away, I had more than one-person approach and say: "Oh you're still here?" I, of course, took that to mean they thought my job was dependent on her which made a certain amount of sense. But they'd protest and say, "No, no, not that," perhaps concerned they'd offended me. "I just thought that you like belonged to her . . . you know, like, sexually."

So we were rehashing those jokes which never fail to move us both to giggles no matter how many times we repeat, when she suddenly got a little more serious and asked, "Well what do you tell them now that we're not working directly together? What do you say?" And I very matter-of-factly responded that I just tell them she's my best friend.

And it's not that she didn't feel the same way about me, I think, but maybe up to that moment she hadn't articulated our love for one another in quite those terms because I remember how moved she was by it even though for me I felt that it was obvious by that point.*

But I have to say, I think I've always been a little bit quicker on the uptake with sensing where our relationship was headed.

Jaime asks: *Why do you think we are so close? What do you remember as early "breakthrough" moments in terms of building trust and intimacy as friends and collaborators?*

What's funny about this question for me is that the key moments for me are almost certainly moments that you don't even remember because we really weren't bonded yet but I was watching you intensely and becoming clearer and clearer that we were related in some ineffable way.

I know the key story I always tell is about hounding you to go to lunch with me but even well before that when I was a fellow at the National Center for Transgender Equality, I got myself involved in the National Transgender Discrimination Survey and would come

---

* It may be worth pointing out here that we both exhibit polyamorous behavior in terms of our best friends as well as our lovers, and that we even share a few other beloveds in our life on whom we bestow this title.

downstairs for those meetings with the express purpose of sitting in the presence of your brilliance.

At that time, I was caught between the dueling desires to be an activist and spending the bulk of my time fighting for liberation or to go into research and find a university-based position that would allow me to live a life of the mind, thinking and writing all day long. And, so when NCTE's Executive Director, Mara Keisling described you and the National LGBTQ Task Force's Policy Institute to me, my immediate thought was, *who is this woman and how do I join her*? But then came the meetings and what really caused my love to climb to the next level were two incidents around open discussion of sex.

The first time was when you had just met someone who was perhaps going to be involved in the survey project (I can't remember who), you kept looking at her and rather than starting off the conversation with the more usual, "You look familiar to me like maybe we've met before or been at the same parties," you said: "I think if you and I made lists of our ex-lovers, we would find connections." I swear that my eyes bugged out of my head (although nobody was looking at the intern sitting quietly in the corner) because on the inside I was screaming, "Yes! That's my community. That's the kind of love network I want to be a part of."

And then a second time we came into a meeting on a Monday morning and everyone else was horrified that you shared your feeling of being particularly grounded in your authentic sexuality after the weekend and it was propelling you forward into this work but I just thought: This person does not know it yet but we are so much the same. So that's what led up to my now infamous pursuit of our first lunch date.

One thing you wrote in your initial reflection that we've talked about before was that I went the extra mile to get you whatever you needed without making you feel like either an idiot or a tyrant. But what's funny about that and what I think is key to what we want to share in this article is that it has never felt like going the extra mile to me. And that's not because I think that I literally haven't gone the extra mile; in reality, I am very aware that I've done things that might annoy me if someone else were to ask. But what is remarkable is that my love for you makes it feel infinitely easier. I actually want to do those things *and* I adore you so much and have such a clear allegiance to your strengths that it makes the idea that you lose receipts seem trivial by comparison.

The other contrast I want to draw here is that activities like helping you find lost emails or reconcile credit card statements has never really felt like "paying my dues." Don't get me wrong, there was a sense of relief when I had interns of my own who could sit with me to do these things, but it really is the love in the equation that made our early years feel different than what I imagine other supervisor–intern or supervisor–employee relationships feel like.

One thing that we also talk about a lot that I can't help but think of here is my relationship with my parents. But I don't mean that I relate to you in a maternal way because I really don't think that's the emotional nature of my love for you despite many people having hypothesized this. Rather, I think my parents primed me for cross-generational relationships because they never talked to me or my sisters like we were any less intelligent or less capable than they were despite our age difference. They shared their interests with us and their professional triumphs and foibles and so when another person with way more experience and history in activism offered me that same love and trust, I was really able to receive it. And run with it and believed in what I had to offer you as well as obviously everything I've learned from you.

I honestly don't know what to say about race in this discussion. I think that the simplest thing to say is that you are a white person I have always felt incredibly safe with around issues of racial justice because you're always clear in every situation with every audience where you stand. But it also goes beyond that.

You've obviously watched me become so much more comfortable in my own skin as a mixed Mexican American and have been an incredibly encouraging voice through it all. I have a very vivid memory of a conversation we had in Kalamazoo during one of my visits when you were encouraging me to move forward with my name change. And it underscores for me your incredible ability to assess a person's journey and verbalize the very thing they know they want next but are deathly afraid of. And I guess as a person going through all the growth I've experienced in my identity in the past 7 years, you never made me feel like "the wrong kind of person of color." In some ways, it was just simpler than with other white people who speak the language of racial justice. For you it always felt like: "I see you and I love you" rather than "I see you and if you behave a certain way in your racial identity, then I will love you."

This is all also related to what I believe is by far your best quality —your commitment toward telling the truth. You used to poke fun at how often I use the word awkward, a vestigial sensitivity I may have continued to cling to after adolescence, a period of incredible awkwardness for so many of us. But you've never been afraid of awkwardness that I've seen. I've watched you bring up the centrality of sex in meetings with people who were utterly horrified, and talk about race in front of white people who looked like their ears were burning at being touched by the words. And I know this commitment to truth telling hasn't always got you rewards but it's always made you proud of yourself and every time I witness it, it makes my love grow deeper because it's what I want too and haven't always been able to do.

I actually used to have these very elaborate, very detailed fantasies when daydreaming in class in high school, in which I would just explode the lecture with the truths that lived in my body but weren't being taught in history class or in English. What if I just outright said that the assignment that we write yet another essay about what it means to "be a man" in such and such novel assigned in my all boy's school was based on a white straight masculinity propped up by sexism? What would happen? I dreamed up lengthy scenarios in which I'd be punished or kicked out of class or given a failing grade or even get physically harmed by the teacher or the other boys in the class. But even though those outcomes feel negative, I reveled in those fantasies. And it felt good to imagine being that honest even if it ended poorly.

And maybe that's a long tangent but it's all to say that I feel that same thrill when you open your mouth in a big group and say exactly what's happening in my head but seems like a taboo otherwise. And it's definitely helped me to feel more confident in externalizing my own truths. Because even though people may object, the earth doesn't stop spinning and the satisfaction is truly unparalleled. To me that's the liberation that you model and that I've been fortunate enough to bear witness to for the past 7 years.

JAIME.

Love as/Is the Work of Revolution

Love destabilizes order
reaches
for what?
the unmade the unsaid the hoped for
the unruly possible—
Justice

Love at work:
laughter
endless ideas
stretching
ourselves, each other

You show me something in your generation
that I cannot see
I share some part of queer history
you've never experienced;
we stitch these together in our hearts
and minds
and dream bigger,
try again
forgive
offer solace
cleave a place of possibility

Love at play:
We cruise the same people
shop in the same aisle of
masculinities
that refuse
to serve this violent order of
things

Refuse
to conform to the
check-off boxes as written

write new ones
break out, laugh
love extravagantly
hurt
paw through the difficult
heal, hope
try again

Love forges family:
my children—
you stand over them,
a watchful
queer uncle bringing gifts
ponies, Harry Potter, fantastical
geographies
my mixed-race daughter has a mixed-race
vigilant travel partner
my white queer son has a sexy queer
confidante, role model, beloved
and I—
the relief of knowing I don't
have to know
everything
as they
secret themselves, carve their quirky
privacies
unknowable in all the ways
that matter
you—my peerless love companion
parsing the magic of
holding on, shaping,
shifting, wishing, passion,
protection, and release.

When we play what's your superpower
the kids roll their eyes when I ask "what's mine"
it's so boring and repetitive:
Love.

When we talk about God and all the stories that
have been made up and passed down through the
ages, they are equally exhausted by my lack of
imagination. The dull predictability:
Love.

But you—you are never bored.
See only the electric, lightning-bolted
fiery wonder of it.
Love.

JACK.

Jaime and I have spent the better part of a decade teaching about sexual
liberation together and one of the topics that emerges consistently
from year-to-year is the question of polyamory. For most people, the
question crystalizes around whether they want to commit to having a
single sexual and/or romantic partner for the rest of their lives—in
other words, whether monogamy is simply a relic of white-supremacist
heteropatriarchy or whether it might, in fact, be right for them.

Of course, Jaime and I, along with our entire cohort of sex radical
facilitators and healers, are happy to share our experiences—for me as
a gay man who has had more sexual partners than the population of
my hometown, and her as a lesbian who came up in a period of beau-
tifully creative experimentation as to the ways we could create families
—radical lesbian cells, non-monogamous women's communities, and
extended queer kinship networks all fueled her formative ideas about
"family." But after all those workshops, classes, presentations, and conversations, what's become clear to me is that the heart of polyamory
isn't simply about having more than one romantic relationship or being
sexually non-monogamous. The heart of polyamory is in the re-
evaluation of which relationships are important to us, and in what
ways.

I guess when I think about friendship as social justice, I feel that
this is indeed the heart of the matter for me. It's not just that friendship
has taught me the finer points of organizing tactics or even that by
Jaime's side, we've worked together as friends to create the world we

want. Rather, it's the way we treat our friends—or, at least the way we strive toward treating each other—is social justice.

Jaime once said, as a part of a wedding blessing: "If two hearts beat as one, then someone is dead." She went on to say that she hoped the public commitments the couple were making toward one another would include commitments to maintain and nurture the friendships that nurtured their relationship and that the day could represent an opening up of possibility rather than the shutting down of possible paths. In other words, justice represents interconnections, not ossification—"two hearts beating as many." It's a way of being in a community rather than valuing only those connected by blood or marriage.

And I think that's my favorite thing about my friendship and partnership with Jaime. We've never been sexually involved but we share as much love for one another as any two people I know.

To Jaime: The highest compliment I can give you is, ironically, the same thing as your one trait that drives me out of my mind. The thing I admire about you most is: You're impossible to satisfy.

Let this not be confused with being impossible to please. You're pleased all the time—tickled by our shared love of action flicks, pleased whenever we see a new publication in print that bears our beautiful collaborative genius, and joyful when we spend time with the kids together. So very often pleased with me.

But pleased is not the same as satisfied. From you I have learned that nothing can ever be enough in reaching toward the just world we imagine and that there's always a higher level to strive for, more to do, and greater heights to push toward.

If you were ever completely satisfied that your work is done, something would surely be wrong—and for that I love you immensely.

CHAPTER TWENTY-SEVEN

Concluding Conversation

NIHARIKA BANERJEA, DEBANUJ DASGUPTA, ROHIT K. DASGUPTA AND JAIME M. GRANT

Our friendships have developed amid multiple life-worlds, diverse eco-logical conditions, and each network has bent/broken/re-made us which has been enabling and disabling at the same time. Across the universe our life forces fly and thrive. Life, after all, is an unruly vector, always escaping empires as well as biopolitical attempts to regulate our bodies and pleasures. In this concluding conversation, we attempt to pour our hearts and souls in the following page, collectively creating a mosaic of words; a milieu; a potentially new order of things.

What does our gut say about friendships? Why friendship? Who are these faces/feelings?

JAIME. Friendship has kept me alive. The deep, abiding friendship of my sister throughout childhood enabled us to critically assess our situation living with depressed, alcoholic, and periodically violent parents who loved us dearly. Daily doses of parental love inter-twined with the impacts of centuries of Irish Catholic subjugation, sexism, and mental illness created a world wherein my sister declared God dead, at the ripe old age of six.

    We saved each other. We played endless games with our stuffed animals that worked through various injustices and humil-iations. These games gave each of us our avocations—one as a writer, the other a social justice advocate. We also strategized constantly—how to stay at the top of our classes? How to work around Mom's fears and rage to get to a party? How to tap into Dad's soft spot when he got home from the pub?

My attachment to my sister birthed a passion for friendship with women that formed the foundation of my adult lesbian identity and pathways. One of my first true rebellions against my mother's crushing authority was to ignore her veto against a birthday party for Lynn Lang, my first grade love. I went to the party and enjoyed it mightily. I am still so impressed with myself that I staved off my anxiety about the certain abuse that would follow until Mom's car drove into the Lang's yard.

ROHIT. Friendship has been an integral part of my life. As a queer and feminist activist and academic, the way I understand friendship and kinship is through the notion of love and solidarity. My friends are objects of attachment but also a constant challenge and critique to the way I see and understand the world around me. It is not just about being a part of each other's lives but also how that changes and transforms us. Here I remember Judith Butler's work on mourning where she argues that the process of grieving and mourning is a way of acknowledging that something has changed fundamentally which will not be the same again. I feel the same about friendships. It fundamentally changes us as people.

Growing up in Calcutta, India, my distance from the larger family structure and my perception of feeling oppressed under it gave way to forging closer relationships with the friendship-family I created outside. This continued when I moved to London 6 years ago, gravitating toward people with not just a similar skin colour or experience as mine but also those who challenged and made me rethink how I viewed and existed within those experiences. Spaces such as the Belsize Park Durga Puja to the Pride Parade in Oxford Circus have all been important milestones only because of the people I got to experience them with.

NIHARIKA. I gave serious thought to the term friendship much later in my adult life. As a form of relationality, it belies so much that I had earlier thought to be essential about friendship, that is, loyalty and love. Desire, solidarity, pain, accountability, work, incompatibility, politics were some of the many forms that friendship also appeared to me in my later adult life across cities and nations and across academic and activist spaces. I now live friendship through non-secure and often unstable ties, bound by desires around surviving and living through oppressive city spaces, everyday loneliness, and benevolent heteropatriarchal structures. When my heart bleeds, numerous faces appear, not to heal but to trace the blood with affective gestures as it travels to meet the earth.

DEBANUJ. In my now, I am creating a loving network of friends with recovering addicts. I am making myself vulnerable in this book and in my everyday life. I surrendered to the rooms of recovery after 17 years of struggling with trauma and addiction in the US. A series of nightmares, painful, and traumatic. Friendships *then* were filled with heartbreaks, being unaccountable and absent from life. In my now, my friendships are across incommensurable corporeal differences. The ties that bind us together are ties forged through our carnal experiences with rotten flesh, trauma, and steps of recovery. I cook and chill with white heterosexual men marked as sex-offenders, African American corporate lesbians, upper-class white gay men, young queers of colour coming through drug courts, penitentiaries and rehabilitation centres. What binds us together is our diseased, criminalized, and traumatized bodies. In our touch, hugs, and silent gestures I feel alive.

Why/when is friendship social justice activism?

JAIME. I think in friendship, social justice is about resisting the ladder of value that posits our friendships as 'less than' romantic attachment. And then drawing on that larger circle of justice seekers to ground us in what's true, what's fair, what the world we aspire to might look like, feel like, taste like. I think it's no coincidence that when you look at how both intimate partner violence and state violence operates—it involves isolating us from our friends. Both individual abusers and government actors understand the power of friendship in affirming our reality, sifting out our critiques of repressive regimes whether at home or at the workplace or city hall, and fuelling our resistance.

It's been a hard learning for me because like most of us, I spent a lot of my life pining after some kind of ultimate romantic attachment. But the truth is, my friendships have always set the bar for me on integrity, mutuality, accountability, and abiding love.

ROHIT. I agree with Jaime about the way in which romantic intimacy and romantic attachment is seen as the ultimate goal to be achieved, one of scarcity which we keep trying to inch closer to. Debanuj and I set about to challenge this in our most recent work on virtual intimacies. This book is a way of bringing these conversations together. I particularly like that Begum and Maher's piece talks of the affective friendship structure within the textile industry and Bangladesh, and how the ravaging effects of globalization and capitalism have also brought these women together to share their collective grief and strength to survive these neoliberal forces.

Similarly, my own piece and the conversation with Rahul and Sunil reflects on the Global Day of Rage—a testament to the transnational potential of queer friendships and activism working toward social justice and creating new forms of public sphere to challenge and continue critiquing the civil society. Ajamu and Jane's piece is a celebration of this friendship when the two began their epic walk from London to Huddersfield (for those who don't know this is a longer distance than London to Paris) aided and supported by their many friends along the way.

NIHARIKA. Our contributors show how social justice lies in our efforts to build communities outside and within normative modes of belonging and togetherness. Friendship provides relief at a time when telling truth about self, determines who will be bestowed with the coveted prize of recognition. Friendship is transformative social justice when we're are able to be together through an ethic of responsibility toward the other (including its failure), share a language of critique, and nurture the social bonds that emerge within the struggles to endure oppressive spaces and benevolent norms.

DEBANUJ. Learning to live accountably with friends is social justice activism. Friendship as I have argued in my essay is a diagonal arrangement between striated bodies. The most unlikely subjects might become close friends potentiating bonds across corporeal differences. The grappling with difference while learning to be with each other potentiates a new order of things. However, this form of activism might not be the 'heroic warrior' kind of friendship such as that of Lord Krishna and Arjuna in Bhagavad Gita. The friendship between Arjuna and Krishna is geared toward fighting a "rightful war." The idea of rightful war was evoked by then President of the United States, Barack Obama in his Nobel Peace Prize lecture in 2009.[1] He spoke about leading and coordinating wars in several parts of the world, and suggested that the concept of a just war holds potential for justice. In my essay, I narrate my journeys with recovering from addiction and trauma. I do not intend to gesture that several addicts and I are in a war against drugs (sounds familiar with President Ronald Reagan's "War on Drugs"). Rather I suggest our struggles with alcoholism, mental illness, chronic diseases and addiction is a continuous, cruddy, everyday form of dying and living. We (as recovering addicts and survivors of trauma) are not waging a war against addiction and trauma. We are gently holding each other's hands, in order to bring us back from the brink of death. In this way our friendship is not a *just war* or a *moral jihad* against drugs.

My relationships with other recovering addicts is neither simply full of revolutionary dreams, or secret plots of overthrowing capitalism, or full of hope and positivity. At times, we struggle with the negativity of pain, lack of fulfilment, intrusive traumatic memories, envy and manipulation. It is in my friend's smile, touch and tears that I find justice. We refuse to let each other die. Our refusal occasions an unruly collective will, a life force that cuts through material differences, creating a cacophonous now. A now that initiates entropic intimacies, bringing us back from zones of decay and abandonment. A now that is different from yesterday and unsure of our futures.

What is the difference between: Friendship and Social Activism? Friendship as Social Activism?

JAIME. I believe this book project has exemplified Friendship *as* Social Activism throughout our process. We came together because of intimacies and trust within our circle of friendship and then drew on our collective aspirations to make visible the hope, creativity and practices of activism we observe in the circles of friendship we individually and collectively inhabit. The contributions are friendship and justice spirals that start with each and all of us and make room for a more just world. It's as simple as the directive I used to give my children when they'd have fits of jealousy when navigating new friends in their mix of playmates—love makes more love.

NIHARIKA. I first recognized friendship as social justice with Sappho for Equality, a collective working for the rights of lesbian, bisexual women and transmen in Calcutta. With them I have been entangled in multiple relationalities that is being forged through the heteronormative orders of the past and present. These friendships have shaken up my familiar relational world, not because I came into queerness (in its political sense) later in life (in my 30s) but because I suddenly found myself in a context where I went through a series of dispossessions around my self as I encountered different forms of finitude around geopolitical access, urban infrastructure, institutional limits, and familial guarantees. My friendships around this collective breach the boundaries of institutional and conventional modes of belonging and hence is both magical and painful. With the help of the contributions and the contributors in this anthology, I think of friendship as social activism in a transformative sense. With them I dream of a renewal of my self (not in a determinate sense) in amid life's manifold precarities.

ROHIT. Friendship as social activism is not just about narrating the ways in which friends have come together to bring about social justice or change but also about how friendship become the catalyst and locus which has birthed several forms of activism as the various chapters in this book demonstrate. Friendship as social activism is also about the creative practices by artists such as Alok who has stoked the imagination of many across the world in various radical QTPOC groups to use art as a form of activism to educate and re-educate and not have to assimilate with the mainstream rhetoric of race and queer politics.

DEBANUJ. Instead of suggesting friendship and social justice as two separate ontological entities, I want us to feel our friendships in our bodies as a form of lived justice. I am a survivor of multiple forms of trauma: adolescent sexual abuse, surviving Kaposi's Sarcoma and Pneumocystis Jiroveci Pneumonia, as well as the loss of home, violence of immigration detention and dealing with addiction. These forceful set of events leave scars, haemorrhages, neural knots covered by the skin-membrane. (My) Body in pain is an abject body inhabiting the interstices of life and death. Painful sensations, traumatic memories that are impossible to narrativize are spaces of abjection. *Disease-drugs-dereliction-expulsion-desperation-touch-tears-storytelling-entanglements-friendships.*

In the above chain of words there is no beginning nor any end. Bodies that are diseased, delinquent, dangerous remain on the verge of expulsion from life of the polis. In trying to give word to pain and trauma, the abject attempts to (re)create a symbolic order. If excruciating pain separates me from (motherly) touch, my friend's touch potentially replaces the need for a return to the mother-figure. In this way friendship institutes a different kind of order. I choose to call this as an order of justice. The essays in this book reveal multiple orders. Hence there is no one way of conceiving of friendship as social justice, rather a multitude of relations that are neither primary nor a revolutionary resolution. I suggest friendship as a becoming where the subject never arrives and in this way initiates potentials for ushering a politics of desubjectivation.

The process of working together on this book—on transnational friendship, new media, etc.

ROHIT. I met Debanuj at a significant juncture in my life. I was going through a breakup and was contemplating making a move to a different city and even country. A mutual friend and scholar Dr Paul Boyce first introduced me to Debanuj who was putting together a panel on viral intimacies at the Ohio State University. I was surprised that despite coming from the same city, working and living in similar spaces and having scores of mutual friends we had never met. Our transatlantic friendship and scholarship has been developed over time as we slowly started to understand how we viewed the production of scholarship, our politics and, most importantly, our shared value toward living through hostile and often oppressive conditions (sexuality, class, and racial). It was during co-authoring an article on virtual intimacies that Debanuj and Niharika invited me to work with them on this book.

Our shared values and intimacies seeps through the writing and editorial process of the book, one that was conceived through multiple Skype conversations, snatches of Facebook messages, countless WhatsApp texts and emails. What attracted me most to the project was being able to challenge the boundaries of academic writing and research and being able to initiate conversation with a diverse group of contributors who were all wanting to do the same—to push the boundaries of what friendship meant and signified and trying to understand these intimate links as activism.

DEBANUJ. Niharika and I started feeling a sense of belonging with each other. I studied Sociology at Presidency College during the 1990s. Niharika-di was my senior. After college, we had lost touch with each other. We had reconnected virtually through Facebook. Niharika-di organized a panel at the National Women's Studies Association annual conference in 2011. The panel featured three of us who had studied at Presidency College during the same time. Our journeys across time and space are different. The reconnections brought back so many memories. Since then we have considered documenting the relationships between friendship and social justice activism. Niharika-di relocated to India in 2015. We are now continents apart. We are now virtually connected. I wake up to her emails and WhatsApp messages. This process mimics our book editing process. We conceived of the original proposal in the summer of 2013. I had requested Jaime to join our editorial team. Jaime and I are intimately entangled in a network of recovery and queer activism. Our idea has always been to produce a collection of love letters, an epistolary written for and by friends whose significant life has been spent in diverse friendship networks.

My friendship with Rohit has developed since 2014. We have both developed a sense of belonging, an affective bond through academic collaborations. Our discussions have been multi-modal-engaging Skype, WhatsApp, Facetime, Facebook, and Instant Messenger. The shared google drive is perhaps our common virtual space. Our editorial decisions and pushing each other to remain as timely as possible has been my largest learning curve. Some of the challenges include irritation with social media glitches; working across multiple time zones; and speaking about embodiment through spaces such as Skype and Facebook. However, as I would wake up to messages from fellow editors in India and the UK, I would feel a sense of belonging that is reflected in our editorial process. Our editorial process has been scattered, in fragments—relocations and everyday demands of parenting, breakups, dealing with health issues, teaching, dissertating created breaks and slippages in the process. In a sense, the body of knowledge encased within the skin of this book, is our collective body.

NIHARIKA. This book I feel is a 'desire line',[2] a wandering away from our conventional institutional expectations to write together about something that each of us are imbricated in. Words right now cannot hold what it has meant for me to think this anthology, organize, and write with Debanuj, Jaime, and Rohit. Amid seismic changes in my life in the last 3 years, this anthology has been a path I have followed together with my collaborators, friends, co-researchers. Travelling this path has opened up other paths for me that remain to be travelled . . .

JAIME. I have loved our process, and appreciated that my peers have done much of the heavy lifting in getting the manuscript over the finish line. I am very close to one of our co-editors and less so to two of my collaborators. We are all working at great distances and our locations have shifted in the course of the work. Isn't this the life of friendship? I've appreciated calls, emails, texts, skypes, and the very occasional in-person hugs, kisses, and roaring laughter. At one juncture, I found myself writing on a shared Google Doc and could see a collaborator, living in a many-hours-different time zone working away just below my forming paragraphs. The distance between both of us shrunk down to a quarter of a page and the intimacy of creating simultaneously in each other's view was lovely. It made me think of what happens when you see a childhood friend after a lapse of a decade and begin talking as though you'd just got off the school bus together.

I also loved putting out the call for contributors in my friendship network, and gathering essays, art, photos, and memories. It's been like scrapbooking on a grand scale, and I imagine seeing the final version—with contributors I am close to alongside essays by friends and colleagues of my co-editors—will also be very resonant with how friendship works. I often find myself sneaking peeks at the friends of my friends—people I don't know who enjoy the love of my friends. I wonder—who are they? What do they care about? Are they loving my friend well? This anthology will answer some of those questions for me, for all of us.

What does our anthology offer as next steps? Why are you committed to idea of friendship as social activism?

ROHIT. Unlike social science projects which offer a tangible set of outcomes and toolkits, this anthology cannot claim to offer any such insights or tools. What it does do is reflect a contemporary moment in time when we came together to think about the transformative nature of friendship, to forge bonds with others who are fighting social injustices. To think of dispossession and how it affects us all. Friendship offers a way of articulating those struggles and thinking.

NIHARIKA. I agree with Rohit that this anthology does not offer a set of concrete modalities or deep insights about how to live friendship as social activism. Along with our contributors we are sometimes consciously, at other times unconsciously, are part of or are creating ways of relating and belonging within institutions that make such relationalities an impossibility in the first place. Our words in this anthology are not only words on a word processor or a printed text but is marked on every body that inhabits these institutional spaces. If each of these narratives are read separately they may be considered individual pieces of one's thought or glimpse of one's life in a specific part of the world. But I hope that at the end of this anthology, we can see our effort to be a collective within biopolitical management of our lives and living—a collective that may not even know itself except through this text, yet together we are drawing visions of friendship as social activism. This anthology then has become an object of friendship as social activism.

DEBANUJ. I do not intend our book to be a diagnosis of what is wrong with the queer/crip/feminist/right to the city/labour movements. Neither is the book intended to be a prescription. As I have stated earlier, the book is an exercise in mutual vulnerability. I have opened up my journeys in recovery. As a newly minted tenure track professor at a major R1 university located in the global north, my next steps are precarious. Instead of obsessing about next steps in life, I have chosen to share lyrical fragments of my now. In this now all that I know for certain, is my friends' touch, smiles, hugs, phone-calls, and texts. Let this book be a 'now'. Let us stay in the now without rushing to usher futurities. I am breaking . . . I am opening . . . eye, now, here, hear now . . .

JAIME. I hope the anthology sparks conversation and also recognition. I think so many of the experiences and sentiments expressed here will resonate for readers—and perhaps help them re-evaluate their hierarchies of value in relationship. I hope a lot of people who live in beloved communities of friends will find affirmation and come out. What would our world look like if our wild, messy diagrams of our lifelong friends and connections became the foundational unit that societies were organized around? I'd like to see the book fuel discussion and movement towards that world.

Notes

1   Barack Obama's acceptance speech is available on YouTube at: https://goo.gl/ZUgMbf (last accessed on 12 August 2017).

2   Sara Ahmed, *Queer Phenomenology: Orientations, Objects, Others* (Durham: Duke University Press, 2006).

Mary R. Adkins-Cartee is a graduate in Society, Culture and Politics in Education programme, University of British Columbia. She is a teacher at T. L. Hanna High School in Anderson, South Carolina.

Ajamu is a London based fine art photographer, activist and academic. He has produced a huge body of work and exhibited in the UK and internationally since 1990. Alongside his artistic practice he has recently commenced an MA in Queer Studies at Birmingham City University. His most significant recent photographic work was a major project entitled Fierce: Portraits of Young Black LGBT People, which exhibited at the Guildhall Art Gallery early 2014 and for which 'rwethereyet' was a significant fundraiser.

Akanksha is actively associated with the women's rights and sexuality rights movements for more than a decade. She has co-founded Sappho for Equality, the only registered organization in eastern India that works for rights and social justice of sexually marginalized women and trans-men. She is the editor of *Swakanthey–In Our Own Voice*, the bilingual, biannual magazine of the organization, co-edited anthologies of queer women narratives *Chhih! Tumi naki* [Shame! Are You A . . .] in Bengali, and conducted a national-level qualitative feminist action research, Vio-Map: Mapping Violence and Violations Taking Place in Lives of Sexually-Marginalized Women to Chart Out Effective Advocacy Strategies.

Maher Anjum is involved with projects in Bangladesh on ethical compliance in the garments sector. She has previously worked with

Department for International Development in the UK, British Council and ITC on various projects.

Aulic is a tri-lingual queer feminist writer born in a city of South Asia. She has published poems, short stories and non-fiction in literary and academic journals.

Niharika Banerjea is an associate professor of sociology at Ambedkar University, Delhi. Working across and drawing from sociology, social anthropology and geographies of sexualities, Niharika writes about gendered institutions, queer-feminist collective imaginaries, notions of community and queer politics in the context of contemporary India. She is currently involved in three collaborative writing projects: 'Making Liveable Lives: Rethinking Social Exclusion'; 'Lesbian Feminisms'; and 'Lesbian Spaces and Community Making in Eastern India'. She identifies as an academic-activist, as a way to critically address familiar binaries between academia and activism—in classrooms, in activist spaces, and in writing practices. A member of the Sappho for Equality, Niharika also identifies as queer, and this identification includes an assemblage of sociopolitical histories of varied journeys, rather than as an already arrived moment.

Paramita Banerjee is a social development professional whose experiences and expertise offer a rare combine of understanding in urban poverty, gender justice and public health. She has been an active participant in the women's rights, queer rights and child rights movements of the country. Paramita has a series of publications to her name, including translations of Bengali poets and writers in English.

Rukmini Banerjee is a queer feminist with a keen interest in narrative structures, embodiments, queer poetry, psychedelic subcultures and pain. She has completed her Masters in Women's Studies and South Asian Area Studies and has worked with Sappho for Equality as a research assistant.

Sumita Beethi is an NGO consultant, social researcher and activist. She is one of the founder members of Sappho for Equality. Sumita has edited 'the other twelve', a collection of first-person narratives by persons institutionalized in state-run mental facilities. Her training in Comparative Literature had enabled her to use literature as a tool for communication and change, through an interactive storytelling process named 'audi-author'. She writes queer poetry, and has published two collections and is currently co-authoring a queer short-story collection in Bengali.

Lipi Begum is lecturer in fashion management at Winchester School of Art, University of Southampton. Recently she was a consultant for the United Nations, Better Work in Textiles and Garments project for the Bangladesh Ready-Made Garment Sector. She is fashion, textiles and design advisor for projects supporting the development of the South Asian creative industries.

Ma Mercedes Alba Benitez is an activist-poet, painter and writer from Guadalajara Mexico. A graduate in literary writing and visual arts from the art school of Julia de Burgos, she is currently based in Finland. According to Mercedes, her 'art and life is a work in progress: a collages of genes, cultures images, languages and dreams of liberty and justice.'

Karni Pal Bhati is associate professor in the English, and current Chair of the interdisciplinary minor, 'Women's, Gender and Sexuality Studies' at Furman University, South Carolina.

Sam Bullington is a shameless dreamer who longs to live in a world filled with kindness, integrity and full recognition of our interconnectedness. He is a transsexual who lives in the Rocky Mountains with his soulmate and four cats. When Sam is not teaching at CU Boulder or the University of Denver, he sings in LGBT choirs, coaches youth basketball, and generally tries to make the world a better place. He is a transsexual who lives in the Rocky Mountains with his soulmate and four cats.

Varsha Chitnis is a PhD in Women's, Gender and Sexuality Studies from the Ohio State University, and in political science from M.S. University of Baroda. Her research interests include South Asian women's histories, women's narratives and caste and gender in India.

Debanuj Dasgupta is an assistant professor in Geography and Women's, Gender, Sexuality Studies at the University of Connecticut. His research and teaching interests are broadly related to neoliberalism, religious extremism and bio-politics in contemporary United States and India, for which he has received the prestigious New Voices Fellowship by the Ford Foundation and the T. J. Reynolds Award in Disability Geographies by the

American Association of Geographers. As the New Voices Fellow, he helped remove the US HIV ban on immigration. His work has been published in journals such as *Disability Studies Quarterly, Contemporary South Asia,* among others.

Rohit K. Dasgupta is a lecturer in the institute for media and creative industries at Loughborough University. He is the author of *Digital Queer Cultures in India* (2017); co-author of *Social Media, Sexuality and Sexual Health Advocacy in Kolkata* (2017) and co-editor of *Rituparno Ghosh: Cinema, Gender and Art* (2015). He is also involved in the trade union and labour movement in United Kingdom and was a Labour Party Parliamentary Candidate in 2017.

Cesare Di Felicantonio is a queer anti-capitalist militant engaged in different social movements. Since the end of 2011, he is enrolled in a PhD programme in Geography at the University of Rome and KU Leuven, that has led him to work with squatting initiatives in Italy and Spain. His research interests include critical political economy, social/economic geography and geographies of sexualities.

Kaciano Barbosa Gadelha is a postdoctoral fellow in Arts at the Art and Culture Institute (Federal University of Ceará, Brazil). He completed his PhD in Sociology at International Research Training Group between Spaces: Movements, Actors and Representations of Globalisation, Latin America Institute, Free University of Berlin. He was part of the (heidy) collective which organized the exhibition "What is Queer Today is Not Queer Tomorrow" at the Neue Gesellschaft für Bildende Kunst in Berlin.

Torsa Ghosal is an assistant professor of English at the California State University, and the associate editor of *Papercuts Magazine.* Her debut novel *Open Couplets* was published in 2017.

Jaime M. Grant is the executive director of PFLAG, where love and friendship is our superpower in the pursuit of justice. Formerly, Grant served as the Policy Institute Director at the National LGBTQ Task Force and the founding Executive Director of the Arcus Center for Social Justice Leadership. In 2011, she was the principal investigator for the National Transgender Discrimination Survey and its report, *Injustice at Every Turn* which revolutionized activism for transgender justice. She has been on the faculty of the National LGBTQ Task Force's Creating Change Conference for almost 30 years.

Alexis Pauline Gumbs is a queer black troublemaker, a black feminist love evangelist, a prayer poet priestess and has a PhD in English, African and African-American Studies and Women and Gender Studies from Duke University. Alexis was the first scholar to research in the Audre Lorde Papers at Spelman College, the June Jordan Papers at Harvard University and the Lucille Clifton Papers at Emory University. She was named one of UTNE Reader's 50 Visionaries Transforming the World in 2009.

Nila Kamol Krishnan Gupta is an independent researcher. They have been an activist on sexuality, gender, mental health, race and ethnicity for more than a decade in LGBT, bi, trans, queer and Asian and black community settings.

Sunil Gupta is a photographer, artist, educator and curator who has lived in London since graduating from the Royal College of Art. He has been involved with independent photography as a critical practice for many years. His latest book, *Queer* was published by Prestel/Vadehra Art Gallery in 2011. Currently he is working on a joint photo-book on LGBT Rights in India with Charan Singh. His work is featured in many public collections including, George Eastman House, Tate Britain and Harvard University.

Jack Harrison-Quintana is a queer Latino activist, demographer and researcher currently serving as the director of Grindr for Equality. A contributing author for *Outing Age 2010: Public Policy Issues Affecting Lesbian, Gay, Bisexual, and Transgender Elders*, in 2011, he co-authored *Injustice at Every Turn: A Report of the National Transgender Discrimination Survey*.

Marai Larasi is the executive director of Imkaan, a UK-based national second-tier organization dedicated to challenging violence against black and 'minority ethnic' women and girls. She has worked in the ending violence against women and girls (EVAWG) field for over two decades, at both operational and strategic levels.

Jeremy Matthew is a final year doctoral student at the department of Culture, Media and Creative Industries at King's College, London, where he is writing his dissertation on the use of social media and online news through mobile devices. He also teaches as a visiting lecturer at the Winchester School of Art, University of Southampton, for the Global Media Management MA programme.

Shamira A. Meghani is a lecturer at the Faculty of Arts, University of Leeds. She has taught at the universities of Sussex and Brighton as well as the Open University, across Schools/Departments of English, Media, History, Sociology and Development Studies.

Shannon Perez-Darby has worked in the Northwest Network of LGBT Survivors of Abuse, and currently serves as legislative assistant to Seattle City Councilwoman, Lisa Herbold. Her articles have been published in several volumes, including *The Revolution Starts At Home: Confronting Intimate Violence within Activist Communities* (2011) and *Trans-Kin: A Guide for Family and Friends of Trans People* (2012). Shannon believes strongly in the power of friends, family and community to transform societal values that support violence and create the conditions to support loving, equitable relationships.

Susan Raffo is a writer-activist and bodyworker. A collective member of the People's Movement Center, Minneapolis, she has several publications to her credit, including the edited volume *Queerly Classed: Gays and Lesbians Write About Class* (1995) *Restricted Access: Lesbians on Disability* (1997) which she co-edited with Victoria Brownworth.

Rahul Rao is a senior lecturer in politics at SOAS, University of London. His research work is based in the field of international relations theory, comparative political thought, gender and sexuality. His first book, *Third World Protest: Between Home and the World* (2010) explores the relationship between cosmopolitanism and nationalism in postcolonial protest. Rahil is currently working on a book on queer postcolonial temporality.

Ignacio G (Hutiá Xeiti) Rivera is a queer, trans, Yamoká-hu/Two-Spirit, Black-Boricua Taíno, performance artist, activist, filmmaker, lecturer and sex educator who prefers the gender-neutral pronoun 'they'. Ignacio is the recipient of the Marsha A. Gómez Cultural Heritage Award for their work on queer, trans, kink and sexual liberation issues. Ignacio is the founder of Poly Patao Productions (P3) and is also one of the founding board member of Queers for Economic Justice.

Kaustavi Sarkar is a dancer-choreographer-educator, performing and teaching Odissi over a decade. As the artistic director of Kaustavi Movement Center, she leads entrepreneurial measures for building an international fraternity dedicated to propagation of Odissi. Kaustavi holds a PhD in Dance Studies from the Ohio State University.

Jane Standing had been CEO at registered charity Centred (formerly Kairos in Soho) for 8 years at the time of the rwethereyet, which was the most significant fundraiser ever undertaken at the organization. Prior to her role there, she had been active in the voluntary and community sector in London for 25 years.

Alok Vaid-Menon is a South Asian transfeminine writer and performance artist.

Amelie Zurn is a social worker and social justice activist supporting the cause of queer liberation, health and sexuality. Beginning her journey as a street activist with OUT!/ACT UP, Amelie used her feminist health-activist tools to help grow the DC AIDS Information Line and other programmes for women living with AIDS. She has also worked with Lesbian Services of Whitman-Walker Health and the Mautner Project helping lesbians with cancer. Recently, she has been nurturing an amazing collective that creates the sexual justice track of the National LGBT Task Force's annual Creating Change Conference.